Mobility, Mobilization, and Counter/Insurgency

MOBILITY, MOBILIZATION, AND COUNTER/INSURGENCY

The Routes of Terror in an African Context

Daniel E. Agbiboa

University of Michigan Press
Ann Arbor

For questions or permissions, please contact um.press.perms@umich.edu

Published in the United States of America by the
University of Michigan Press
Printed and bound by CPI Group (UK) Ltd, Croydon, CR0 4YY

First published February 2022

A CIP catalog record for this book is available from the British Library.

Library of Congress Cataloging-in-Publication data has been applied for.

ISBN 978-0-472-13290-4 (hardcover : alk. paper)
ISBN 978-0-472-03892-3 (paper : alk. paper)
ISBN 978-0-472-12978-2 (e-book)

To my mother:
Esther Glory Agbiboa (Nipogo)
who embodies the possibilities of mobility.

Contents

Digital materials related to this title can be found on the Fulcrum platform via the following citable URL: https://doi.org/10.3998/mpub.11472497

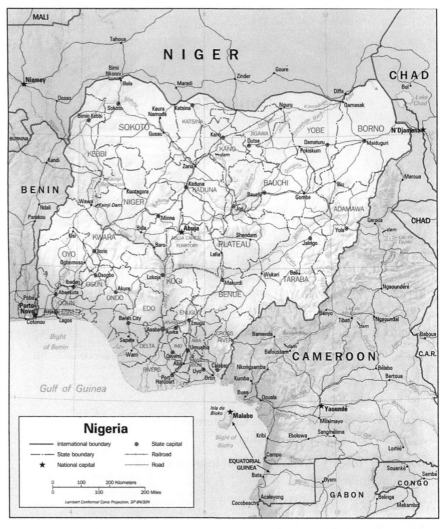

Fig. 1. Map of Nigeria. (Public domain image from the Library of Congress, Geography and Map Division. Available at https://www.loc.gov/item/93681863/.)

Acknowledgments

I first started thinking about a book on mobility and insurgency after local authorities across northern Nigeria banned a major source of survival for existentially immobile young men, motorcycle taxis (*achabas*), on account of their subversive mobilities. Over time, it became increasingly clear to me that the roots and routes of armed conflicts were generally disconnected in the extant literature, despite a substantial degree of overlap between the two. Against that backdrop, this book sets out to reclaim the logic of mobility in matrices of armed conflicts, using the case study of one of the world's deadliest jihadist groups, Boko Haram.

The book is empirically grounded, while also representing a broader theoretical project that critiques the popular representation of conflict terrains as spatially fixed geographical containers for insurgent and counterinsurgent processes, and geography as a neutral backdrop in which terrorist activities occur. The intersecting or multiple interacting mobilities analyzed in this book challenge the essentialist, functionalist, and characteristically Western representations of movement in Africa as one-sided, anarchic, and dangerous—in short, to borrow Robert Kaplan's (1994) phrase, as "loose molecules . . . clearly on the verge of igniting." By focusing on the region of Africa's Lake Chad Basin (Nigeria, Cameroon, Niger, and Chad), this book reconfigures the margins of the "new mobilities paradigm," which invariably takes the Global North as the primary site of research and interest. Yet, as Peter Adey (2006, 83) reminds us, mobility "means different things, to different people, in differing social circumstances."

Timeless lines from Frank Sinatra's song "That's Life" bring home my experience of navigating the fast and slow lanes of writing this book.

You're riding high in April, shot down in May
But I know I am gonna change that tune
When I'm back on top, back on top in June

I have perched atop the broad shoulders of many academic institutions and scholars during the long and often bumpy road of completing the book. I am very appreciative of the intellectual and personal support I have received from my colleagues at the Department of African and African American Studies at Harvard University; the Jimmy and Rosalynn Carter School for Peace and Conflict Resolution (formerly the School for Conflict Analysis and Resolution) at George Mason University, where I was assistant professor (2017–19); and the University of Pennsylvania's Perry World House, where I completed a postdoctoral fellowship (2016–17).

I thank the Harry Frank Guggenheim Foundation (Distinguished Scholar Award) and Harvard University (FAS Tenure-Track Faculty Publication Fund) for funding the research on which this book is based. A two-week research trip to the Melville J. Herskovits Library of African Studies at Northwestern University allowed me to access a wealth of local materials no longer available in Nigeria, particularly local histories and official pamphlets on mobility, cross-border trade, banditry, and governance in the Lake Chad region. The wonderful Florence Nthiira Mugambi happily hosted me and facilitated my access to library resources.

During fieldwork in northeast Nigeria, I benefited from the kindness of many. I especially thank all the participants in that research, including the road transport workers and unionists in northeast Nigeria who generously took time off from work and sometimes during work, to share their personal stories and insights about the Boko Haram insurgency and its impact on their workaday world. The voices, experiences, and agency of those "silent victims" and "heroes of the road" have deeply enriched this book. I am particularly grateful to Umar Abdu Mairiga, my research assistant par excellence, who, as ever, helped to coordinate and translate interviews and focus group discussions.

Since I completed my doctoral study at the University of Oxford, my teaching and research have pivoted on the straddled themes of mobility, power, and politics. I thank my brilliant and engaged students at Harvard and George Mason University for challenging my thinking in this field and for pointing me toward new and rewarding directions and interpretations.

During the writing process, I gained a wealth of insights from a number of international conferences and research seminars where I presented aspects of this book. I am grateful to Rivke Jaffe for inviting me to the

Urban Security Assemblages Conference at the University of Amsterdam in February 2019, where I benefited from insightful discussions with such brilliant minds as Diane Davis, AbdouMaliq Simone, Atreyee Sen, Laurens Bakker, Tessa Diphoorn, Nida Yasmeen Kirmani, Steffen Jensen, and Maya Mynster Christensen, among many others. I am grateful to Kyoto University's Center for African Studies for inviting me to speak at the international symposium "African Potentials and the Future of Humanity" in January 2019. Special thanks go to Motoji Matsuda, Itaru Ohta, and Hirano-Nomoto Misa for their support since our first meeting at the Fourth African Forum in Yaoundé, Cameroon, in 2015. I was greatly honored to give a lecture as part of the Dean's Seminar in African Politics at George Washington University's Elliott School of International Affairs in February 2019. I offer my sincere thanks to members of the Dean's Committee who organized the seminar, especially Cynthia McClintock, Erick Kramon, Khadidiatou Ndiaye, Paul Williams, and Sharon Wolchik. Paul Lubeck of Johns Hopkins University invited me to present my work in the Research Seminar Series held at the School of Advanced International Studies in March 2018. I thank all of the participants at that seminar for their perceptive comments and feedback.

I also benefited from participating in the workshop "Charting Research Priorities" at the West African Research Center in Dakar, Senegal, in July 2018. I am grateful to the United States Institute of Peace and the RESOLVE Network for inviting me to be part of that working group, with particular thanks to Bethany McGann and Kateira Aryaeinejad. In May 2018, I presented my research at the Oslo Migration Conference, "Vulnerability, Protection, and Agency," organized by the Peace Research Institute Oslo and the University of Oslo. There, I benefited from interactions with Jorgen Carling, Marta Bivand Erdal, and Maja Janmyr, among other participants. Also in May 2018, I gave a public lecture at Vilnius University's Institute of Asian and Transcultural Studies in Lithuania. I am thankful to members of the AfriKo team who organized that event, especially Karina Simonson, Mante Makauskaite, and Eugenija Kovaliova. As a consultancy platform, incorporated in Lithuania but putting African professionals in productive interaction with professionals in the Baltic states, AfriKo epitomizes the power of mobility to generate zones of connectivity through unexpected encounters. In July 2021, I presented aspects of this book in the global roundtable discussion on "Im/mobility Politics and Climate Change Response-ability," organized by Lancaster University's Centre for Mobilities Research and partners. I thank participants at that roundtable, especially Monika Buscher and Mimmi Sheller, for a fruitful conversation.

The entire editorial team at the University of Michigan Press was enormously helpful and meticulous in putting the final product together, from the proposal through the review and publication stages. I owe profound thanks to the editorial director, Elizabeth Sherburn Demers, editorial assistant Haley Winkle, and to production editor Mary Hashman; it was wonderful to work with them. I also thank the multiple anonymous readers for the press whose insightful comments and suggestions contributed to the depth of this book. A very special thank-you goes to my copyeditor, Meridith Murray, who is "a little bit of a crank" when it comes to proper punctuation. I am grateful to Wale Adebanwi, Ebenezer Obadare, Olly Owen, Abiodun Alao, Cyril Obi, Emmanuel Acheampong, Kenneth Amaeshi, Terrence Lyons, and Jacob Olupona for their quiet inspiration. My doctorate supervisor and mentor, the one and only Abdul Raufu Mustapha, passed away just after my graduation in 2017. He was a true model of scholarly excellence and remarkable clarity of thought and expression— and of humility, to boot.

I cannot sufficiently thank Mollie Laffin-Rose Agbiboa, my wife and lifelong friend, who put up with the ups and downs of the writing process and the related mood swings and prolonged absences. Without your support, this book could never have been written. I cannot forget the occasions when your fierce brilliance and remarkable knack for words offered me a ladder to climb out of the writing hole into which I sometimes fell. And to my son, Fintan Laffin Agbiboa, the source and summit of my *joie de vivre*. I thank my mother, Esther Glory Agbiboa ("Nipogo"), and my siblings, Ann, Philo, Joy, and Patrick (Osi), for always being there, especially during those times when (I feel that) I am not moving well enough. My late father, Chief Fintan Agbiboa, you remain supportive in death as you were in life.

I tip my hat to what could have been and to what is yet to come.

Introduction

The Neglected Linkages between Mobility and Insurgency

> When a nation is lost, the underlying cause of the collapse is always that she cannot handle her transport. Everything in life, from marriage to manslaughter, turns on the speed and cost at which men, things, and thoughts can be shifted from one place to another. If you can tie up a nation's transport, you can take her off your books.
>
> Rudyard Kipling[1]

On September 11, 2001, nineteen terrorists[2] hijacked four planes in the United States and used them to kill nearly three thousand people. Those agents of extreme fear sought not just to cause death and destruction but also to immobilize international capital and to instill the fear of moving. Since those attacks, security discourse has featured mobile technologies and systems prominently as the locus of terror, with militant groups (e.g., Al-Qaeda) brazenly advocating the wielding of cars and trucks as "mowing machines" to mow down the enemies of Allah (Yahaya 2010). Recurrent and deadly mobile attacks have heightened the securitization of fear,[3] evidenced by national policies of containment and control that treat mobility[4] as both an imminent and an immanent threat and that regard mobile lives as both a risk and at risk. In the aftermath of 9/11, the mobile subject was "a becoming bomb" in the eyes of the state, and mobility transformed from public safety into a national security threat (Packer 2006). At the same time, migration shifted from an economic and cultural threat into a physical one. Depending on the context, migrants were treated either as criminals or as victims (Vogt 2018; Lahav 2013).[5]

Informed by a paradigm of suspicion, the visceral process of controlling movement in the post-9/11 era was best exemplified by biometric borders (Amoore 2006), bio-spatial profiling (Kaufman 2016),[6] and the indefinite detention of could-be terrorists (Ahmed 2004a). Signing the US Homeland Security Act of 2002, President George W. Bush proclaimed a new mobility agenda primarily aimed at maintaining an open border for tourism, business, and "good" immigrants while excluding undesirable elements, such as terrorists, drug dealers, and other criminals (Lahav 2013, 148). The result was a panopticon state and an "auto-control society" (Packer 2006), in which borders, checkpoints, and transit routes reinforced, reproduced, and intensified vulnerability for stigmatized, racialized, and disposable groups (Mbembe 2018).

Since the launch of the open-ended "war on terror," certain civilian populations in transit have been reduced to bare life, as aggressive control over mobility and motility—the capacity to be mobile—increasingly becomes the major concern of a securitarian governmentality. Mobility and mobile lives in the modern Western world are mainly seen as threats to be controlled, straightened out and disciplined (Cresswell 2006, 26). Amid growing fear about migrant invasion and terrorists slipping through immigration nets, disciplinary and discriminatory technologies of surveillance and control have become the axis around which the politics of modern government rotates (Pickering and Weber 2006; Vigneswaran and Quirk 2015). Checkpoints, for instance, have become a place possessed by biopower, where mobile bodies are subjugated, controlled, and defined in terms of threats (Foucault 1990, 144; Ivasiuc 2015, 53). Such biopower reflects the exclusionary nature of modern liberalism, particularly its unbridled power to conjure up new meanings of what is normal and what is deviant (Amir and Kotef 2017), as well as to determine what should count as legal norm and what should be excluded, who is to be thoroughly inspected and who is to be permitted faster movement (Pallitto and Heyman 2008, 319).

Hagar Kotef (2015, 54) retraces the history of liberalism, that is, the liberal subject and its illegal "other," through the corporeality and regime of mobility in which the free movement of some delimits and denies the existence of others. Two examples are most illustrative. The first is Israel's mobility regimes, where roads, barriers, and checkpoints fragment and regulate mobility for some groups (the Palestinians) and enable it for others (the settlers and Israeli security forces) (Weizman 2007). Sri Lanka is another example, where unequal access to political power and patronage networks between Muslims and Tamils are concretized at military checkpoints where Muslims can cross to do business in Colombo—Sri Lanka's commercial capital—more smoothly than Tamils (Klem 2011, 740). In those and other cases, mobility has become the benchmark for differentiating between inside and outside (Ahmed 2004b, 37), reinforcing Zygmunt Bauman's argument that in today's "liquid modernity," mobility has climbed to the most coveted of all values, and the freedom to move has become a primary source of stratification (1998, 2).

The above depiction of mobility throws into bold relief the paradoxical and highly stratifying nature of globalization, evidenced by its simultaneous creation of spaces of flow and closure intended to constrain the movement of people judged to be undesirable or surplus to requirements. Globalization "divides as much as it unites," and "what appears as globalization for some means localization for others; signaling a new freedom for some, upon many others it descends as an uninvited and cruel fate" (Bauman 1998, 2). Recognizing that paradox shines a spotlight on the fundamental questions raised by anthropologist Bruce Whitehouse: "Why is it that, even as lives are becoming increasingly mobile, the process of identity construction for many people has become increasingly circumscribed by territorial boundaries? If globalization is associated with deterritorialization, how do we explain concurrent processes of reterritorialization around the world?" (2012, 23).

That dialectic of flow and fixity lays bare the complex ways in which mobility intersects with the spatialization and materialization of power, inequality, and revolt, giving rise to what James Holston (2008) calls "insurgent citizenship." The sense of mobility is embedded in the word *insurgence*, from the Latin word *insurgere*, meaning to rise up in revolt. Pramod Nayar (2017) coined the term *insurgent celebrityhood* to describe the inextricable link of mobility with dissidence, a mobility that enables the mobilization of protest, dissensus, sentiments, and political activism. In a like vein, Antoinette Burton and Tony Ballantyne (2016) invite readers into a narrative of world history from below, in which agitators, rebels, strikers, insurgents, and unorthodox visionaries operate according to an organizing logic of mobility. Thus, mobility is shown to be at the core of dissent and disruption, the tactics that people at state margins or urban peripheries adopt in the face of unequal power relationships and entrenched systems of inequality.

As governance through mobility—or governmobility (Bærenholdt 2013)—has shifted from public safety to national security writ large, mobile lives have again emerged as productive allies in the war on terrorism, extending the state's surveillance capacity. This rise of the security paradigm as an organizing logic of contemporary social life is exemplified by the surveillance assemblage that followed 9/11, when US Homeland Security enlisted more than three million truck drivers in its Highway Watch[7] program to serve as "eyes and ears" of security agencies, claiming that truckers are "everywhere" and "naturally very aware of suspicious activity and behavior" (Donohue 2008, 252). Through such a program, mobile subjects are relied on to report suspicious goings-on to law enforcement agents so that another 9/11 can be avoided. In other words, the post-9/11 securitarian state expects mobile subjects to be many things at once: "watchmen, suspects, and everyday citizens whose de-differentiation and territorial fluidity grants an almost ubiquitous surveillance potential" (Reeves 2012, 342). Ironically, the state's rallying cry "See something, say something" fosters fear while also reassuring mobile subjects that public safety is top on the national security agenda.

The Mobility-Insurgency Disconnect

Scholars have theorized mobility as the *axis mundi* of freedom and modernity, perhaps the single most important factor for change in the twentieth century (Gewald et al. 2009, 5). As a key technological extension of free human movement (Goodwin 2010), motorized transportation was fundamental to the development of twentieth century mobile society, in which people imagined their futures enabled by technology (Hart 2016, 27). Moreover, technological revolutions in transportation and communication systems released human interaction and the flow of goods and services from the existing spatial and temporal constraints. A prime illustration is northern Nigeria, where the introduction of motorized transport in the 1920s—including the completion of highways from Maiduguri to Kano and to Jos in 1947 and the extension of the Nigerian railway to Maiduguri in 1964—transformed the fish trade from Lake Chad (Mukhtar and Gazali 2000, 83). Another example is India, where the coming of the first passenger train in 1853 cemented the status of the train as the cornerstone of progress and modernity (Aguiar 2011, xii).

In an insightful article, Hagar Kotef and Merav Amir argue that early liberalism saw freedom as essentially freedom of motion: "It configured autonomous subjects as moving beings, it imagined freedom of thought primarily through the metaphor of moving bodies, and it limited the power of the state and the law above all by maximizing free movement of individuals" (2011, 63). In France, for instance, the car was seen as a key sign of independence and freedom in a repressive society (Menoret 2019, 135). Similarly, in South Africa, minibus taxis (*kombis*) became a powerful symbol of post-apartheid freedom and a vital arena for black economic empowerment (T. Hansen 2006, 187).

At the same time, mobility is experienced as a contradictory resource that can create extensive systems of oppression under the illusion of freedom and self-determination. Nick Gill et al. observe, "There is as much un-freedom in mobility as there is in fixity" (2011, 4). In that light, a growing corpus of works has cautioned against the tendency to romanticize mobility, that is, the enduring tendency to equate mobility with progress, freedom and change (Cresswell 2006, 43). Writing about India, Aguiar (2011, xxi) argues that if the notion of modernity is expanded to include people excluded and disempowered by a culture of mobility, then the colonial trope of movement as emancipation pales significantly. On the relationship between mobility and immobility in Palestine, Jess Bier challenges the assumption that the ability to travel is always a privilege. "Many Palestinians," he writes, "must go abroad to find work or visit family members who themselves cannot enter the Occupied Territories. So extensive international mobility can be a symptom of, rather than a remedy to, challenges to Palestinian stasis within the West Bank" (2017, 58).

Such scenarios suggest that mobility and immobility, always relationally dependent, should be seen not as diametrically opposed but as "dynamic constellations of multiple scales, simultaneous practices, and relational meanings" (Sheller 2018, 2). That symbiosis has been acknowledged by a number of scholars. Jennifer Turner and Kimberley Peters (2017, 3) argue that sites of immobilization and stasis (e.g., prisons) are central to the way that we make sense of mobilities and mobile experiences, both practically and theoretically. Similarly, Noel B. Salazar and Alan Smart (2011, iv) observe that the very processes that facilitate movement and global connections also promote immobility, exclusion, and disconnection. Gina Porter et al. argue that understanding how immobility is created necessitates keeping an eye on the power of discourses and practices surrounding mobility (Porter, Hampshire, Abane, et al. 2017, 60).

Until now, studies on mobility and insurgency[8] have been disconnected. Mobility researchers have paid scant attention to insurgency, and conflict scholars have been weirdly silent on how insurgent violence is constantly reconfigured as it is shaped by and diffused through a series of (im)mobile entities. Although scholars have explored various theories and empirics in relation to the political geographies of armed insurgency, the conjunction with mobility—specifically the manner in which spaces and places are made, imagined, contested, and enforced (Gupta and Ferguson 1997, 47)—remains terra incognita. An example is Mimi Sheller's meticulous examination of "the triple mobility crisis" of the contemporary era: climate, urbanization, and refugees. Sheller calls our attention to "how power and inequality inform the governance and control of movement, shaping the patterns of unequal mobility and immobility in the circulation of people, resources, and information" (2018, 32). Yet Sheller overlooks the mobility injustice caused by terrorism and insurgencies and by government failure, despite their embeddedness in the mutually reinforcing relationship between spatiality and injustice, what Mustapha Dikeç calls the "spatiality of injustice and the injustice of spatiality" (2001, 1792).

In this book, I aim to reclaim the logic of mobility in matrices of armed conflicts, with northeast Nigeria and the Lake Chad Basin (Cameroon, Niger, and Chad) as a regional focus. Despite mobility's centrality to the maneuvers and strategies of both state and nonstate armed groups, mobility concerns have remained tangential to how we come to think and write about wars in the contemporary world. The extant literature on internal wars harp ad nauseam on the roots of armed conflict while glossing over its routes and trajectories. As James Clifford puts it, "Roots always preceded routes" (1997, 3). Scholars thus miss the complex ways in which state and nonstate actors, as well as local populations, interact with and socially navigate around mobile infrastructures (e.g., roads and checkpoints) that facilitate terror and seizure (Masquelier 2002; Lombard 2013). To date, few studies have provided a systematic analysis of the mobility-insurgency nexus, including its ramifications for diverse people and places located in the fast and slow lanes of everyday life. By and large, researchers have neglected to ask either what a study of mobility can offer to our understanding of contemporary wars or how and why mobility is mobilized in creating and sustaining configurations of securitarian governmentality. They have neglected to address a question James Clifford (1997, 3) raised regarding travel in conflict zones: "But what would happen if travel were untethered, seen as a complex or pervasive spectrum of human experiences?" When Peer Schouten (2019, 2021) argued that roadblocks have garnered meager attention from studies concerned with political order and armed rebellions in the Central African Republic, he was hinting at that disjunction between mobility and the micropolitics of rebel governance and conflict financing. Similarly, when Denis Retaille and Olivier Walther

(2013) observed, in discussing the Malian conflict, that "mobility is every-thing," they were alluding to the fundamental role (if undervalued) that transportation and mobility play in the evolution and mutation of radical Islamist organizations in Sahel-Saharan Africa.

The mobility-insurgency disconnect is symptomatic of binaries of dual-ism and difference in social science research, particularly between fixity and motion (Tsing 2005), local and global (Ballantyne and Burton 2009), mobilities and mobilizations (Jaffe et al. 2012), movement and material culture (R. Kelly 1992), transportation and human geography (Salazer and Smart 2011; J. Shaw and Hesse 2010), and historical studies of transport, mobility, and migration (Pooley 2017). A growing number of mobility studies have questioned that neat organization of mobilities into separate spheres. If mobilities constitute a key component of people's social and geographical locations, they argue, why are they frequently treated in isola-tion from the complex interplay of political, social, cultural, and economic relations of power that shape one's being and becoming, one's security and potential for displacement? (Hyndman and de Alwis 2004, 540). Regarding the divide between transportation and human geography, Jon Shaw and James Sidaway pointedly ask,

> Is it an overstatement to suggest that much transport geography has taken place in a disciplinary backwater, only marginally associated with key social, political and cultural imperatives that shape and are shaped by systems of transport and travel? Has this in turn led to consideration of transportation being underplayed more generally in human geography at least in analytical terms? (2011, 504)

Nearly two decades ago, Susan Hanson criticized the moribund nature of the field of transport geography which, she claims, remains stuck within the analytical framework of the 1960s (2002, 469). In his early work, John Urry questioned the "a-mobile" nature of much social science study, which fails to recognize that space matters and that spatial variations can alter both the object of and methodology for research (1981, 462). In a similar vein, Tim Cresswell laments the fact that despite its centrality to today's world (particularly our lived experience and representation of it), the meaning of mobility has failed to recognize and engage the heterogeneous nature of space and, instead, remained wedded to "a kind of blank space that stands as an alternative to place, boundedness, foundations, and stabil-ity" (2006, 2).

Bringing Mobility Back In

Given the centrality of mobility to today's increasingly mobile and inse-
cure world, this book breaks the silence of mobility in studies of internal wars in Africa and the Global South generally. It makes a case for a
hybrid approach that bridges that disciplinary divide in order to build the
"meaningful two-way dialogues" and "shared research agendas" that Peter
Merriman et al. (2013, 148) called for, thereby strengthening the hybridity
and multiplicity at the heart of mobilities. While admitting that "the theoretical and methodological conventions of one discipline can appear bewil-
dering and unsatisfactory to another," Jim Conley and Arlene McLaren
argue that the complex nature of mobility necessitates the multidimen-
sional lens of various disciplines. "Working across disciplines," they argue,
"allows for greater insight into how automobility is entangled with material and social life globally and in specific cultural contexts" (2016, 2). That
hybrid approach is crucial, considering that physical and social mobility are
deeply imbricated and coproduced (Kaufmann et al. 2004, 748). In Bor-
dieuan topology, physical space functions as a framework for the structure
of the social world (Fogle 2011, xiv). On the symbiosis between physical
and social mobility, Vincent Kaufmann et al. write,

> First, both forms of mobility are concerned with structural change
> and social transformation. Second, both are concerned with precon-
> ditions and consequences of movement; spatial mobility includes
> transport and communication systems as reactants to, or modera-
> tors of, time and space, while social mobility proposes reciprocities
> between social background, institutional arrangements, inheritance
> and achievement. Third, both emphasize the importance of space
> (social vs. geographic) and time (temporal effects on social position
> and structure vs. speed of displacement of goods, information and
> people). (2004, 748)

By interrogating the neglected linkages between (im)mobilities and
insurgencies—two topics that have shared little of the same space in extant
literature—this book aims to move the fields of mobility and armed conflict
into a position of "productive discomfort" (Herzfeld 1992, 16), cognizant
of the fact that "mobilities research is itself on the move" (Falconbridge
and Hui 2016, 1). Theoretically, the book draws on the "new mobilities
paradigm" (Sheller and Urry 2006)—which locates mobility and immobility "at the center of constellations of power, the creation of identities and

the microgeographies of everyday life" (Cresswell 2011, 551)—to critically examine the protracted war on Boko Haram in northeast Nigeria and the Lake Chad Basin since 2009. This analysis extends to the lived experiences of mobile subjects who are caught in the crossfire between armed insurgents and state security forces. The book departs from predominantly sedentarist theories of armed conflicts that privilege spatial fixity or bounded places or that reduce mobility and migration to illogical one-way flows that rarely stray far from fleeing situations of extreme poverty or civil war (Choplin and Lombard 2014, 60).

The Lake Chad Basin is approached in this book as a region where the principal form of territoriality is itinerant and nomadic (Mbembe 2002a, 69; MacEachern 2018; McDougall and Scheele 2012; Wilson 2017). For centuries, the Lake Chad region has remained a focal point for hybrid people and cultures (Tijani 1980, 122; Kyari 2007). Settlements in the region came in several waves, beginning with what was essentially fishing migration in the 1950s, before accelerating, due to the Sahelian drought, from the 1970s through the 1980s (Magrin and Pérouse de Montclos 2018, 35). From the Hausa to the Kanuri, the Buduma, the Junkun, and the Igbo, the flow and interaction of people in the Lake Chad region was facilitated by the translocal nature of familial, religious, and ethno-linguistic groups and identities (Boesen et al. 2014, 5). In that riparian region, the idea of "place" is not delineated by points and lines: What mattered the most was the intersectionality and intensity of flows, and the inventive responses they seem to generate. Such multiple interacting mobilities constitute a break with simplistic (Western), one-sided representations of movement in Africa as anarchic and dangerous (e.g., Kaplan 1994).

By analyzing the intersecting (im)mobilities that drive insurgent violence in northeast Nigeria, I hope to demonstrate how the micropolitics of mobility is central to the transformation of the Boko Haram insurgency, including the diffusion of its message and methods. The micropolitics of mobility are seen here as the inherently transformative powers of seemingly daily events and encounters en route (Bissell 2016, 395). This book's focus on Africa, specifically the intensely mobile Lake Chad region, provides a long overdue corrective to extant literature on mobilities, which too rarely expand beyond cultures and canonical discussions of mobility in Western societies, despite the fact that "mobility means different things to different people, in differing social circumstances" (Adey 2006, 83). Research suggests that Africans, men and women, have historically dwelled in motion. More than any other part of the world, Africa is constantly on the move (Adepoju 1995, 87; van Dijk, Foeken, and Til 2001, 14). As David Rain's study of circular labor migration in Sahel-Saharan Africa powerfully shows,

> Throughout Africa, it is natural to move. *Cin Rani* [seasonal migration] and other movements that are partially determined by the climate are common here, for the environment in many places does not permit sedentary living. . . . To the migrants I met and talked with, moving is as commonplace as eating; those who move are no more remarkable than those who eat. (1999, 4)

Understanding Mobilities

When it comes to defining or applying the notion of mobility, researchers run the risk of overstretching its analytical purchase, thereby producing a vacuous signifier. Mobility is nothing if it means or applies to everything (Adey 2006). Tim Cresswell has identified three central and interconnected dimensions of mobility: (1) physical movement (getting from one place to another), (2) the representations of movement that give it shared meaning, and (3) the practice of movement as experienced and embodied (2010, 19). One can extend Cresswell's representations of movement to include "the forms of communication, alliance and exchange enabled through the circulation of images and information" (Jaffe et al. 2012, 644). For example, to articulate creative ways of harnessing technology-mediated communication to express and address the everyday challenges and constraints of socio-physical mobility, young men in urban areas in Mozambique often use the idiom of "traveling while sitting down" (Archambault 2012, 401).

In perhaps the most comprehensive definition of mobility, John Urry (2008) identifies it with five important forms: physical travel of people (e.g., for work, leisure, family life, pleasure, migration, and escape); physical movement of objects (e.g., flows of economic goods; objects delivered to producers, consumers, and retailers); imaginative travel (e.g., through images of places and peoples via television and other media, or "armchair traveling"); virtual travel (e.g., city tours on the internet, often in real time); and communicative travel (e.g., through person-to-person messages via email, letters, telephone, fax, and mobile phone) (Ohnmacht et al. 2009, 10). Terrorism inserts itself within those overlapping flows and intersecting mobilities. Susan Ginsberg explains, "Terrorism by a few and migration by many are twin offspring of modern mobility. Both are outcomes of rapid communications, accessible information, and speedy and expanded transportation—all achievements of the 20th century that promote the global movement of people" (2006, 9). In the same vein, Tom Ridge, former US secretary of homeland security, argued that "as the world community has become more connected through the globalization of technology, transportation, commerce and communication, the benefits of globalization available to peace loving, freedom loving people are available to terrorists as well" (cited in Kaufman 2016, 73). Pushing the analysis further, Mike Davis calls attention to the way that today's terrorists take advantage of the seamless merger of modern technologies: "The car bomb plus the cell phone plus the Internet together constitute a unique infrastructure for global networked terrorism that obviates any need for transnational command structure or vulnerable hierarchies of decision-making. Cells or clones can now synchronize car-bomb attacks across continents without any personal contact or obligatory commander-in-chief" (2007, 11–12). That behavior echoes the rise of what counterterrorism expert Marc Sageman (2008) calls "leadership jihad."

Given the manifold security threats facing today's mobile and proximate world (from terrorism to pandemics), states are increasingly withdrawing into the "safe haven of territoriality" (Bauman 2000, 214, 221), giving rise to what Anthony Richmond (1994) graphically calls "global apartheid." As Sharon Pickering and Leanne Weber have illustrated, the stratifying nature of mobility in the contemporary era bodes ill for the poor and marginalized, especially migrants in transit.

> Unauthorized border crossers have asphyxiated in lorries, been blown-up in minefields between Greece and Turkey, been crushed to death in the undercarriages of trains and frozen in the wheel compartments of planes. They have leapt to their death from balconies trying to elude immigration authorities, and their bodies are now washed ashore with casual regularity on Mediterranean beaches. They have perished in the Arizona desert, risking the most dangerous crossings to avoid armed border patrols and vigilante groups, taken their own lives in detention centers, and have died at the hands of border guards, police, people smugglers, private security guards, immigration authorities and violent racists. (Pickering and Weber 2006, 10)

As a relational and experiential phenomenon (Adey 2006, 83), mobility both subverts and reinforces power relations and class dynamics (Mains and Kinfu 2016, 650). Mobility is a resource to which not everyone has equal relationship (Skeggs 2004, 4). Studies have demonstrated that the freedom and the distribution of benefits deriving from mobility are cloaked in vast inequalities (UNDP 2009, 10). Given its embeddedness within the production of power and relations of domination, mobility is necessarily political. A case in point is the Central African Republic, where control over transportation and trading routes has become a focal point of the ongoing civil war. There, rebels and state armed forces carve positions of power out of the capacity to disrupt circulation (Schouten 2019). Offering another example are Africa's desert-based societies, where being mobile is a necessity. At the ungoverned—or alternatively governed—desert's edge, survival and power rests squarely on the capability to control movement, both one's own and that of others (Rossi 2015, 168).

Mobile Infrastructure, Power, and Contestations

Granted that power and resistance are coterminous, the negotiation of mobility intensifies the production of power relations. Foucault explained, "The individual, with his identity and characteristics, is the product of a relation of power exercised over bodies, multiplicities, movements, desires, forces" (1980, 74). Such power relations are most visible in infrastructure, understood here as "built networks that facilitate the flow of goods, people, or ideas and allow for their exchange over space. . . . They comprise the architecture for circulation, literally providing the undergirding of modern societies, and they generate the ambient environment of everyday life" (Larkin 2013, 328). Generally, infrastructures are contested sites where various actors with unequal access to power and resources cooperate, compete, and collide. Roads, for example, are disputed spaces where cars and people, governments and publics, and the spiritual and the material, intermingle and confront one another (Mbembe and Roitman 1995, 329).

The study of mobility assembles three key aspects of infrastructure: infrastructural power, or how infrastructure constitutes a privileged institutional channel for regulation (Mann 1984; Bachmann and Schouten 2018); infrastructural warfare, which describes the deliberate targeting of urban infrastructure (Rodgers 2012, 430); and infrastructural lives, denoting the everyday experience and politics of urban infrastructures (Graham and McFarlane 2015; Graham 2006a). In Africa, for example, the erratic nature of infrastructures has turned its cities and city life into contradictory spaces structured by flows and blockage, presence and absence, and mobility and stasis (Mains 2012; De Boeck 2015, 3). Related to that development is the way that mobile infrastructures such as borders have become sites and gateways of extortion and impunity—in short, of marking conflict and "policing mobilities" (Christensen and Albrecht 2020, 390).

The System of Automobility: Cars, Class, and Privilege

The system of automobility raises persistent and pertinent questions of the inequality trap, aspiration, and rank, while offering new insights into the intersectionality of social class, power, and privilege (Green-Simms 2017, 4; Lawuyi 1988). In much of the developing world, a car constitutes an object of fantasy, and whether or not a person owns one implies class status (Mbembe and Roitman 1995, 330; Adichie 2013, 544). Discussing the world of the Yoruba taxi driver in southwest Nigeria, Olatunde Lawuyi states, "The travelers themselves know that, if angered, the driver may refuse to take them to their destinations, for a certain power inheres in the owner's control of the vehicle and in a sense makes him a privileged citizen" (1988, 5).

The car is both a vehicle for and a symbol of social mobility. Jeremy Packer (2008) shows how the ownership of Cadillacs by African Americans—as a sign of affluence and a way to express themselves—was perceived by the police and the overriding white culture as a core marker of criminality, gangsterism, and welfare embezzlement. Cadillacs came to represent a particular car's driver as black and, thus, as an intruder on "white space" (Macek 2006, 127). Furthermore, Packer (2008) explains how concerns over "traffic safety" provided cover for efforts by a panoptic government to discipline a marginalized and immobilized (black) population.

As the foregoing examples suggest, cars take on values that transcend their utilitarian function, and the system of automobility produces a "hybrid assemblage of specific human activities, machines, roads, buildings, signs and cultures of mobility" (Urry 2004, 26). Igor Kopytoff (1986, 67) has urged scholars to track the cultural biography of cars, because of its capacity to generate rich cultural data about how it was acquired, where the money came from, the buyer-seller relationship, the various uses of the car, and the identity of its passengers and borrowers.

Roads and the Politics of Power and Control

> Without roads which one is free to use at will, men might almost as well be castaways on a desert island.
>
> Dewey 1954, 60

No mobile infrastructures offer better examples of the complexity of motion and stasis than roads, variously described by anthropologists as "vectors of capital" (Jeganathan 1997, 222), objects of fascination and terror, and spaces of fear and desire (Masquelier 2002, 831). Road infrastructure is essentially a contested site where power is exercised and negotiated. In British and French-ruled Africa, roads were constructed not just to serve the practical purpose of transporting but also as a "measure of control and reprisal in the context of disciplining a subject population" (Gewald, Luning, and van Walraven 2009, 5). Discussing the French military's project of colonial conquest in the late nineteenth century, Tasha Rijke-Epstein writes,

> Road building was perhaps the infrastructural activity that most aptly epitomized the colonial conquest in the eyes of French military officers. Roads served as a living artefact that testified to the primal presence, aspiration to omniscient powers and technological prowess of the French colonial force. Creating a road was one of the most obvious materializations of the figurative work of colonial domination over places and peoples. (2018, 358)

It is particularly revealing that the foremost challenge faced by the colonial government in Africa from the nineteenth century onward was keeping people in (the same) place. This was difficult to achieve because they were constantly on the move; "you cannot build an order on the basis of that which is unstable" (Mbembe 2018). A case in point is apartheid South Africa, which struggled to enforce its system of racial segregation and political separation through operationalizing thousands of entries and crossings (Kotef and Amir 2011, 63). Roads helped the colonial state in Africa to extend and enforce its will and control at a symbolic and functional level (Gewald et al. 2009, 4).

In northern Nigeria, for example, roads came to embody the transformative power of mobility. In a piece published in early 1937, Nigeria's first prime minister, Sir Tafawa Balewa, praised the British colonialists for transforming the country, particularly in respect to the preservation of religion and the expansion of the economy. Note the pride of place that the prime minister gave to the infrastructure of roads.

> In no time [after the conquest of the entire land], we started seeing our country enter *baske* [enlightenment/modernity]. Our trade and economy grew; roads opened and people from other lands started

coming to our country. Roads that facilitated safe travel opened everywhere and we got a better and easier means of transporting goods. Channels of knowledge opened to us and our religion was strengthened as a result. Before the European conquest, only a few could make the pilgrimage to Mecca. Now, due to the opening of roads many are making the pilgrimage annually. This is indeed a great blessing for us. (Ochonu 2006, 118–19)

During the Great Depression, from 1929 to 1939, northern Nigerian roads were proclaimed by the colonial administration as critical to other social investments. "Material developments, which would speed up administrative, cultural and economic progress," were said to be "held up by complete lack of a road system" (Ochonu 2006, 131–32). In southeastern Nigeria, colonial administrators regularly blamed transportation problems for the low proportion of oil to kernels in exports and were keen to emphasize "the special problems involved in transporting kernels through narrow rivers and creeks by canoe" (Lonsdale and Peel 1988, 52). Describing a road construction project in rural Borno State in northeast Nigeria, Gina Porter writes,

Within days of a road construction team setting up camp in a new area, flimsy shade covers would be erected and women from nearby settlements would begin to set up food stalls. This was often followed by the construction of first temporary, then permanent, dwellings: settlements subsequently rapidly established themselves along the new all-season paved roads. The small collection of food stalls, following the opening of the road, could rapidly transform into a thriving new market, which would link into the city markets down the road. It is not surprising that road construction—viewed from the tar—is often seen as the harbinger of positive change in regional economies, and with positive benefits for women. (2012, 5)

Beyond Nigeria, Peer Schouten (2021) has empirically analyzed a complex system of roadblock politics in the Central African Republic. There, he notes, control over passage points along strategic trading routes became a vital source of logistical, especially financial, power and an object of struggle. All of the foregoing examples support the argument that control over movement has always been critical to the formation of subject positions and the shaping of not only political orders, but also war economies.

The "Mobilities Turn"

Mobility did not start in the twenty-first century, since humans and nonhumans have always moved. Yet today's complex entanglement of movement, power, and politics is most powerfully articulated by the new mobilities paradigm (Sheller and Urry 2006). Originating in the social sciences from the "spatial turn" (Lefebvre 1991; Massey 1984), which emphasized the place of space in the construction of society, the "mobilities turn" is the argument that the concrete mediations of mobility and immobility are central to many lives and many organizations (Hannam et al. 2006, 1). As explained by Sheller, mobility research focuses on

> the constitutive role of movement within the workings of most social institutions and social practices, and focuses on the organization of power around systems of governing mobility, immobility, timing and speed, channels and barriers at various scales. It focuses not simply on movement per se, but on the power of discourses, practices, and infrastructures of mobility in creating the effects of both movement and stasis, demobilization and remobilization, voluntary and involuntary movement. Such discourses, practices, and infrastructures are culturally shaped by what we can think of as mobility assemblages—constellations of actors, actions, and meanings that are influenced by mobility regimes that govern who and what can move (or stay put), when, where, how, under what conditions, and with what meanings. (2018, 19)

Mobility constitutes a key arena where state and nonstate actors exercise a significant degree of power and authority. As such, mobility embodies the melding of the center and the margins. In short, "Mobility makes states" (Vigneswaran and Quirk 2015, 7).

Theoretical insights from the turn in the social sciences toward all things mobile have been applied to a wide range of disciplines, including sociology, anthropology, history, gender studies, social work and social policy, and disability and health studies. Such applications confirm the analytical appeal of mobilities studies across disciplinary boundaries (Pooley 2017, 253). Despite the flourishing of mobilities publications since the new mobilities paradigm was announced, critical security studies have not incorporated mobilities, and security scholars have not explicitly referenced the "mobilities turn" (Leese and Wittendorp 2017,

173). That neglect is rather puzzling, since "issues of security, securitization and surveillance have become significant in the contemporary world and . . . have brought about interesting overlaps between such areas and mobilities scholars" (Sheller and Urry 2006, 16). When mobility does appear in civil war and insurgency studies, it is either treated as a secondary concern or reduced to migration (Pickering and Weber 2006), as part of what Benita Parry calls a "rapt interest of Western academics in migrations and exiles" (2004, 73). Yet mobility studies and critical security studies share ideological grounds in at least five thematic areas: power and government, spaces of regulation and intervention, freedom and control, infrastructures and justice and ethics (for an excellent discussion on all those areas, see Leese and Wittendorp 2017).

Cognizant of the thematic overlaps, the present study explores the constitutive role of mobility in armed insurgency, using the case of Boko Haram in northeast Nigeria and the Lake Chad Basin. For this study, that riparian zone is appropriate because it has always been a translocal space of flows and flux, where regional interaction is the prevailing state of affairs (Scheele 2012, 13). A central goal of this book is to probe the role of mobility as a neglected aspect of insurgency and counterinsurgency and, in so doing, to reconfigure mobility as the central object of conflict inquiry rather than as a mere offshoot of a set of other historical, social, political, and economic processes. In a special issue on (im)mobility in the journal *Identities*, the editors acknowledged, "None of the contributors began the research reported here by thinking about mobilities as such. Instead, issues related to (im)mobility arose from research on other topics: tourism, migration, and global flows of commodities" (Salazar and Smart 2011, vi). The present study's approach stands in sharp contrast to typical earlier works that thus "stumbled upon" mobility.

Objectives and Context

This book aims to bridge the gap between mobility and insurgency/counterinsurgency by studying up close how the Boko Haram insurgency developed around and was simultaneously transformed by the system of automobility, by which I mean the "simultaneous dependence on the materiality of cars and roads and circuits of sociality, labor, migration, and politics" (Bedi 2016, 392). Since 2009, Boko Haram has inspired a large corpus of works focusing on its origins and grievances (Mustapha 2014; Thurston 2018;

MacEachern 2018), its message and methods (Kyari 2014), its mobilization patterns (Higazi 2015), its gendered dimensions (Matfess 2017; Agbiboa 2021), and the role of civilian defense groups in its operations (Agbiboa 2020). Insightful as those works are, they generally overlook the system of automobility that drives the insurgency and, more broadly, the governance and control of movement in the region. While the role and impact of automobility has featured in a modicum of works on Boko Haram (e.g., MacEachern 2018; Seignobos 2015), the insurgency has rarely been interrogated as "a 'style of analysis' in which mobilities are treated critically and in context" (Falconbridge and Hui 2016, 3). Yet issues of mobility and access are central to human geography, because of their capacity to reconfigure and shift the types of questions asked and, therefore, the insights gained (Shaw and Sidaway 2011, 505; Wittendorp and Leese 2017, 7). By studying conflict through the lens of mobility, new questions are asked, established themes are reimagined, and new empirical sites are explored.

Primed with the above concerns, this study has three interconnected objectives: to analyze the evolution and mutation of Boko Haram in light of how the sect interacts with mobility and mobile infrastructures, to gauge the extent to which the governance of mobility has been a central factor in the war against Boko Haram since 2009, and to assess the impact of Boko Haram's mobile warfare and the state's regulation of mobility for people whose livelihood rests squarely on movement and access. Furthermore, this study seeks to understand how those mobile people in extremis are negotiating a daily life that is fraught with multiple risks, from travel to places and people. This book is thus a tripartite analysis of the vital role that mobility assumes across the operations of jihadi insurgents, state security forces, and everyday people for whom mobility is survival, especially in the context of spiraling violence and precarity. My aim in this book is to advance our tenuous grasp of how constellations of mobility and immobility shape insurgency and counterinsurgency, including how individuals and groups are subjugated and controlled as suspect communities and objects of surveillance when exercising their right not just to free movement but also to nonmovement. The state is recast here as a mobile, rather than moored, entity—one that is "capable of mirroring the mobility of subjects in the regulation of them" (Gill, Caletrio, and Mason 2014, 6).

The above objectives are grounded in the most adversely affected states in northeast Nigeria: the capital cities of Maiduguri in Borno State, Damaturu in Yobe State, and Yola in Adamawa State. Those states are frequently traversed by Boko Haram's highly mobile and loosely knit cells (Curiel, Walther, and O'Clery 2020). Those predominantly Muslim capitals have been in the throes of Boko Haram's violent insurgency, mutatis mutandis, since the July 2009 uprising that resulted in the extrajudicial killing of Boko Haram founder Mohammed Yusuf and about eight hundred of his followers. Combined, the states of Borno, Yobe, and Adamawa account for an estimated 92 percent of internally displaced persons in northern Nigeria, with women making up 52 percent of that category (Pillay 2018). Since July 2009, in what the United Nations deems the "worst humanitarian crisis on the African continent" (UN News 2016), Boko Haram has probably killed a hundred thousand people, displaced 2.1 million, and plunged 5.1 million into acute food insecurity. Research in 2020 showed Boko Haram conducting at least two attacks each day, killing nearly eleven people daily (Curiel et al. 2020, 5).

The majority of people fleeing the violence now live among host communities that are poor and destitute themselves, intensifying the competition for already scarce resources. In Yola, refugees now exceed the city's estimated population of four hundred thousand (Mark 2015). The insurgency has resulted in serious damages to physical infrastructures and social services across northeast Nigeria. A 2015 assessment by the Nigerian government shows that the economic impact of the conflict is extensive, reaching US$9 billion across all six northeast states. Two-thirds of the damages, at a cost of US$5.9 billion, are in Borno, with damages in Adamawa and Yobe accounting for $1.6 billion and $1.2 billion, respectively. Damage to transport infrastructure is put at US$525.8 million: $73.8 million in Adamawa, $306.1 million in Borno, $116.9 million in Yobe, and $29 million in Gombe (World Bank 2016).

The "bad neighborhood" effect of Boko Haram's sphere of operation in the Lake Chad Basin—a porous region and safe haven for smugglers and road bandits—has ensured the organization's transmogrification into a violent regional militia, evidenced by its cross-border attacks and its 2015 splinter group Wilayat Gharb Ifriquiya (Islamic State West Africa Province, or ISWAP). Research suggests that roughly a third of Boko Haram cells move across Lake Chad borders (Curiel et al. 2020, 16). The prevalence of forced migration in the Lake Chad Basin suggests that its porous borders "are as much nodal points in multiple circuits of movements of goods, services, ideas and people, as they are anchor points for livelihood practices that are more settled, more locally embedded and oriented" (Pieterse 2010, 208). Lake Chad borders have become fluid places where the state is unable or unwilling to exercise its full authority, perhaps because there is a lot to be gained from maintaining gray or twilight zones of law and lawlessness, of order and disorder—"returns made from controlling uncertainty, terror, even life itself" (Comaroff and Comaroff 2006, 5). Furthermore, the regionalization of the Boko Haram insurgency has been especially boosted by the Chadian wars, the armed conflict in Darfur, and the fall of the Gaddafi regime in Libya, all of which have coalesced to make transformative technologies (e.g., guns, cell phones, and motorbikes) cheaper and more accessible (MacEachern 2018, 135).

Modern Chariots: Automobility, Toyota, and "New Wars"

"New wars" provide a canvas on which play out the complexities of the intimate relationship between cars and people (Miller 2001, 16). Mary Kaldor (1999, 84) disputably used the term *new wars* to describe untamed, chaotic wars in the post–Cold War era in which the distinctions between state and nonstate, civilians and combatants, are blurred and messy. The "new war" thesis has withstood criticisms from such scholars as Edward Newman, who argues that "all the factors that characterize new wars have been present, to varying degrees, throughout the last 100 years" (2004, 185). From the "technicals" armed with machine guns in Somalia, through the "Toyota wars" in Chad, to Boko Haram's mobile warfare in Nigeria, a fundamental characteristic of contemporary wars, specifically guerrilla or irregular warfare, is "permanent, rapid movement" (Klute 2009, 196). As Mao Tse Tung put it, "Our strategy should be to employ our main forces in a broad, flexible, but never fixed front—a strategy, if successful, that needs a high degree of mobility even in difficult terrain, and that is characterized by fast attacks and retreats, rapid concentration and dissolving of troops. It will be mobile war to the greatest extent—and no static war" (cited in Klute 2009, 196). To control movement is to control power and place. In light of the speed, maneuverability, flexibility, and surprise that constitute the hallmarks of irregular, guerrilla warfare, states fighting terror are increasingly forced to rethink their military strategy. In 2004, Donald Rumsfeld, then US secretary of defense, urged, "Our [new defense] strategy requires agile, network-centric forces that can take action from forward positions (rapidly reinforced from other areas) and defeat adversaries swiftly and decisively" (US Department of Defense 2004, 13).

Since the nineteenth century, automobiles have played a fundamental role (if largely unacknowledged) in relations of power and control of place. In Arabia, for example, cars were a major source of colonial power. The revolt of the Ikhwan militia, created in the 1910s to conquer the Arabian Peninsula, was suppressed in 1929 with the help of British armored cars and aircraft, resulting in the consolidation of the Al Saud's power and the birth of Saudi Arabia. No wonder the Ikhwan saw automobiles as "the invention . . . of the devil" and thought "planes flew contrary to Allah's will" (Menoret 2019, 132). The spatial advantage afforded by automobiles is exemplified by members of the Islamic State of Iraq and Syria (ISIS), whose success largely rests on their ability to "operate along internal supply lines that cross the Iraq-Syria border, allowing them to move men and material to different areas of the battlefield as needed. Mostly this movement is achieved by means of trucks, buses and smaller, mobile technical (pickup truck) and motorcycles" (Stewart 2014).

First produced in the 1960s, the Toyota Hilux, a compact pickup truck commonly used in the developing world, has become the vehicle of choice for most violent extremist groups, partly due to its durability.[9] That quality was put to the extreme test in 2006 by the British TV show *Top Gear*. The show's producers bought an eighteen-year-old Hilux diesel, with 190,000 miles on the odometer, for fifteen hundred US dollars. "They then crashed it into a tree, submerged it in the ocean for five hours, dropped it from about ten feet, tried to crush it under an RV [recreational vehicle], drove it through a portable building, hit it with a wrecking ball, and set it on fire. Finally, they placed it on top of a 240-foot tower block that was then destroyed in a controlled demolition. When they dug the pickup out of the rubble, all it took to get it running again were hammers, wrenches, and lubricant. They did not even need spare parts" (Somaiya 2010). Andrew Exum, a former US soldier, highlighted the popularity of the Hilux in war zones: "It's the vehicular equivalent of the AK-47. It's ubiquitous to insurgent warfare. And actually, recently, also counterinsurgent warfare. It kicks the hell out of the Humvee" (Engel 2015).

Among insurgent groups such as the Taliban, Al-Qaeda, Al-Shabab, and Boko Haram, the Hilux is so popular that it has become almost part of their brand. The Taliban's pickup trucks are not only good for carrying large numbers of people and weapons but also provide ideal platforms for intimidation and enforcement. Land Cruisers and Hiluxes made the Taliban "ready to leap down and beat women for showing a glimpse of ankle or to lock a man in a shipping container for three weeks until his beard grew to the approved length. Or, most dismal, to drag an accused adulterer or blasphemer to the soccer stadium for execution" (Burns 2001). The relationality of mobility and the intersecting flows of place are most visible in how the Taliban and Al-Qaeda came by their war machines: "Corrupt importers in Pakistan order vehicles by the hundreds, mostly from distributors in Dubai or Kuwait, and register them for transit in Afghanistan.

In practice, the vehicles 'fall off the back' of transporters along the way, in provinces of Pakistan adjacent to the border. There, free of duty and tax, they are sold at a fraction of the official price" (Burns 2001).

Commonplace in northeast Nigeria are internet-dispersed photos and videos of masked Boko Haram fighters carrying AK-47 rifles and driving in or standing in front of Toyota trucks with mounted weapons. George Klute discusses how such war machines transformed the pace and nature of guerrilla wars in the post–Cold War era. Klute sheds light on how Toyota pickups were transformed into "modern chariots" and wielded to lethal effect in the Tuareg rebellions and desert wars in Mali and Niger in the 1990s (2009, 141). During combat, Tuareg rebels made clever use of their superior driving skills and the prevailing dust-laden winds of the Sahara to create dust storms, offering cover to combatants as they attacked and retreated. The confused victims were left in a "haze of dust." Toyota pickup trucks not only dominate Third World battlefields but are vital to the illicit business of smuggling migrants and goods across the Sahel-Sahara. A prime example of that use comes from the notorious town of Agadez, located on the edge of the Sahara in northern Niger and widely perceived as a "hub of smugglers," where fast and easily maneuverable Toyota pickups are routinely used to discretely circumvent checkpoints and to reach the southern part of Algeria and Libya (Brachet 2018, 24).

Security/Mobility, Transport and Revolt, and Mobility without Mayhem

Over the last decade, at least three books have sought to explain the relationship between mobility, immobility, and security. Those book-length analyses suggest a growing interest in how mobility is mobilized in conflict zones. Ab initio, not one of those three books focuses on Africa, a continent where, as argued above, mobility constitutes a way of life and death.

In their edited volume *Security/Mobility: The Politics of Movement* (2017), Matthias Leese and Stef Wittendorp integrate research that explores the political regulation of movement with research that engages the material enablers of and constraints on such movement. At its core, *Security/Mobility* aims to "highlight and scrutinize the politics of movement—manifesting itself in questions of who can be mobile, in what ways, when, and under what conditions—and the sites where those politics materialize and unfold their effects" (6). *Security/Mobility* rethinks diverse but complementary subjects that encompass internet infrastructure, the circulation of data, discourses of borders and bordering, bureaucracy, and citizenship. Although *Security/Mobility* recognizes that insurgents and terrorists constitute the ultimate threat to the contemporary world and that the threat is inextricably linked to the flows of global movement (4), the book does not tell us exactly how state and nonstate armed groups interact with mobility or how civilians in conflict zones socially navigate mobilities that are "always contingent, contested, and performative," that are "never free but are in various ways always channeled, tracked, controlled, governed, under surveillance and unequal" (Sheller 2018c, 34).

In *Transport and Revolt: Pigeons, Mules, Canals, and the Vanishing Geographies of Subversive Mobility* (2015), Jacob Shell argues that the decline of specific transport modes is attributable, at least partly, to the fears of revolt that such modes elicited among the status quo. Shell claims that certain modes of transportation present opportunities for "subversive mobilities" that pose a threat to a ruling political regime (4). Shell's notion of subversive mobilities offers a useful lens for analyzing the Nigerian government's response to Boko Haram's mobile warfare, particularly the banning of popular forms of movement and livelihoods (e.g., motorcycles and horses) on account of their potential for subversive use. Shell's case studies focus mostly on animal-based modes of mobility (e.g., elephants, carrier pigeons, sled dogs, and camels), which are "less legible." The current book expands the focus to mechanical modes of mobility that are more legible (e.g., motorcycles), while also drawing on the literature on embodied transport, including knowledge of body-vehicle hybrids (Spinney 2006; Bissell 2014) and the linkages of bodies, technologies, practices, and beliefs to the contexts in which they appear (Larkin 2008, 10).

Transport and Revolt provides a powerful lens for examining how mobilities are (re)shaped by complex hybrid geographies (of humans and nonhumans) that "contingently enable people and materials to move and to hold their shape as they move across various regions" (Sheller and Urry 2006, 215). Those geographies are reminiscent of the Deleuzian concept of the "war machine," a formation that assembles bodies, objects, and their respective vitalities in contingent social arrangements. Danny Hoffman (2011) deploys the notion of the war machine to show how young, marginal men in Liberia and Sierra Leone were assembled to work, socialize, and make war during civil wars. Notably, *Transport and Revolt* does not draw on the new mobilities literature, as Shell himself admits (Attoh et al. 2017). Instead, it interrogates the radical works of historians Peter Linebaugh and Marcus Rediker (2000), concerning the diffusion of radicalism among dispossessed groups in the Atlantic world of the eighteenth century, and

James Scott's (1998, 2009) famous work on the need for modern states to rearrange societies and their spatial infrastructure as "legible." In contrast, the present study is inspired by the "mobilities turn" (Sheller and Urry 2006), as an analytical lens to employ in making sense of the mobilization of and against mobility in the war on Boko Haram, including the daily experiences of mobile subjects as they struggle to survive against all odds.

In *Mobility without Mayhem: Safety, Cars, and Citizenship* (2008), Jeremy Packer examines how mobile people in America came to be viewed as a threat to self and society and how safety discussions often pathologize all mobile workers as susceptible to rage and as potential terrorists. Packer's work builds on an earlier article, "Becoming Bombs: Mobilizing Mobility in the War on Terror," in which he explores earlier forms of governing mobility and the rationale for doing so. His analysis extends to how and why those forms were radically altered post-9/11, through implementations of homeland security measures that legitimized the treatment and control of the mobile subject as an immanent threat. *Mobility without Mayhem* makes a convincing case for tracing the transformation of automobility from its original linkages to the "desire for freedom" to its framing as a "becoming bomb" that needs to be regulated.

Inaccessibility and the Diffusion of Insurgent Violence

The increasingly mobile nature of contemporary warfare necessitates new approaches to conflict that go beyond the view of place as fixed and focus on place as a product of multiple and intersecting flows, a "complex web of relations of domination and subordination, of solidarity and cooperation" (Massey 1994, 81). Conceived as such an approach, this study draws on a logic of diffusion (Zhukov 2012) and inaccessibility (Tollefsen and Buhaug 2015), in which the spread of violence is constrained by the connective topology of the physical space it impacts. Yuri Zhukov observes, "Where insurgents can easily travel from restive to peaceful locations, and where accessible targets are of high intrinsic value, violence can be highly contagious" (2012, 144). By collapsing all places into zones of connectivity, the system of automobility is able to provide low-cost routes for insurgent groups to move personnel, ammunitions, information, spare parts, foodstuffs, fuel, and other essentials key to sustaining, relocating, or interrupting the cycle of violence. The networked interaction of insurgent activities is made possible through movement and access. It is no accident, then, that Ernesto "Che" Guevara's manual on guerrilla warfare argued that armed insurgents are favored by "zones difficult to reach, either because of dense forests, steep mountains, impassable deserts or marshes" (1961, 29). A case in point is the Sambisa Forest in Nigeria's northeast region, where Boko Haram has found a safe haven. The thick and thorny Sambisa covers an area stretching sixty thousand square kilometers. Since 2014, Boko Haram has shifted its operational base to that labyrinthine forest, from which the organization launches its attacks and recruits nearby villagers.

Theoretically, this book draws on the seminal study by Andreas Tollefsen and Halvard Buhaug of how considerations of inaccessibility impact opportunities for armed insurgency as well as efforts toward community stabilization. Two key determinants of inaccessibility take center stage in this expansion of their work. The first is physical inaccessibility, which relates to the distance from the point of origin and the terrain that has to be traversed, as well as proximity to an international border (Tollefsen and Buhaug 2015, 9–10). Physical inaccessibility is relevant to armed rebellion in at least two ways.

> First, rough terrain provides opportunities for establishing safe havens, undetectable and unreachable by governmental forces. Likewise, seeking refuge across the border—and/or enjoying tacit or direct support from a sympathetic neighboring government—facilitates training, regrouping, rearming, and trade. . . . Second, insurgents may take advantage of terrain to inflict disproportionate damage to the regime. . . . The effectiveness of a regular army is restricted in rugged landscapes; swamps, jungles, and mountain ranges present major obstacles to armored vehicles and other heavy equipment as well as putting a strain on supply lines, and dense forest canopies hinder aerial detection. Moreover, rebels often have greater local knowledge, which further amplifies the asymmetrical nature of insurgency. (Tollefsen and Buhaug 2015, 11)

In Borno State, most local-level stabilization depends on the military ensuring access to strategic roads, and humanitarian efforts have pivoted to local government areas that are physically accessible, including Maiduguri, Mafa, and Biu in Borno State. The situation is not helped by the Nigerian government's announcement in August 2019 that it was withdrawing its troops from far-flung outposts in the countryside and gathering them into fortified settlements called "supercamps." Those camps are inside of garrison towns, where soldiers settled thousands of local populations in recent years—either after Boko Haram chased those populations away or when soldiers burned villages and rounded up inhabitants, saying that doing so would secure the countryside. The military retreat has given free rein to armed opposition groups (Boko Haram / ISWAP) in rural areas, while also spotlighting the fundamental role of pro-government militias who have emerged in protection of their local communities. Those militias include the *yan gora* (the Civilian Joint Task Force), the *yan banga* (vigilantes), and the *kungiyar maharab* (hunters).

A second determinant of inaccessibility is sociocultural inaccessibility, which relates to key aspects of human geography, including ethnolinguistic diversity and characteristics of locals as well as their political and economic status. Sociocultural exclusion and alienation from the core increase latent conflict risk through their influence on identity formation and perception of collective grievances (Tollefsen and Buhaug 2015, 15). Nowhere is that influence more evident than in the northeast Nigeria—a region plagued by poverty, bad roads, and environmental risks. Bounded by Cameroon (for 1,690 kilometers) in the east, Niger (for 1,497 kilometers) in the north, Benin (for 773 kilometers) in the west, and Chad (for 87 kilometers) in the northeast, a defining feature of this region is its sociocultural porosity. Boko Haram has cashed in on the sociocultural affinities that Cameroon, Niger, and Chad share with northeast Nigeria, to facilitate the smuggling of weapons and recruitment of fighters. In that way, the Salafi-jihadi group emulates a number of other insurgent movements, including the Revolutionary United Front in Sierra Leone, Cambodia's Khmer Rouge, and the Turkish Kurdistan Workers' Party, or PKK.

Mobility as a Dimension of Fieldwork:
Toward a Mobile Ethnography

Mobility not only constitutes the main subject of this study but also structures its methodology. The data for this book derives from field research conducted periodically between 2017 and 2019 in Borno, Yobe, and Adamawa—three states most adversely affected by the Boko Haram insurgency. Following an escalation of the crisis that killed thousands and displaced millions, the Nigerian government declared a "state of emergency"[10] in all three states. Data were collected through ethnographic methods, particularly in-depth interviews, focus group discussions, informal conversations, oral histories, and several hours of observation at checkpoints operated by a local security assemblage of soldiers and militias (vigilantes and hunters) helping to identify and arrest Boko Haram

Fig. 2. Borno Express Transport Corporation, Main Terminus, Jos Road, Maiduguri. (Photograph by Daniel E. Agbiboa.)

members. Interviews occurred in bus stations operated by various transport unions, including the National Union of Road Transport Workers (NURTW), the Road Transport Employers Association of Nigeria (RTEAN), and the Nigeria Union of Petroleum and Natural Gas Workers (NUPENG). In Borno State, interviews took place at the Borno Express Main Terminus along Jos Road, Kano Motor Park, the Gamboru Ngala Road Park, the RTEAN office along Kashim Ibrahim Way, and Tashan[11] Baga. In Yobe State, interviews occurred at Damaturu Motor Park, Yobe Line Terminus, Yobe Mass Transit, and Central Motor Park along Kano Road. In Adamawa State, interviews were conducted at Jambutu Motor Park, the Mbolo Transport Association, and Adamawa Sunshine Drivers in Jimeta. I traveled on precarious roads from Gombi to Madagali and from Mararraban Pella through Maiha and Mubi, interviewing intrastate and interstate drivers.

With the consent of my informants, I initially recorded interview sessions to assist the natural limitations of my own memory and note-taking.

However, most road transport workers, especially truck drivers, did not want to be recorded, with some suspecting that I was an undercover security agent. The anxieties of those operators are understandable since, in the wake of Boko Haram, road transport workers have been scapegoated as potential terrorists or suppliers of arms and foodstuffs to Boko Haram camps. Every time I brought out my digital sound recorder, those interviewees became palpably edgy. As a consequence, I adjusted my approach and started to take detailed handwritten notes after all interviews. That method proved easier and less obtrusive, as many of my interlocutors were more forthcoming in an unrecorded interview setting. Hence, for the rest of my fieldwork, I used methods similar to those Robert Desjarlais describes in his award-winning *Shelter Blues: Sanity and Selfhood among the Homeless.*

> I spent much of my time hanging about, listening to conversations, and then finding a place to write down the gist of these exchanges. . . . My notes on these conversations, which typically contained quasi-verbatim accounts, lacked the precision that tape or audio recordings could have provided. However, as many anthropologists have found, especially those who have worked among homeless populations, the advantages of unassuming participation in daily activities, during which one can develop lasting, informal ties with people, often outweigh the benefits of information obtained through surveys and more intrusive methods. (Desjarlais 1997, 41)

Taking to the road—in particular, dwelling at checkpoints located at the precarious and shifting margins of the state—enabled me to closely observe and describe the mobile subject on the move, the circulation of power relations across space, and how place shapes the tactics and maneuvers of people in transit. Treating mobility as an important dimension of fieldwork helped me to recognize the geometries of power relations that situate mobile subjects and groups within an unpredictable context of terrorist violence, victimization by security forces and bureaucrats in uniforms, and government failure. I took regular field notes of observations, reflections, and informal conversations with my interlocutors. At the analysis stage, those notes both contextualized and supplemented the interview material. That approach is inspired by Julien Brachet's (2012) notion of mobility as essentially a field site, that is, as a privileged moment of observation and discussion. Akhil Gupta and James Ferguson call for scholars to "forge links between different knowledges that are possible from different locations and trace lines of possible alliances and common purposes between them" (1997, 39). In response, this study adopts a "mobile ethnographic" approach, which "involve[s] 'walking with,' or travelling with people, as a form of sustained engagement within their worldview. Through such 'co-present immersion' the researcher moves with modes of movement and employs a range of observation and recording techniques. It can also involve 'participation-while-interviewing,' in which the ethnographer first participates in patterns of movement, and then interviews people, individually or in focus groups, as to how their diverse mobilities constitute their patterning of everyday life" (Urry 2007, 40). By participating in a moving field site (e.g., following drivers around and asking questions, listening, and observing en route), I gained a deeper understanding of the lived realities of mobile subjects. That "go-along" approach (Kusenbach 2003) afforded rare access into the transcendent and reflexive aspects of mobile experiences in situ. Working in and within movement allows us to experience the ephemerality of the relations between mobile individuals and state agents, particularly as it relates to everyday practices of control, taxation, illegality, and coercion (Brachet 2012, x).

I made my field site the very movements and stoppages of mobile subjects on dangerous roads, including the risks those movements produce and around which they are configured. By interrogating mobility as a spatial dimension of fieldwork, I operationalized the call by Gupta and Ferguson for researchers to rethink the "idea of 'the field'" as a form of mobile dwelling that legitimizes knowledge derived from shifting locations instead of bounded fields (1997, 31). According to Martin Heidegger, to dwell is to "reside or to stay" and "to be at home within a place" (1993, 361). Given their dwelling in motion, mobile subjects embody a hitherto untapped wealth of situated knowledge about Boko Haram members and the activities of security forces, knowledge that can dispel the various "conspiracy theories" (Mustapha 2014) that obscure (rather than clarify) the truth about the emergence and persistence of the Boko Haram crisis.

This study also draws on my own cumulative observations of the evolution and mutation of Boko Haram. I have followed the Salafi-jihadi group since mid-2009, when its founder, Mohammed Yusuf, was extrajudicially killed in police custody, an event forcing the group underground. My analysis of Boko Haram's mission relies, further, on several open sources: they include the group's *tafsir* (sermon); the doctrinal publication *Hadhihi Aquidatuna wa Minhaj Da'awatuna* (Our creed and the method of propagation), which calls for a return to the pristine age of Islam (Salafism);[12] and several audio messages and flyers (as translated in Kassim and Nwankpa 2018).

The data gathered during my field research were triangulated with popular discourses about Boko Haram's origins, grievances, and patterns of mobility and mobilization. I am aware that "discourses, by way of hegemonic closures, fix meanings in particular ways and, thus, exclude all other meaning potentials" (Jorgensen and Phillips 2002, 186). Such exclusion is particularly likely in states of emergency such as Borno, Yobe, and Adamawa. Marian Aguiar argues that understanding terrorist violence requires a close study not only of its material effects but also of how it is represented and interpreted in popular imagination (2011, 150). As such, this book takes seriously the plethora of rumor, humor, ridicule, and conspiracy theories surrounding (the war on) Boko Haram in northeast Nigeria and the Lake Chad Basin. Those "subjugated knowledges" (Foucault 1980)[13] are crucial for at least two reasons: first, they are a means through which people in conflict zones deconstruct and construct meaning out of a lived reality that is decidedly dangerous; second, they have powerful capacity to express local fears and concerns around terrorism, political violence, and everyday insecurity.

The Road Ahead

This book is divided into six chapters. Chapter 1 explores the origins and social dynamics of a unique cohort of "dirty workers" (Hughes 1951) who were among the first social categories to join Boko Haram: namely, drivers of motorcycle taxis (*achabas*). The chapter argues that with the onset of structural adjustment and widespread economic crisis in the 1980s, *achabas* became a source of survival and recognition for unemployed youth waiting for adulthood. It discusses how the movement of *achaba* drivers—and therefore their daily survival—was constantly interrupted by corrupt and trigger-happy security personnel. That interruption nurtured in *achaba* drivers a deep sense of resentment toward the state.

The analysis of *achabas* sets the scene for chapter 2, which examines the relationship between local immobility and mobilization of disaffected youth into Boko Haram, with particular focus on the peripatetic Koranic students, the *almajirai* (sing. *almajiri*). Like *achaba* drivers, the *almajirai* of northern Nigeria consist exclusively of marginal young men who eke out a living under circumstances of great disadvantage and massively limited possibilities. The *almajirai* are seasonal migrants (*yan ci rani*) who historically moved from the countryside to urban areas in search of livelihood opportunities. Like *achaba* drivers, they linger at the bottom of society and are habitually scapegoated for the crisis of Boko Haram. Many *almajirai* were compelled to join Boko Haram as a way out of their own existential immobility, that is, their sense of lacking progression. Chapter 2 reinforces Anna Tsing's observation that "mobility means nothing without mobilization" (2005, 215), which emphasizes that moving from one place to another is not enough, in itself, to enact change. In a northern Nigerian context characterized by desert encroachment, a youth bulge, and few job opportunities, Boko Haram found a fertile ground for youth mobilization at the precarious margins of the state.

Chapter 3 explores the neglected linkages between state traffic law and its manner of enforcement, on the one hand, and the escalation of Boko Haram, on the other. Boko Haram's preexisting animosities toward the Nigerian state turned into an armed insurgency following the Maiduguri uprising in July 2009, culminating in the extrajudicial killing of its founder, Mohammed Yusuf, and hundreds of his followers. The catalyst for that uprising was the (manner of) enforcement of a new helmet law in Borno State in 2009, which mandated that drivers and passengers of motorcycle taxis wear crash helmets. Boko Haram members, many of whom were *achaba* drivers, refused to wear helmets, not only because they believed it was against their religion, but also because helmets were expensive.[14] To explain why Boko Haram escalated in 2009, chapter 3 adopts a conflict spiral model (Pruitt and Kim 2004, 96–99), which posits that conflict escalation results from a vicious circle of action and reaction. The state's contentious tactics around the enforcement of the helmet law, coupled with the nature of the mobile police as agent provocateur, educed a contentious retaliatory or defensive reaction from Boko Haram jihadists, which provoked further contentious behavior from state security forces, completing one circle of the conflict spiral and starting it on its next iteration. The spiral model of conflict is fundamentally a bilateral reaction model, because each party is reacting to the other party's prior actions. Once started, conflict spirals are extremely difficult to stop, because each side feels that failing to retaliate will be perceived as a sign of weakness.

The extrajudicial killing of Yusuf and approximately eight hundred of his followers in the July 2009 violence forced Boko Haram to go underground, only to resurface in 2010 with a psychology of vengeance and an austere line of Salafism. Chapter 4 explores the manner in which the post-2009 Boko Haram mastered the art of mobile warfare, wielding automobility and speed as a lethal weapon against security forces, politicians, and anyone reluctant to back its cause. Motorcycles (*achabas*) allowed Boko Haram fighters to assemble and disperse quickly into surrounding bushes and mountains. At the same time, Boko Haram exploited the extremely porous borders, large areas of desert,[15] trading routes, and sociocultural affinities of the Lake Chad Basin, to smuggle arms, recruit fighters, launch attacks, and evade the eyes of the state and of vigilante groups. Chapter 4 contends that Boko Haram's mobile tactics reclaim long-established ways in which *achabas* were central to the success of smugglers of the Lake Chad Basin, furnishing its members with more flexibility to operate farther away from their frontier sanctuaries. The chapter's analysis extends to the resistance of local populations caught in the crossfire between Boko Haram's mobile warfare and the indiscriminate violence of the Nigerian military, with specific focus on the emergence of the Civilian Joint Task Force.

With cognizance of the argument that mobility is vacuous without a critical scrutiny of the spatial, infrastructural, and institutional factors that configure and constrain mobilities (Hannam et al. 2006, 3), chapter 5 explores how the Nigerian state mobilizes (against) mobility in its counterinsurgency operations. The chapter argues that the state, in its bid to deny Boko Haram movement and flexibility, viewed automobility as essentially a potential bomb and lumped mobile subjects into a suspect community. Subsequently, roadblocks, curfews, verification, and punitive measures were applied to coerce and constrain movement of goods and services within and across borders. Beginning in 2010, affected states in northern Nigeria banned the operation of *achabas* along major highways and within inner cities, in an effort to thwart Boko Haram's mobility. The ban of *achabas* criminalized the primary source of livelihood for thousands of able-bodied young men, without providing a viable alternative. It played into the hands of Boko Haram, by allowing that group to mobilize the new crowd of the dispossessed, thereby reinforcing the insecurity and unpredictability the motorcycle ban was meant to address. The securitization of mass transit spaces in the wake of Boko Haram's mobile warfare had a snowball effect on extortion by security forces and human rights abuses, as soldiers, police officers, and militias increasingly turned checkpoints into private tollbooths, with impunity. In lieu of *achabas*, authorities sanctioned the use of registered tricycle taxis (*keke napeps*) as a safer option for getting around. Anyone not traveling by tricycle, truck, or protected convoy was suspected of being a Boko Haram insurgent, with several tragic instances of innocent people being killed by soldiers as they rode their *achabas*. Chapter 5 explores how, in the name of Operation "Lafiya Dole" (Peace by Any Means), mobile people are increasingly regulated as objects of surveillance when exercising their freedom to move. Further, it looks at the ways in which mobility makes it possible to analyze biopower, the control of bodies and lives in crisis.

This book's conclusion advances some final reflections on the broader theoretical and empirical implications of the ideas presented in the study, particularly how and why mobility is mobilized in insurgencies and counterinsurgencies, by state and nonstate actors. Through a tripartite focus on militants, the military, and mobile subjects, the conclusion shows that the terrain for critical engagement between mobility and conflict is very fertile. This book only scratches the surface.

ONE

Dangerous Work(ers)

Youth, Motorcycles, and Stuckedness in Nigeria

Youths[1] in Africa are experiencing a chronic crisis of being and becoming. A lived experience of precarity[2] condemns many young men and women in contemporary Africa to a permanent state of youth and immobility (Watts 2018). The lifeworld of the African youth is increasingly marked by what anthropologist Ghassan Hage calls "stuckedness," the "sense of entrapment, of having nowhere to go" (2003, 20). That feeling of "not moving well enough" (Jansen 2014) or of "moving around with little reward"[3] (Langevang and Gough 2009, 753) recurs ad nauseam in accounts of the African young and their "youthscapes and escapes" (Porter, Hampshire, Mashiri, et al. 2010). Across the continent, youths, especially young men, generally articulate their daily frustrations in the idiom of mobility and immobility (Archambault 2012, 393).

A few examples are noteworthy here. Daniel Mains (2011) examines how young men in Ethiopia struggle daily to construct optimism in an environment where hope is undercut by economic uncertainty and cultural globalization. Marc Sommers (2012) interrogates the realities of young men in Rwanda who are stuck as they strive, against near-impossible odds, to become adults. Henrik Vigh describes how youth in Guinea Bissau seek to escape a social position characterized by "marginality, stagnation, and a truncation of social being" (2006, 37). Karen Hansen discusses how the socio-spatial experiences of young men in Zambia are "delaying their entry into adulthood" (2005, 13). Adeline Masquelier describes how the involuntary immobility associated with un(der)employment "kills the pants" of bored young men in Niger Republic who are forced to pause their future because they lack sustainable livelihoods (2019, 2).

Alcinda Honwana (2012) uses the terms *waithood* and *youthmen* to describe an indefinite and frustrating period between childhood and adulthood in Mozambique, South Africa, Senegal, and Tunisia, caused by a combination of failed neoliberal economic policies, bad governance, and political instability. Such liminality is at the epicenter of mobility, which has been recognized as an in-between marked by "both spatial and temporal aspects that generate possibilities for the transformation of bodies and identities" (Ghannam 2011, 792). Those "ambivalences of mobility" (Wilson 2017) underline the "being-in-the-world" micropolitics through which global security is enacted. As Maya Christensen argues in her chronological account of the recruitment, deployment, and deportation of ex-militia men in Sierra Leone, "The supply of global security depends on a form of local immobility: on a population that is 'stuck,' yet constantly on the move to seize opportunities for survival and recognition" (2015, 23).

A common thread running through the aforementioned youth studies is the way in which "the language of stasis captures young men's failure to meet social expectations measured against the universal telos of development" (Masquelier 2019, 3). Such language of stasis provides a useful frame for understanding why youth join armed insurgent groups and how those groups thrive on their power to mobilize locally immobilized youth waiting for adulthood. In this chapter, I probe the emergence, perceptions, and practices of a cohort of "dirty workers" closely connected to the rise of Boko Haram: namely, drivers of motorcycle taxis (*achaba* in northern Nigeria, *okada* in southern Nigeria).[4] The concept of "dirty work" was broached by Everett Hughes (1951) to describe occupations and labor conditions seen as disgusting or degrading. A favorite target of police enforcement and extortion, *achaba* drivers are marginal[5] youth who get by on Nigeria's dangerously potholed and bottlenecked roads. Across northeast Nigeria, daily encounters between drivers and security forces manning checkpoints and roadblocks are ordinarily "tense affairs because they are marked by an exhibition of aggressive and counter-aggressive moves. They show that power is not used but misused" (Mele and Bello 2007, 445).

While *achabas* represent efficient mobility for ordinary people looking for a way around endless traffic gridlocks ("go-slows"), the movement of *achaba* drivers is regularly interrupted by money-eating and trigger-happy state security forces, at numerous checkpoints ostensibly set up to neutralize Boko Haram's mobility. In practice, those predatory checkpoints serve to keep drivers stuck in traffic, which makes it easier to extort them. So conceived, *achaba* drivers may be seen as moored in the very process of moving. Unlike studies that have shown how road stops (e.g., for truck drivers) are spaces for the enactment of hospitality (Molz and Gibson 2007, 14) and "road comforts" (Beck 2013, 443), the mooring of *achaba* drivers in northeast Nigeria is a function of extortion and coercion (Mele and Bello 2007). For many operators, therefore, mobility is experienced as "a resource and a burden at the same time, as both a form of agency and a limiting structure" (Jaffe et al. 2012, 649). For road transport workers, the coupling, over time, of their mooring—what Allen Xiao (2018) calls "interfered rhythms"—with day-to-day extortion of their hard-earned income has contributed to an antigovernment mentality and a culture of resistance. The widespread corruption engenders resentment among citizens, while compromising the state's ability to police insecurity. Furthermore, the *achaba* drivers' existence between urban and rural classes, especially their routine traversal between spaces of luxury/wealth and deprivation/inequality, serve as constant reminders of the systems of exclusion and exploitation to which they are subjected (cf. Sopranzetti 2014, 125). Those reminders deepen their anger toward the state and encourage feelings of difference and antagonism. The anger felt by *achaba* drivers toward corrupt and time-wasting mobile police on the road likely helped Boko Haram's antigovernment ideals to gain traction in the *achaba* community and may have influenced many operators to identify with the group.

Members of terror groups often belong to the section of society that supports or shares the grievances and message of the terrorist group (Browne and Silk 2011, 97). Based on in-depth interviews with 495 voluntary recruits into Boko Haram and other violent extremist groups, one study found that state violence and abuse of power play a decisive role in why people decide to join armed opposition groups (UNDP 2017). In like vein, a field report by Mercy Corps (2016, 14) found that "Boko Haram took advantage of deeply held grievances around government inadequacies to gain a foothold in communities." Boko Haram founder Mohammed Yusuf often condemned the extortion, violence, and impunity of the police and military. Consistent with his intent to "develop emotions of injustice" among the commoners, "the stoking of hatred and calling for violence proved crucial elements in his discourse" (Apard 2015, 43–44).

This chapter focuses specifically on the origins of *achabas*, their role as a lifesaver for many jobless young men, and the dangerous environment in which *achaba* drivers ply their trade on a daily basis. My focus predominantly on motorcycle taxis rather than any other means of transportation in Nigeria has two reasons. First, *achabas* have historically been a popular source of economic survival for marginalized young men in northeast Nigeria (at least until the ban of *achabas* in 2009). Second, *achabas* are the preferred means through which Boko Haram diffuses its insurgent violence. By looking up close at the workaday world of *achaba* drivers, especially at the contested nature of their relationship with the state, it is possible to deepen our understanding of Boko Haram's grievances, its mobile warfare, its road knowledge, and its bouncebackability.

The Emergence of Motorcycle Taxis in Nigeria

A long tradition in the study of human geography establishes visceral connections between lack of physical mobility and the experience of social exclusion (Kain 1968; Hanson and Hanson 1980). One study of the relationship between youth, mobility, and rural livelihoods in West Africa found that the lack of access to affordable and available transportation reduces one's life chances from birth and even before (Porter, Blaufuss, and Acheampong 2007). In other words, mobility "constitute[s] a significant stratifying force through which unequal life chances are being continuously reproduced" (Manderscheid 2009, 7). Studies conducted more recently have demonstrated that the degree of mobility (physical or virtual) impinges on "the extent to which shared experiences can produce a sense of solidarity or a collective identity, which can be mobilized to increase levels of autonomy" (Jaffe et al. 2012, 649).

Since the 1980s, the majority of urban Nigerians have relied on cheap motorcycles with two-stroke engines for their daily commute, the common man being too poor to own a car. Produced by foreign manufacturers (e.g., Honda and Yamaha) and imported secondhand, *achabas* emerged as a popular means of mobility for lowly Nigerians during a time of massive urban population growth, when increased demand for mobility widened the gap between supply and demand. For instance, in Kano, the commercial nerve center of northern Nigeria, the population increased from nine hundred thousand in 1983 to four million in 2012. Before motorcycles were available, bicycles and donkeys constituted the primary forms of mobility for country dwellers (e.g., farmers) and poor inhabitants of outlying urban areas in northern Nigeria (Udo 1970, 184). The coming of *achabas* revolutionized the transport industry, positioning them as a central means of movement and survival for ordinary citizens trapped in a cycle of "transport poverty."

Although transport by *achabas* has never been officially recognized as an income-generating activity in Nigeria, authorities have tolerated their presence on the road. In that sense, the use of *achabas* mirrors Nigerian society, where legality is a fluid concept: what is considered legal is not necessarily licit and where what is illegal is not always illicit. Such an "ethics of illegality" (Roitman 2006) is exemplified by the way that *achaba* drivers, who survive by smuggling gasoline (*zoua-zoua*) along the porous Nigeria-Cameroon borders, imagine their illegal activities as legitimate forms of economic extraction from a vampiric state, one that is simultaneously present and absent in their lives (MacEachern 2018, 128–30). Deprived of their navigational capacity (Appadurai 2004)—that is, their capacity to aspire toward a meaningful future—many *achaba* drivers are caught between daily survivalism and a distant apocalyptic horizon (Masquelier 2019, 14).

Structural Adjustment Program and Existential Immobility

The culture of *achaba* in Nigeria is part of a broader informal transport industry that emerged in sub-Saharan Africa in the 1980s, as a local response to government failure to provide adequate and affordable transportation services for the masses (Cervero and Golub 2007). In particular, the proliferation of *achabas* in Nigeria is traceable to the neoliberal structural adjustment program (SAP) introduced by General Ibrahim Babangida's military regime in mid-1986, to address the economic crisis that greeted a collapse in oil prices. Nigeria's oil boom lasted from 1974 to the early 1980s, before giving way to serious recession and debt crisis in the mid-1980s. The International Monetary Fund and the World Bank advanced the SAP as a panacea to the economic crisis in Nigeria, and the program's early phase saw implementation of currency devaluation, elimination of subsidies, and reduction of state intervention in the economy. However, those implementations led to the devaluation of the real incomes of the Nigerian working class, so much so that it became very difficult for salary earners to survive on their real earnings, forcing many hard-pressed civil servants into multiple modes of livelihood, self-identification, and expression (Mustapha 1992; Skinner 2015, 3). Jean and John Comaroff framed the contradictions of the market economy as a "world in which ends far outstrip means, in which the will to consume is not matched by the opportunity to earn, in which . . . the possibility of rapid enrichment, of amassing a fortune by largely invisible methods, is always palpably present" (1999, 293).

Following an abrupt reversal in their living conditions, daily life became increasingly precarious for many Nigerians. With the dwindling economic and traditional support base occasioned by structural adjustment, youth were pushed to the limits of survival on the fringes (Momoh 2000, 181). The lack of social services and rising educational costs intensified by the withdrawal of the state from social provisioning made it difficult, if not impossible, for Nigerian youths to attend or remain in school. The situation was not helped by the lack of gainful jobs available after graduation (Ya'u 2000). As Adeline Masquelier argues, "youth who sought upward mobility through schooling can no longer expect to be automatically recruited by the state, as was once the case" (2019, 1). Such disempowering circumstances revived fearful decolonization discourses portraying African youth as "a smoldering fire ready to burn African urban areas" (Bay 2006, 10). For example, Nigerian newspapers of the 1990s and early 2000s painted a general picture of moral panic about the youth predicament in that era. An article titled "Nigerian Youths: What Hopes, What Future?" lamented,

> Formerly a vibrant force for positive social changes, today's Nigerian youth has been clobbered by societal contradictions unto at best a supine state of schizophrenia and at worst unto a state of dare-devilry with increasing properties for anti-social activities. . . . With its army of unemployed but qualified and able-bodied youth, Nigeria could be said to be sitting on a tinder-box. (*Post Express*, May 23, 1998, cited in Beekers 2008, 27)

The SAP introduced a mobility dimension to exclusion in Nigeria. By exclusion, I mean "the process by which people are prevented from participating in the economic, political and social life of the community because of reduced accessibility to opportunities, services, and social networks, due in whole or in part to insufficient mobility in a society and environment built around the assumption of high mobility" (Kenyon et al. 2002, 210–11). Specifically, the withdrawal of the state from social provisioning had a negative impact on the transport sector. The lack of funds available for road maintenance caused transportation infrastructure to deteriorate rapidly, while the rising cost of imported vehicles caused a decline in vehicle purchases. The demand for spare parts decreased, and the World Bank was pressured to force cuts to fuel subsidies (Porter 2012, 6). On top of those challenges, Nigeria was hit hard by high inflation, which raised the price of imported vehicles and made it difficult to replace worn-out vehicles with newer-looking ones. For instance, vehicle imports plummeted from 15,750 units in 1979 (during the oil boom) to only 2,729 units in 1986, when the SAP was implemented (Samaila 2015). The number of buses in circulation was affected severely. For instance, the state official statistics for Kano show registration of five thousand buses in 1982 and 565 in 1986 (*Kano State Motor Vehicle Statistics* 1986, 4–5). That drop is in marked contrast to the halcyon years of the oil boom, when car ownership was so high that even relatively poor farmers could afford an *achaba* (Guyer 1997, 86). Official records show that the number of registered cars in Nigeria during the decade of the oil boom doubled between 1976 and 1982. That unprecedented scale was due largely to massive pay increases in the public and private sectors. At that time, even Nigerians who could not afford a car of their own had the means to pay transportation fares (Porter 1995, 4).

From the mid-1980s, the federal government attempted to address the problem of reduced mobility amid the economic crisis through efforts, such as the Urban Mass Transit Programme introduced in 1988, that proved ineffective. To supplement their meager wages, low-income workers increasingly converted their private cars to commercial use. But those car owners were reluctant to take their cars beyond paved roads, because of the difficulties of obtaining spare parts and because of the soaring cost of pre-owned vehicles in Nigeria. If drivers could manage to find enough business on paved roadways, they were reluctant to subject their vehicles to the dangers of off-road routes (Porter 2012, 16). As a result, people living in peripheral regions and off-road communities found it very difficult to bridge spatial distances and improve their chances of upward social mobility, and their predicament gave rise to further exclusion and inequality. Women in particular were adversely affected by poor roads and transport services, which impinged on their access to markets, services in health and education, agricultural extension services, and banking facilities and credit. It is not unusual to see women carrying heavy loads along busy paved roads because they cannot afford to pay for transportation (Porter 2012, 32). Their situation reinforces the argument that "being mobile and immobile are important factors of social differentiation and a generator of patterns of inequality" (Ohnmacht et al. 2009, 20).

Mobility and the Politics of Survival and Recognition

Andrew Walker describes *achaba* drivers as "men who have not been put to work in factories, or farms, who cannot enter the civil service, who in many cases are even denied the rights to full adulthood within a hierarchical society because many cannot marry" (2016, 137–38). Rather than frame *achaba* drivers as men in crisis, I want to treat crisis as context, as a terrain of action and meaning (Vigh 2008, 8). My interest is in the series of operations in and through which *achaba* drivers make do against all odds. As a lived experience, crisis is woven into the fabric of the workaday world of Nigerian drivers; crisis is approached as an intrinsic part of the banal and thus as unsurprising (Mbembe and Roitman 1995, 326). Against the backdrop of risk, insecurity, and radical uncertainty, many youths in extremis turned to the informal transport sector in droves, offering services at bus stations and driving *achabas* as a way out of their precarious existence. For single young men waiting for adulthood, *achaba* driving became a way to "overcome insecurity and boredom by fashioning new spaces of belonging" (Masquelier 2019, 4). The turn of youth to *achaba* work reinforces the argument that transportation and mobility in Africa provide a route out of poverty and are central to attaining successful, sustainable livelihoods (Porter, Hampshire, Abane, et al. 2017).

The Lake Chad Basin has one of the highest demographic growth rates and one of the youngest populations in the world, with countries such as Niger posting a median age of 14.8 years old (Magrin and Pérouse de Montclos 2018, 41). That youthful age structure creates enormous needs relating to access to fundamental services, including education, health, and integration into the labor market. Moreover, even prior to the coming of Boko Haram, the lack of opportunity for employment among local youth played an important role in rural crime (Saïbou 2010) and the emergence of "men in arms," for whom violence became a "practical occupation" (Debos 2011, 409). From the 1970s through the 1990s, northern cities such as Maiduguri saw considerable dislocation and ad hoc urbanization. In particular, youth struggled with un(der)employment at "precisely the time when hereditary Muslim rulers were losing their long-standing powers of surveillance and control" (Thurston 2018, 31). In major cities such as Kano, a blend of high population growth, desertification, moribund infrastructures, and shortage of investment stretched the carrying capacity of the rural economy to its limit, provoking a hemorrhaging of young, jobless, and unmarried men from vastly rural communities into urban centers in search of gainful jobs and access to formal education as a means of survival (Meagher 2013, 170; Kane 2003, 233). The turn of youth to cities as a survival strategy reinforces the argument that "for many people across the world, moving into the city from rural areas or smaller towns is a first step in achieving social mobility" (Jaffe et al. 2012, 644). Yet urban life does not offer guarantees of financial security for rural migrants. Urban youth often have to forge a path through precarity, understood here as the manner in which the subjectivities of youth are fostered out of a profound and radical sense of insecurity and uncertainty (Pratten 2013, 246).

In many northern Nigerian cities, *achaba* work became the saving grace of the commoners, providing jobs and rescue from the "curse" of idleness for an estimated one million unemployed persons, including retrenched employees, failed traders, struggling pensioners, and Koranic students (*almajirai*) streaming into the city from rural areas (Meagher 2013). In (northern) Nigeria, "to be idle is to be lazy. It is also to be weak and potentially susceptible to moral decay, or worse. Rather than seeing idleness as a by-product of structural inequality, many elders associate it with thievery and delinquency" (Masquelier 2009, 4). Demographically, 88 percent of *achaba* drivers fall in the age bracket of eighteen to thirty years, and only 47 percent have received any type of formal education (Meagher 2018). *Achaba* work generally attracts both Muslim and Christian populations, as evinced by the religious stickers displayed on the bodies of commercial *keke napeps* (tricycle taxis) across northern Nigerian cities. In Maiduguri, over 58 percent of *achaba* drivers in 1999 were school dropouts or unemployed graduates who found themselves in the business without training (Abbas 1999). According to one respondent, Umar Barau, a transport union leader in Yobe State, *achaba* work was started by the *talakawa* (commoner) as a means of economic empowerment for the jobless. Barau tells me that,

> The truth is that any Nigerian you see or meet driving *achaba* is as a result of unemployment. . . . It is the sons of the poor that are jobless who created the job of *achaba* driving. We have people with different qualifications in this trade: people with first degrees, Masters, Secondary and Primary School Leavers, etc. who are all here in this job and struggling to survive. We sat, initiated and developed this concept [of *achaba*] to have something doing until something concrete comes up. That is why we are telling the world on a daily basis that before the government created poverty alleviation, *achaba* association, started by sons of less privilege people, started poverty alleviation in Nigeria.

In northern Nigeria, a man's social and marital status is closely related; becoming a man depends on the availability of resources to marry and to provide for dependents. By keeping a household, a man acquires "wealth in people" (Guyer 1995) and "becomes a respectable person, that is, a person who receives social recognition from others, including peers and elders. . . .

By the same token, those who cannot secure livelihood are doomed to social immobility. They cannot hope to attract a wife until they have better prospects" (Masquelier 2019, 15). The physicality of the crisis (e.g., lacking the resources to marry a wife or provide for dependents) reduces people to a precarious condition that affects not only how they define themselves but also how they are defined by others (Mbembe and Roitman 1995, 330). Moreover, in a northern Nigerian region that is predominantly Muslim, "the consequences of being *stuck in youth* extend well beyond earthly life. Since unmarried Muslim youths are said to receive fewer divine rewards than married men for their five daily prayers, wifelessness can potentially compromise their chances of entering paradise" (Masquelier 2019, 17). *Achaba* work is thus fundamental for unmarried men, as it enables them to pay the often-inflated cost of bride price, marry a wife, and acquire the status of *masu gida* (household heads); in short, *achaba* work enables young men stuck in waithood to become *homi completo* (complete men). During my fieldwork, many transport workers told me that *achaba* work was their primary source of income and enabled them to get married and keep their families. Umar Mohammed, a former *achaba* driver who now serves as the chairman of one of the associations for drivers of *keke napeps* in Damaturu, recalled, "I joined this [*achaba*] work after I completed secondary school and could not be gainfully employed. I was one of the boys that embraced this as a means of social livelihood, and I am very proud of it, as I got married and built all my houses through this job, including the one I am in now."

Drivers generally forge their positive self-image out of their *achabas*, the material symbols of their survival and respectability. That symbolism partly explains why many drivers invest a great deal of resources in decorating their automobiles. Across northern Nigeria, it is common to see road transport workers using dusters to wipe dirt from their vehicles at the slightest opportunity, particularly while stuck in traffic. That practice shows "a sense of self-accomplishment that a rider derives from owning or riding a well-decorated tricycle" (Williams et al. 2019, 25). In relation to Makeni in Sierra Leone, Michael Burge argued, "Bike riding is about building up one's personhood as a responsible and full member of society, an adult, in continuous check and balance with the environment. . . . [By] riding a bike, young men had found a way to overcome at least partially the social inertia of not becoming adults, caused by the lack of resources" (2011, 60). The popularity of *achabas* among youth stems from relatively low start-up capital and maintenance costs and from the feeling of economic freedom and autonomy afforded by motorcycle ownership. As one scholar explains, "The promise of earning a fast buck in a job that does not require formal training, the cool style of the drivers, and the sheer promise of a world flush with quick cash and potential have made the industry a highly attractive place for many young men" (T. Hansen 2006, 187).

The majority of drivers either acquired their *achabas* through hire purchase or simply run their motorcycles for owners, to whom they must make a daily local return. Typically, an owner purchases an *achaba* for an estimated N 400,000, then loans it out to drivers at a cost of around N 672,000, with the agreement that the driver remits N 14,000 balance on a weekly basis (or N 2,000 daily) over a twelve-month period. Often, a driver is unable to meet the financial agreement and is at risk of losing the *achaba* and all the money paid for it so far. That difficulty explains why some drivers have turned to loans offered by Boko Haram to enable them to complete payments and own the *achabas* they drive. Given the immense pressure to complete payment, *achaba* drivers have little option but to work fifteen to twenty hours daily—"24 hours on the Road," as one sticker puts it. "Before the *achaba* ban was enforced in 2009," said Garba, a driver of a *keke napep* from Mubi, "it was only sleeping that separated me from my motorcycle."

Corruption, Coercion, and Delay Tactics

The demand for bribes (also known as *dash*, *kola*, or *egunje*) from transport workers at roadside checkpoints is a widespread phenomenon linked to security officers on transit and trading routes across the Lake Chad Basin. Most of the illegal payments are commanded by mobile police, military personnel, custom agents, traffic inspectors, municipal officials, and transport union officials. In northeast Nigeria, they are mostly commanded by the mobile police. Olivier Walther et al. explain, "Some security officials elicit a fixed fee at each roadside checkpoint, mainly from small traders and migrants, while others extract informal payment from individuals whose vehicles fall short of the regulations. Lastly, some officials establish long-term relationships with large traders and regional transporters to facilitate the passage of prohibited imported goods" (2020, 5–6). Those corrupt practices account for significant road delays and increase the cost of transporting. For every hundred kilometers traveled in West Africa, truckers transporting goods often lose forty-six minutes (6).

Despite working long hours, many *achaba* drivers are left frustrated by their meager takings. "*Achaba* is just daily income," a driver in northern

Nigeria said, adding, "What you get today you use today, and tomorrow you start again from scratch" (Meagher 2018, 210). The low income of *achaba* drivers is linked to the intimidatory tactics and extortionate powers of transport union officials—for example, the National Union of Road Transport Workers and the Road Transport Employers Association of Nigeria—and also to the violent and delaying tactics of police officers carrying AK-47s at roadside checkpoints. A former *achaba* driver from Yola noted, "There are losses from bad roads like Borgu and Numan Roads, but losses from checkpoints are higher than loss from bad roads." Describing the usual method of extortion, a driver from Maiduguri said, "A police can arrest you on the basis that you have parked in some 'no parking zone.' The police will insist that you drive him to the nearest police station. Along the way, the police will then ask you to stop and haggle with you just like petty traders do in the market until a settlement is reached. A civilian cannot win in any argument with a uniformed security personnel."

Any reluctance by transport operators to *dash* (bribe) officers on the road is often settled by force. It is very common for a soldier or police officer to open fire on vehicles when drivers refuse to surrender a portion of their hard-earned money, showing how "poverty and political violence share a common target, the bodies of those less powerful" (Kirsch 2002, 58). One tanker driver in Yobe State recounted, "Police are known for killing drivers because of N 20. It has happened in Kaduna, and even in this town policemen have killed drivers who refused to give them N 20 bribe. . . . A road safety officer will look at you and say you have to pay N 50,000 for an offense when your tires are fine. You are using your seat belt correctly. And your particulars are intact." During my fieldwork in Borno State, drivers shared harrowing stories of *achaba* drivers who were severely beaten or shot to death by soldiers and police officers for refusing to pay bribes of US$1 or less, coded as "water money."

At most highway checkpoints in northern Nigeria, it is common to see a solider poking the muzzle of his AK-47 into the eyes of a driver refusing to supply the exact bribes required. Refusal or hesitation to pay a bribe can be a costly mistake, resulting in lengthy delays at checkpoints, detention at the agency office, vehicle impoundment, or tire deflation. That threat explains an argument Mbembe and Roitman make about African roads: "Those who follow the rules scrupulously sometimes find themselves in a snarl, facing figures of the real that have little correspondence to what is publicly alleged or prescribed. . . . Every effort to follow the written rule is susceptible to lead not to the targeted goal, but to a situation of apparent contradiction" (1995, 342). "They are not fair to us at all," a driver said, explaining, "They usually carry out regular raids and arrest us for no crime. I once paid N 10,000 to bail myself. This is our main problem here" (Abubakar 2015). In light of such difficulties, local residents often compare driving work to "death-worlds" that confer on drivers the status of living dead (Mbembe 2003, 39).

In northeast Nigeria, security personnel are often prepared to smash windshields or remove windshield wipers or fuel tank covers when drivers refuse to *dash* (bribe) them. The delay tactics of mobile policemen are a major source of frustration for *achaba* drivers. "At some checkpoints, if you don't settle them, they can delay you for three to four hours before you will be released," said Musa in Maiduguri. "Due to all the delays, a two hours' journey will take you ten hours," another driver said. There is little chance of escape from the delays unless drivers pay the required cash bribes. The following passage best captures the typical scenario of delay tactics on Nigerian roads:

> After the inspection of documents, the police officer asks the taxi driver to put his foot on the brakes. If the brake lights fail, the poor driver falls through the trap. If not, the inspection continues. Everything is subject to it: tires, brakes, shock absorbers, headlights, blinkers, bumpers. Tired of insisting, the cops have recourse to their last card, the missing fire extinguisher and first-aid kit, before asking all of the passengers for their papers. The second device is simply to waste time. The policeman stops a taxi, asks for "the documents" and moves away from the vehicle. He talks with his colleagues without even deigning to glance at the papers. Hurried and tired of waiting, the passengers get out of the taxi one by one and hitch rides with other cars. . . . As soon as the taxi driver gives "500," the policeman returns his documents and the pigeon is free to fly away and be plucked elsewhere. (Mbembe and Roitman 1995, 344)

The corruption and insecurity reinforce the contradictory nature of mobility as a source of both freedom and coercion—in short, as "the ultimate form of displacement" (Masquelier 2019, 2).

Mobile Networks of Solidarity

Despite their location at the bottom of Nigerian society, the power of *achaba* drivers lies in their sheer numbers and capacity for collective organizing, as illustrated by what Sara Ahmed calls "fellow feeling" or "feeling-in-common" (2004, 36). Accidents involving cars and *achabas* in Nigeria promptly draw scores of supportive *achaba* drivers. A trader in Maiduguri said, "I have seen instances when they [*achaba* drivers] gang up in support of their colleague, even if it is he who is at fault." That statement is confirmed by the popular image of *achaba* drivers as people who "seem to become provoked at the slightest misunderstanding" (Habib 2010).

As a closely integrated travel community, *achaba* drivers belong to neighborhood associations that serve as an "infrastructure of support" (Masquelier 2019, 6), providing networks of solidarity, accumulation, and protection. Such associations are directed by social relations of patronage informed by notions of trust and mutual dependence. A transport union leader in Maiduguri told me, "If one of us gets into an accident, it is our job to look after him in the hospital and take care of his bill and to take him home. If there is any problem between our member and mobile police—you know this job involves a lot of youth bound to slipups—it's our job to resolve the problem. Also, if your machine got damaged or malfunctions, the union will give you N 2,000 on credit for you to repair the damage and pay back N 1,000. If your wife delivers a baby and you bought a ram for the naming ceremony but couldn't afford biscuits or kola nuts, the union can help you out." Thus, far from being "atomized individuals" with similar positions brought together through space (a passive network), *achaba* drivers represent individuals with similar positions brought together deliberately (an active network) (Bayat 1997, 65).

Dangerous Mobilities: Roads and the Liminal Space of Driving

While roads remain one of the most distinctive signs of modernity, they are also spaces for dangerous mobilities. Nigerian roads in particular are liminal spaces embodying "all the basic contradictions of the experience of modernity itself, of its inescapable enticements, its self-consuming passions, its discriminatory tactics, its devastating social costs" (Comaroff and Comaroff 1993, xxix). For many Nigerians, traveling is a source of persistent fear, due mainly to the dangers associated with it. Many have lost their lives on Nigerian highways. Novelist Ben Okri (1992) graphically describes Nigerian roads as infrastructures that "swallow people." While roads bring jobs, consumer goods, economic freedom, and prospects, they are also sites of death and destruction (Soyinka 1965; Mbembe and Roitman 1995, 328). An age-old Yoruba saying describes roads as the "long coffin that holds fourteen hundred corpses." A columnist for the *Osun Defender* compared the scale of deaths caused by bad roads in southwest Nigeria to the Boko Haram insurgency that kills innocent lives on a regular basis. The columnist adduced the case of Lagos–Badagry Expressway, which has become a death trap in recent years.

> From Seme, the Nigeria-Benin Republic border to Volkswagen in Ojo local government area of Lagos State, there are over 10,000 potholes and several other valleys that are big enough to consume a car. Ordinarily, from Seme border to Mile 12 is not supposed to be more than 45 minutes for any vehicle speeding at the moderate of 80km per hour, but due to the horrible condition of the roads, commuters spend more than 4 to 5 hours lurking one another up in hundreds of the bad spots on the road. As a matter of fact, vehicles plying the road get spoilt so easy, thereby making owners spend lot of hard-earned money in repairing their vehicles. (*Osun Defender* 2012)

For many Nigerians, *achaba* drivers epitomize not only the dangers of road life but also the die-hard figure of the average Nigerian in times of crisis. Although *achaba* drivers have a reputation for recklessness, their labor fills a vital gap in spatial mobilities, providing door-to-door services, often on unpaved roads. In northern Nigeria, where both roadside and many off-road villages are in bad condition, *achabas* serve as a lifeline for villagers (Porter 2012, 8). The usage of *achabas* blurs the distinctions between public and private life. An *achaba* driver told me, "By using my motorcycle to take my children to school and my wife to market, I have been able to save more money and cater better for my family, as I do not have to pay the high bus fares for myself, my wife, and our children." Through *achabas*, people are also able to maintain networks of social communication and conviviality. But, despite the positive contributions of *achabas*, their contributions to urban insecurity have come to typify their workforce. Across Nigeria, most general hospitals have a dedicated "*achaba* ward," where victims of *achaba* incidents are treated. In Maiduguri's General Hospital, for example, the special "Jincheng Ward"—named after the popular Jincheng motorcycles—is dedicated to *achaba* victims. Hospital records show that 75 percent of corpses in the mortuary belonged to *achaba* drivers or passengers (*Dan-Borno* 2010). For many road transport workers, then, *achaba* work remains "a last resort because of the high risk involved in it. You could collide with a car, bus, tipper or trailer, or even your fellow *achaba* driver" (Abubakar 2015).

Motorcycle accidents are partly a result of unlicensed drivers on the road, most of whom received training "on the job" (Cervero 2000). They are also partly due to the influence of drug and alcohol abuse, speeding, and bad roads (Mburza and Umar 2008, 176). Many drivers do not deny driving under the influence; however, they claim that drugs and alcohol help them to manage stress and maintain a sense of control. Leaders of *achaba* unions often blame northern Nigeria's decrepit roads, rather than the recklessness of drivers, for frequent gridlocks and road accidents. The leader of an *achaba* association said, "Our problem here is that of roads. The roads the government built since 1982 have not been rehabilitated. The roads used by motorists are the ones used by *kura* people (cart pushers), *mai ruwa* people (water vendors), wheelbarrow pushers and my members, the *achaba* operators. And the roads are not wide enough to contain the vehicles. This is why you see this congestion. It is not caused by the population of my members alone. This is why a lot of road accidents involving my members happen" (Abubakar 2015). Despite the risks associated with using *achabas*, many Nigerians continue to use them for lack of a better alternative. In rural communities in Borno State, for example, women generally viewed *achabas* as indispensable when medical emergencies arise, particularly during the rainy season, when vehicles struggle to navigate muddy and pothole-stricken roads (Porter 2002).

Against the backdrop of delays, dangers, and blatant extortion, *achaba* drivers often find themselves "moving around with little reward" (Langevang and Gough 2009, 753). To make the most of their time, which is money, those transport operators must constantly find a way around bottlenecked roads. One way of doing so is through the driver's possession of context-specific knowledge and the art of making do (Bissell 2009, 188; Crang 2000, 150). Success involves knowing how to weave in and out or get around people and things, and "experience on, and familiarity with, the road gives rise to an array of dispositions and arts of negotiation that are constitutive of subjectivities of conflict" (Mbembe and Roitman 1995, 329, 340). The situation echoes what Caitlin Cahill (2000, 253) calls "street literacy," that is, an embodied knowledge of urban spaces and how to move around them under different conditions. Such street literacy requires extensive social networks through which drivers are able to gather information and resources (Evans et al. 2018, 683). Put differently, street literacy configures the road as "a site of bricolage that allows for both pragmatism and acts of imagination" (Masquelier 2019, 6).

Another way in which drivers negotiate the dangers of the road is through regular (paid) consultations with two sets of marabouts: *malaman tsibbu* and *malaman duba*. The former provide drivers with health advice, prayers, and charms (*laya*) that are widely believed to ward off evil spirits on the road and to guard against bribe-eating and trigger-happy soldiers and mobile police officers, highway robbers, and armed insurgents on roads more and less traveled. Many drivers, especially long-haul truckers, are concerned about the most favorable time to set out on a journey; hence, they seek knowledge and information from the *malaman duba* regarding safe travel and clearing (un)seen obstacles en route. The *malaman duba* uses his "knowledge of stars to cast horoscopes, prescribe ritualistic acts, say prayers, read verses from the Qur'an and give advice on the avoidance of certain places and people, together with the best time for departure . . . which enables them to . . . achieve success" (Swindell and Iliya 2012, 244).

The need to avert road dangers through divine intervention and fortification has a long history in West Africa. In her account of the social lives of Ghanaian drivers, Eugenia Date-Bah (1980, 525) found that owners of passenger vehicles were often "supplicants at shrines because of a paranoiac fear of failure, perceiving themselves as the objects of envy of those who wanted them to have financial disaster." Similarly, in her work on everyday security in Ghana, M. J. Field found that lorry owners are always conscious of themselves as objects of envy (1960, 134). As a result, they regularly take their lorries to shrines for protection against enemies of progress and purveyors of financial disasters. In Ben Okri's novel *The Famished Road* (1992), the social status of Madame Koto—the proprietor of a local bar and brothel, whose knack for business and friends in high places make her the most powerful person in the locality—is cemented when she acquires a new car. She approaches a traditional herbalist who promises that the car will bring prosperity and plenty of money.

> Anyone who thinks evil of you, may this car run them over in their sleep. This car will hunt out your enemies, pursue their bad spirits, grind them into the road. Your car will drive over fire and be safe. It will drive into the ocean and be safe. It has friends in the spirit world. Its friends there, a car just like this one, will hunt down your enemies. They will not be safe from you. A bomb will fall on this car and it will be safe. I have opened the road for this car. It will travel all roads. It will arrive safely at all destinations. (Okri 1992)

One study of the road experiences of Yoruba taxi drivers in southwest Nigeria found that 80 percent of Muslims and 60 percent of Christians displayed protective charms in their vehicles, a turn to symbolic action in the face of insecurities (Lawuyi 1988). For Lagos, the study found,

Armed robbers may attack and steal the vehicles. The roadside mechanic may have mistakenly connected two wires that could ignite and burn the vehicle. Nobody can predict when accidents will occur, as drivers in a hurry overtake dangerously. The *juju* [charm] in the vehicle serves to remind the drivers of their power to escape from any danger . . . make drivers disappear into thin air when accidents occur. Alternatively, they may prevent accidents. They also bring wealth by attracting passengers. Through their mystification the *juju* makes it possible for the individual to survive the disruptive processes created by national and international tensions, which affect economic processes. . . . The *juju* themselves are not mechanical. (Lawuyi 1988, 4)

Gendering Mobility: Motorcycles, Movement, and Morality

Doreen Massey emphasized the politics of mobility and access, arguing that "some are more in charge of it than others; some initiate flows and movement, others don't; some are more on the receiving end of it than others; some are effectively imprisoned by it" (1993, 61). That argument highlights two salient points: first, the close relationship between power relations and the production of space; second, the embeddedness of mobility within the political. I add a third point, the interconnectedness of mobility and morality. As David Morley argues, discussions about mobility tend to have moral overtones of one sort or another (2000, 238). All three points mentioned above are most exemplified by Nigeria's predominantly Muslim north, where mobility is, above all else, a fundamental space for the monitoring, enforcement, and safeguarding of public morality, especially of the social interactions between men and women.

Joshua Grace has argued that discourses about the physical limitations of women's automobility are "less about what women can do with motor vehicles and more about perceptions of what motor vehicles would do to women and, by extension, society" (2013, 414). The contested issue of women's right to use mass transportation services is most evident in the states of Kano and Zamfara. In those states, Sharia penal code is integrated into the criminal laws, and a vigilante group (*hisba*) exists to enforce the law (Adamu 2008, 148). In northern Nigeria, the popular practice of men and women sitting very close to each other on *achabas* or the notion of women sitting astride a motorcycle taxi was interpreted by authorities as an offense to public morality and decency. Husbands, in particular, disapproved of such type of iniquitous mobility. The acting director general of the Sharia Commission in Kano commented, "Everyone knows the type or manner in which women sit on motorcycles and it looks quite adulterous because women sit quite close to achaba riders with their bodies touching each other. If mere looking can lead to adultery, then the manner in which women sit on motorcycles can increase the rate of adultery" (*Weekly Trust*, cited in Adamu 2008, 148). That comment particularly reveals how the moral geographies of place and mobility interact to inscribe women motorcycle passengers with an "immoral intent" (Rana 2018, 264). Furthermore, it underscores a deep attitudinal culture in the predominantly Muslim north in which men typically arrogate control over women's morality and mobility, both of which are inextricably linked in local imagination; husbands, for example, generally forbade their wives from traveling far from home.

Restriction on women's travel distance is closely entwined with a dominant male ideology that women are likely to indulge in promiscuous activity in distant places where their identity is concealed or unknown (Porter 1995, 13). That notion reinforces the argument that "mobile things were masculine things" and that "women in motion were prostitutes" (Grace 2014, 415, 471). In rural Borno, women were generally prevented from traveling to the capital city of Maiduguri to purchase vital goods for resale, and the few women who engaged in such trade relied on their husbands or male relatives to obtain trade items for them. Women's success in trade was widely seen as dangerous because it gave them more freedom and independence (Porter 1995, 9). Yet, as shown by one study of transnational women traders in Kinshasa in the Democratic Republic of Congo, it is not so much a woman's financial independence that provokes moral anxiety; to the contrary, what draws "criticism, gossip and suspicion" (Braun 2019, 379) is the motility made possible by her extended social network (her ability to be mobile). Gina Porter has empirically shown how rural women's travel to distant places severely affected their reputation in Borno State, because of the close association of long-distance travel with immorality (2012, 6). Further afield, a study of the nexus between gender and mobility in Indonesia finds that post-1997 narratives of women's mobility have increasingly pivoted to normative judgments regarding young women's independent mobility and sexual behavior. The study shows that "tracing the shifting and contested meanings of 'good girls,' 'obedient daughters,' 'virtuous women,' and 'respectable places' . . . brings into focus the ways in which the cultural struggles over gender norms influence the causes and consequences of mobility" (Silvey 2000, 145).

In the case of the Nigerian states of Kano and Zamfara, women were banned from using *achabas*, and authorities proposed three alternatives: "first, to declare such an act as anti-sharia, and therefore to prohibit the practice; second, to provide women with an alternative means of transportation [i.e., tricycles and women-only buses]; and third, to encourage female motorcyclists" (Adamu 2008, 148). While the governments of Zamfara and Kano adopted the first two proposals, the third was quickly jettisoned as a further offense to public morality. In May 2004, the Kano State House of Assembly passed its Traffic Amendment Law, which forbade women from using *achabas*. The state then imported about sixteen hundred three-seater motorized rickshaws (known as *adaidaita sahu*, meaning "conforming to the right path"), which, unlike *achabas*, preserved the sexual segregation of men and women. The law punished defaulters with six-month imprisonment and a fine of N 5000 (US$37). A *hisba* group of nine thousand was inaugurated to stop all *achaba* drivers carrying women passengers unrelated to them. The *hisba* was entrusted with the powers to fine *achaba* drivers and confiscate their motorcycles. In that example, "we see not only how space is appropriated, used and managed, but the working out of an uneven citizenship and its contradictory features of inclusion and exclusion" (Monroe 2009, 263).

Over two thousand *achabas* were confiscated by the *hisba*, who often ordered women off them. A report by the Human Rights Watch alleges widespread abuses by the *hisba*, including summary and extrajudicial arrests and floggings, stopping vehicles carrying men and women and forcing the women to disembark, disrupting conversations between men and women in public places on the grounds of alleged immorality, the seizure and destruction of alcoholic drinks and the causing of damage to the vehicles transporting them, and the violation of the rights of people to privacy (Mustapha and Ismail 2016, 3). Excluded and enraged, *achaba* drivers and owners took to the streets in (violent) protest, attacking members of the *hisba* and setting fire to the state-endorsed tricycle taxis. That reaction reinforces the nexus between precarity and forms of sociopolitical agency. As Judith Butler tells us, when the bodies of those rendered disposable collect in public view, they are saying, "We have not slipped quietly into the shadows of public life; we have not become the glaring absence that structures your public life" (Puar 2012, 168).

The *achaba* protests were largely economically driven, as *achaba* drivers stood to lose substantial income if the law held. Women constituted the vast bulk of *achaba* passengers. Also, in barring women from riding with men, the law deepened the inequality between men and women. Merritt

Polk notes, "Despite the complexity of reasons underlying social inequali-ties, if social equality is the goal and spatial equality is the means then equal access to transportation technologies can be seen as a necessity" (1998, 208). The law banning *achaba* drivers from carrying women passengers met with such resistance that the governor at the time, Ibrahim Shekarau, had to relax it in his second term, to avoid alienating the large Muslim *achaba* constituency. Whether or not to carry women passengers was then left to each operator's conscience (Meagher 2018, 193).

Perceptions of Road Transport Workers

During my fieldwork, drivers of *achabas* and *keke napeps* often complained about disrespectful passengers and private car owners who viewed them as "common drivers," womanizers, or drug addicts. "People think we are use-less people," said Mohammed, a former *achaba* driver in Yola who now runs a *keke napep* business. "*Keke napeps* are sold at N 665,000 and motor vehicles sold at maybe N 700,000," he noted, "but the dilapidated car owner will shout at you saying, 'look at this useless man scratching and damaging my car with a *keke*.' This is despite the fact that the difference in the price of the two vehicles is really not much. In the event of an accident with a *keke napep*, people used to claim that the *keke napep* owners are rascals." Such negative perceptions partly explain why road transport workers struggle to construct a positive self-image based on the good characteristics and rewarding nature of the business. Many drivers see their business not as a "real trade" but as a provisional one that they do for lack of a better alter-native (cf. Olvera et al. 2016, 172). *Achaba* drivers I spoke to in northern Nigeria often maintained that they were only in the business because they had many (hungry) mouths to feed.

Beyond Nigeria, the negative perceptions of motorcyclists are widely documented. The United States is a case in point. From the 1960s onward, front pages of notable magazines such as the *New Yorker*, *Newsweek*, and *Time* were awash with images of rebel outlaw motorcycle gangs terroriz-ing placid communities (H. Thompson 1966, 38–39; Wolf 1991). In Hol-lywood movies, motorcyclists were portrayed as "Hell's Angels," "Wild Angels," "Angels Unchained," and "Hell's Bellies." In the novel *In Cold Blood* (1966), by American author Truman Capote, the depiction of the psychotic murderous personality of Perry Smith, the crazed killer, relied heavily on Smith's apparently having been a motorcyclist (Maxwell 1998, 274). Study-ing motorcyclists in postindustrial urban America, Andrew Maxwell found that "perhaps the most powerful, and inaccurate, constraint in delimiting the motorcycle community is the assumption of non-riders that all motorcyclists are, were, or potentially can be, rebellious outlaw bikers" (1998, 273). Along a similar line, in his *Mobility without Mayhem*, Packer argues that the popular imagination of motorbikes in the United States as inherently "risky" derives from an implicit and fluid notion of riders as "dirty, rough-neck, outlaw types" (2008, 125). He further argues that the popularity of motorbikes among youth (particularly young men) in the 1960s spawned public concerns about the dangers associated with bike riding. Consequently, blatant "discrimination and police brutality against bikers" were "often masked as safety concerns" (Packer 2008, 129; Macek 2006).

Jennifer Hart (2016) describes how public transport in Ghana is dominated by young men generally framed as "criminals, cheats, and bad citizens." Historian Kenda Mutongi (2006, 549) argues that drivers of *matatus* (minibus taxis) in Kenya were commonly seen by commuters and Kenyans of all ranks as "political thugs who exploited and mistreated passengers and participated in gang or mafia-like violence." Matteo Rizzo points to the permanent everyday discourse in Tanzania's Dar es Salaam that criminalizes drivers of *dala dalas* (minibus taxis), blaming them for the dysfunctionalities of public transport (2011, 1187). Mariama Khan describes how cross-border drivers in Senegambia were often subjected to social stereotypes, epitomized by the Wolof saying that "the *chauffeur* [driver] is not dependable" (2018, 113). In Togo, there is a certain social stigma linked to driving motorcycle taxis (*oléyia*), which explains why it is often seen as a temporary way of making ends meet (Olvera et al. 2016, 172). In South Africa, drivers of *kombi* taxis are "caricatured as notoriously aggressive, arrogant and paranoid" (Czegledy 2004, 80). In African countries that have endured bloody civil wars (e.g., Liberia and Sierra Leone), motorcycle work provides unskilled former combatants with a regular source of income, "without calming the fears of a resurgence of past violence" (Olvera et al. 2016, 166).

Ironically, the vast majority of road transport workers in northeast Nigeria resented their bad image as *yan tasha* (motor park touts), which they interpreted as an affront on their social persons and livelihoods. Those drivers described themselves as respectable and responsible citizens who are often victims of security force harassment and prejudiced public opinion. In the states of Borno, Yobe, and Adamawa, the susceptibility of drivers to abuses from security forces—including extortion, coercion, delay, and shootings—have only escalated following their suspected links to Boko Haram. For drivers there, fear and insecurity have become a way of life.

Moving beyond the origin of motorcycle taxis and the figure of the commercial motorcyclist in (northern) Nigeria, the next chapter shifts analytical focus to the social dynamics of Boko Haram. Particular attention is put on that group's mobilization of immobile and disaffected local youth, especially the peripatetic Koranic boys popularly known as the *almajirai* (sing. *almajiri*). Many *achaba* drivers were previously *almajirai* and used to beg for alms at motor parks and bus stops across northern Nigerian cities. A popular response during my interviews with *achaba* drivers in the states of Borno, Yobe, and Adamawa was "I started from Koranic school and ended up as a driver." That fact is generally missing in most analyses of the *almajirai* that harp excessively on its coming anarchy.

TWO

Local Immobility and Mobilization into Boko Haram

Radical Islamist movements in Africa generally draw their recruits from two primary constituencies, the disaffected urban poor and the pious middle class (Kane 2003). The former are marked by precarity and lack of social mobility—what Murray Last (2012) calls material and spiritual insecurity—while the latter are alienated from power structures (Bayat 2007; Lubeck 1985). Simply put, alienation and frustration are central to the appeal of Islamism among urban youth (Kepel 1994, 249). A prime example of that appeal is visible in Egypt, where rapid urban growth without equal opportunities for social mobility—which was available to earlier generations—created potential constituencies for religious (Islamic) radicalism among urban youth (Eickelman and Piscatori 1996, 117). Consequently, urban youth with blocked social mobility and limited capacity to aspire pushed for "a comeback to a puritanical and egalitarian way of life, reducing the social gap by taking from the rich and giving to the poor, lowering the overall level of expectations, and thus limiting tensions and bitterness" (Sivan 1985, 126).

Islamic scholar Ousmane Kane contends that "urban youth tend to be attracted to anti-establishment ideology" and that they "nourish the full range of human desires—material, moral and spiritual. In a world that curtails their autonomy and blocks their aspirations, they strive with the means at their disposal to affirm and consolidate their existence in the world" (2003, 230–31). That argument is confirmed in northern Nigeria, where reformative Islamic ideologies led by major Islamist organizations—

including Yan Izala, Tijaniyya, Qadiriyya, Jama'atu Nasril Islam, Maitatsine, and Boko Haram—continue to weaponize marginalized young men and women with an anti-establishment ideology. For many un(der) employed youth in northern Nigeria, the failure of Western-imposed institutions (*boko*) to satisfy their material and spiritual needs inspired them to embrace the path of societal purification and reform (*tajdid*).

Across West and Central Africa, Islamist reformist organizations have deliberately targeted or appealed to the poor and marginalized in urban and rural communities, including young women. With little hope for upward mobility, marginalized youths are often inclined to ideologies that hold the promise of a better life, in this world or the next. A prime example from West Africa is the Katiba Machina. As one of the most influential jihadist movements in central Mali, the Katiba Machina has targeted the most vulnerable in society,

> offering them a means of escaping a situation of despair and directionlessness to the dead certainty of violent resistance. By seeking to recruit in the poorest and least educated areas, they target destitute young men some of whom perceive that they do not have anything to lose by joining the movement as combatants, and are considered to be more malleable to religious indoctrination. (Rupesinghe and Boas 2019, 9)

Jihadist movements aside, Rene Lemarchand has argued that a fundamental social reality that generated the disasters of the African Great Lakes region has much to do with the emergence of a huge class of "masterless men," a social category by which he means "excluded youth in an economically stagnant region, who have been the foot-soldiers of war as well as the diggers of minerals" (cited in Trapido 2015). Addressing the mobilities of youths in waithood, particularly their physical mobilities and their representations, can result in "mobilization towards collective claim-making as well as individual attempts to achieve social mobility" (Jaffe et al. 2012, 644). The bottom line is that mobility and mobilization are mutually reinforcing.

Following a discussion of the origins of Boko Haram, starting with the Maitatsine uprisings, this chapter focuses on how Boko Haram mobilized a social category of disaffected and locally (im)mobile youth in northeast Nigeria, with emphasis on the *almajirai* (peripatetic Koranic students). My overriding objective here is to demonstrate how mobility and mobilization are deeply intertwined in the context of insurgency and how local (im) mobility is a tool not only of political mobilization (e.g., Sopranzetti 2014, 122) but also of insurgent mobilization and the diffusion of violence. As noted in the preceding chapter, many operators of *achaba* were once *almajirai* who begged for alms at motor parks, before transitioning into informal jobs as "motor boys" (bus conductors) and then "masters" (drivers/owners). In chapter 1, I focused on the origins of *achabas* and the immobilization of *achaba* drivers. In the present chapter, I expand that focus by looking at the figure of the *almajirai*. Like *achaba* drivers, the *almajirai* are linked closely (if dubiously) to the Boko Haram crisis (Hoechner 2018). Many Boko Haram fighters are said to have come directly from the *almajirai* and the Kanuri community (C. Cohen 2015), although it is clear that many non-Kanuri persons have joined the group.

The *almajirai* are exclusively young boys who find themselves in an environment of limited opportunities for economic survival and social becoming. They are seasonal migrants (*yan ci rani*) who move from rural to urban areas in search of livelihood opportunities. Like *achaba* drivers, the *almajirai* linger at the bottom of Nigerian society; they are not only stigmatized as dirty workers but also scapegoated as Boko Haram's foot soldiers. In examining the *almajirai* and their relationship with Boko Haram, it is necessary to shed light on how the experience of local immobility often compels marginal men to join armed opposition groups as a way of economic survival and social recognition. It is important to precede that analysis with discussion of the precursors of Boko Haram in northern Nigeria.

The Maitatsine Uprising, 1980–85

Between December 1980 and April 1985, several cities in northern Nigeria experienced disturbances between a millennial sect called Maitatsine and the Nigeria Police Force. The violent uprisings were led by Muhammed Marwa (also known as Maitatsine), a one-eyed Islamic *mallam* (teacher) who migrated from the border town of Jappai in northern Cameroon and settled in Yan Awaki Ward in Kano State sometime in the 1940s. There, Marwa became an Islamic zealot intent on purifying Islam, which, in his view, had come under the corrupting influence of modernization and westernization (Hickey 1984, 251). The Maitatsine uprising bears the hallmarks of the Islamic millennial tradition, and of the Mahdist movement, which was a central factor in the nineteenth-century history of Islam in the northern region (Clarke and Linden 1984, 109; Loimeier 1997). Marwa vehemently opposed the Sufi Tijaniyya and Qadiriyya brotherhoods, calling their members *kafir* (infidels). He would say to them, "Wanda bata yard ba Allah ta Tchine" (May Allah curse he who disagrees with His version). Nigerian historian Toyin Falola describes Marwa as a Koranic preacher with an eccentric personality.

> Forceful, persuasive, and charismatic, Marwa rebelled against many opinions popular in Kano Islamic circles, denouncing certain parts of the Holy Quran and even criticizing the Prophet Mohammed. Opposed to most aspects of modernization and to all Western influence, he decried such common technologies as radios, wristwatches, automobiles, motorcycles, and even bicycles. Those who use these things or who read books other than the Quran were viewed as hellbound "pagans." (Falola 1998, 146)

As eccentric as Marwa's personality was, his message and methods did not necessarily constitute a radical departure from those of previous Islamic movements (Pham 2006), such as the Jama'at Izalat al Bid'a Wa Iqamat as Sunna (Society of Removal of Innovation and Reestablishment of the Sunna), Yan Izala for short,[1] a reformist Islamist movement founded by anti-Sufi and Salafist leader Sheikh Abubakar Gumi. In Kano, Marwa attracted commoners, *talakawas*, with his radical message that not only denounced (as *kafir*) affluent local elites, including rulers (*saratua*) and big men (*manya-manya*), but also opposed Western (*boko*) influence and secular authorities (Lubeck 1985; Hickey 1984, 253).

The social base of Maitatsine's following of well over six thousand members consisted predominantly of the *almajirai*, the nomadic Koranic boys who attach themselves to any learned *mallam* in a time-honored tradition of apprenticeship. The rural-urban migration of the *almajirai* typically followed seasonal agricultural patterns: "As dry season job opportunities (reliant on higher rainfall levels) die out, expectations change and harvest become even more unpredictable, many people are seeking alternative ways of ensuring food security and meeting their cash needs. Given the dearth of off-farm income possibilities in much of the rural Sahel, people travel to towns or centers of economic activity to earn money" (Oppong 2017). In Hausa, seasonal migrants are referenced as *masu abinchin rani* ("men who eat away in the dry season") and are called *yan ci rani*. In a less common sense, seasonal migration may be seen as a rite of passage for young adult males—*yan tuma da gora*, which refers to "sons who jump with a gourd"[2]—known among the Hausa as *yawon dandi*, the walk of the world (Swindell and Iliya 2012, 243; Olofson 1976). Unlike the Western *flaneur*—the detached observer and gentleman stroller of modern city life emblematic of nineteenth-century French literary culture—the *masu abin-chi rani* had a dual advantage: "The young men would leave the village and go to the town to earn their living thus leaving fewer people at home to eat the grain remaining from the previous harvest. In the town, the young men would practice an occupation (perhaps one they had already learned), get temporary work or engage in trading. If they could, they would send money or goods (e.g., seeds or tools) to the family in the village, thus supporting the family at home" (McIntyre 2014, 109).

Similar migratory habits occur in interior parts of West Africa, such as Burkina Faso, where persistent socio-economic pressures at home and opportunities at the places of destination inspired young men to wander (Anarfi 1995, 70, cited in Oppong 2017). Such wandering should be separated, however, from the popular practice of "stuck" and seemingly idle young men in Niger, who spend most of their time at the *fada*, a "youths-cape" where young men waiting to be employed and to start earning wages assemble to forge new spaces of sociability and belonging (Masquelier 2019, 3). The figure of the *almajiri* in Nigeria bears a striking resemblance to that of a nomad as defined by Rosi Braidotti.

> The nomad does not stand for homelessness, or compulsive displacement; it is rather a figuration for the kind of subject who has relinquished all idea, desire, or nostalgia for fixity. This figuration expresses the desire for an identity made of transitions, successive shifts, and coordinated changes, without and against an essential unity. The nomadic subject, however, is not altogether devoid of unity; his/her mode is one of definite, seasonal patterns of movement through rather fixed routes. It is a cohesion engendered by repetitions, cyclical moves, rhythmical displacement. (Braidotti 1994, 23)

In the late 1970s, Nigeria experienced a major decline in its rural world, to the extent that many *almajirai*, who ordinarily remained in urban areas only for the duration of the dry season, began to settle there (Lubeck 1981).[3] That tendency shows how staying put can become a source of social mobility (E. Jackson 2012). No culture is in stasis, and traveling and dwelling exist in a complex, interdependent relationship (Clifford 1997). Marwa is said to have recruited from that large and ready reservoir of "displaced yet morally self-conscious" *almajirai* (Lubeck 1985, 371) straining to maintain a dignified and purposeful life against multiple odds. To those *yan ci rani*, Marwa offered shelter, security, camaraderie, and alternative ways of socially navigating the city. Although the Nigerian military eventually suppressed the Maitatsine uprising, hundreds more people died in reprisal riots over the next five years, especially in the states of Kaduna, Yola, and Gombe (Kane 2003, 98–99; Tamuno 1991).

The similarities between Maitatsine and Boko Haram are striking, prompting one of Nigeria's former heads of state (1966–75), General Yakubu Gowon, to describe Boko Haram as "a disturbing repeat of the 1980 Maitatsine Uprising" (Public Library of US Diplomacy 2009d). The leaders of both anti-establishment groups built a strong reputation among the *talakawas* as radical Muslim preachers capable of challenging a hopelessly corrupt ruling elite in Nigeria. Like Maitatsine, which set up a separate community disdaining modernity and globalization, Boko Haram established a revolutionary Islamic community, in rural Kanama in Yobe State in 2003–4. From there, Boko Haram launched deadly attacks on police stations (Higazi 2015, 306). Both Marwa and Mohammed Yusuf, the founder of Boko Haram, resented abuses by security forces, and after those leaders were extrajudicially killed, their followers launched a "holy war." That war's reprisal attacks suggest that the use of brute force to quell dissenting voices only fuels "self-righteous revenge" among remnants of the suppressed groups (Last 2014, 50). Murray Last (2014) argues that Maitatsine and Boko Haram represent the continuation of a long tradition of dissidents; those organizations are not a new phenomenon, nor will they be the last of their kind. Notably, both Maitatsine and Boko Haram originated in an urban environment, departing from the rural impetus of earlier uprisings (Thurston 2018). Irrespective of their incoherent objectives and brutal methods, Africa's postcolonial rebel movements are symptomatic of an urgent urban malaise that needs to be addressed (Mkandawire 2002, 181).

Similarities aside, Maitatsine and Boko Haram also exhibit significant points of departure. At the theological level, the Boko Haram movement is distinct from Maitatsine, the founder of which developed idiosyncratic readings of the Koran and claimed to be a prophet (Thurston 2018, 25). John Paden observed another distinction between the two groups, arguing that unlike adherents of the Maitatsine movement, Boko Haram followers embrace technology, as seen in their dependence on motorbikes, automatic weapons, and information media. Further, Boko Haram espouses a fundamental orthodox theology, as opposed to the extreme beliefs of Maitatsine, which promotes a brand of Islam even more reactionary than that of the fundamentalists (Paden 2012, 47).

The Emergence of Boko Haram

The first generation of Boko Haram was largely comprised of sons of the social upper class with an aversion for Western education (*boko*). The current iteration of Boko Haram—known as the cult of Yusuffiya prior to 2009—is a continuation of northern Nigeria's long tradition of dissent and dissidence (Last 2014), which thrives on mobilizing commoners against un-Islamic and anti-Islamic systems (Thurston 2018, 2). The charismatic Salafi preacher Mohammed Yusuf—born in Yobe State on January 29, 1970—founded Boko Haram in 2002 near the Maiduguri Railway Terminus, with the goal of setting up an Islamic caliphate that was strictly administered based on Sharia. Boko Haram is an offshoot of Ahlus Sunna, a Nigerian network set up by graduates of the Islamic University in Medina and devoted to teaching and implementing the Wahhabi *da'wa* (missionary call) against the traditional scholars and the Sufi orders, as well as to lobbying politicians for the implementation of Sharia in public life (Brigaglia 2012b, 37).

Yusuf was educated in the tradition of the Yan Izala Islamic reform movement. Established in 1978 in the city of Jos by Shaikh Ismaila Idris, with funding from Saudi Arabia, the Yan Izala originally sought to fight what it perceived to be the un-Islamic innovations (*bid'a*) of the established Sufi orders in northern Nigeria. The groundwork for the Yan Izala was laid by the influential Shaikh Abubakar Gumi who, beginning in the 1960s, publicly eschewed Sufism and called for a return to Islamic puritanism. Following Gumi's death in 1992, intra-Salafi competition led the Yan Izala to splinter into several movements with varying levels of motivations and tolerances for a modern secular state (Kane, 2003: 122). From the 1990s, the Yan Izala saw the rise of a second-generation of young (and middle-aged) scholars, the vast majority of whom had studied at Medina thanks to generous scholarships from Saudi Arabia. This generation returned to northern Nigeria with high hopes, only to find the first generation of Gumi's followers still dominating the Izala hierarchy, occupying fundamental positions of teaching and leading prayers. These second-generation, returnee scholars were frustrated that their "Yan-Izala-style" modern Islamic education neither translated into leadership positions within the Yan Izala nor gainful career opportunities outside of it. Growing intergenerational tensions within the Yan Izala compelled several young generation scholars to withdraw from Gumi's Yan Izala to establish their own independent clusters and to compete for followers in a crowded religious "marketplace." These scholars leveraged the prestige of their Saudi Arabia education, especially their fluency in spoken Arabic and erudition in Salafi and Wahhabi doctrines, to build a strong social base (Thurston, 2016: 10; Loimeier, 2012: 145).

Yusuf was a student of Ja'far Mahmoud Adam, an influential Kano-based Izala sheikh in the Islamic Movement of Nigeria. Like Ja'far, Yusuf was very much part of Nigeria's wave of Islamic reform. "This was a man that is very knowledgeable in Islamic Fiqh, Hadiths, and Jurisprudence with a clear voice that people enjoy listening to," said Muhammed, a former student of Ja'far in Kano, whom I met in Maiduguri. Muhammed explained, "He was an *ulama* (teacher) that doesn't accuse anyone, no matter your sect, orientation or belief. These were some of the reasons that youths generally leaned towards learning from him."

As a representative of Ahlus Sunna in Maiduguri between 1999 and 2002, Yusuf was a familiar face on local television and radio, where he preached and delivered lectures. In 1994, he was appointed emir of the Movement for the Revival of Islam, a campaign critical of both the traditional Muslim leadership under the sultan of Sokoto and new modernizing groups such as Yan Izala. Even to this day, most Nigerian Salafis are vehemently opposed to Boko Haram (Thurston 2018, 24). By 1999, Yusuf was appointed to Borno State's Sharia Implementation Committee. He soon became critical of how Sharia was managed by the committee, which he accused of corruption and apostasy (*Vanguard* 2009): "Yusuf had developed a 'rejectionist' position according to which the present, government-run Sharia courts are illegitimate because they operate under a non-Islamic, secular government" (Brigaglia 2012b, 38). While Ja'far and Yusuf shared an ideology rooted in the Salafi/Wahhabi *da'wa*, the two would eventually split on matters of strategy. Yusuf's rejectionist position seemed too extreme to Ja'far, and to many others in the Ahlus Sunna, who ultimately believed that Sharia needed to be enacted within the legitimate government. Having interviewed Ja'far in 2002 (before he was murdered in April 13, 2007, by gunmen reportedly sent by Yusuf), Andrea Brigaglia explains,

> Ja'far was in fact engaged in pushing towards an increased Islamization of the political institutions of the country, while Mohammed Yusuf advocated the necessity of a radical withdrawal from anything related to the Nigerian state, including working for the police, participating in the government, working in the administration of Sharia within the framework of the state, and studying in formal educational institutions (hence the nickname Boko Haram,

i.e., "modern education is forbidden," that the movement involuntarily gained after it started to preach against attending government
schools and universities). (2012a, 22)

Following the split from Ja'far, Yusuf founded Boko Haram in 2002.
The group initially adopted the moniker "Nigerian Taliban" and set up
a camp in rural Kanama in Yobe State, at the edge of the Sahara Desert,
which it dubbed "Afghanistan." Those name choices indicate some level of
ideological influence from jihadist groups such as Al-Qaeda and the Taliban, and followers of Yusuf self-consciously imitated the dress and public
image of those groups and combined Salafi puritanism with utopian ideal-
ism (Watts 2018). "When Boko Haram started expanding," a resident of
Maiduguri told me, "we noticed changes in their mode of dressing with
turban, long robes, ankle-length trousers and something like a petticoat,
similar to what people in Afghanistan and the Middle East used to wear.
They carried backpacks, and we don't know what's inside. These bags were
like children schoolbags."

Like Maitatsine, Boko Haram was a product of an intolerant and austere
Salafist strand challenging the Sufi hegemony that began in West Africa
in the 1970s (Mustapha 2015).[4] The name by which Boko Haram members self-identify, Jama'atu Ahl as-Sunnah Lidda'awatih Wal-Jihad, signals
a rejection of the Western-style modernity that underpins the Nigerian
government. Yusuf said, "We are for jihad, and our jihad is meant to put
an end to democracy, to western education and civilization. The jihad is
intended to make us return to the original state of Islam" (Zenn et al. 2013,
50). Before his extrajudicial death in police custody on July 30, 2009, Yusuf
noted, "Western education is mixed with issues that run contrary to our
true beliefs in Islam. . . . Our land was an Islamic caliphate before the British colonialists turned it to an infidel land. The current system is contrary
to true Islamic beliefs" (*Daily Trust* 2009). As part of his Salafi teachings,
Yusuf sought to return to the Quran and Hadith as the source and acme of
knowledge, which is reflected in his assessment of Western vaccines.

For Yusuf, modern vaccines are not better than Prophetic medicine,
adding that "black seed," the water from the Zam-zam well near the
Ka'ba in Mecca, and olive oil are Islamically proven medications. He
also stated that he had read on the Internet that modern vaccines
have side effects; hence prophetic medicine is better than modern
vaccines. Here Yusuf seems to be echoing the rejection of polio vac-
cination by some Muslims. Yusuf grandly declared these medical

concepts and theories contrary to Quran and Sunna; learning them [or using them] is thus haram [forbidden]. (Anonymous 2012, 125, cited in Renne 2014, 474)

Until his murder, Ja'far distanced himself from the extremist drift that he realized Yusuf's Boko Haram was taking. In his published speech "Boko da aikin gwamnati ba haramun ba ne," Ja'far clarified the permissibility of studying in public institutions and working for the state (Brigaglia 2012a, 22). Muhammed Abdullahi, the former director of the Religious Affairs Ministry in Borno State, maintains that the ministry considered Yusuf to be "overzealous" and often encouraged him to "calm down" (Public Library of US Diplomacy 2009d).

Boko, *Yan Boko*, and the Sokoto Caliphate

Boko Haram originally emerged as a protest against political corruption and bad governance in northern Nigeria, which the movement sought to remedy through a demand for an Islamic state under strict Sharia law (Meagher 2014, 2). In the eyes of the sect, Nigeria's woes are traceable to its *yan boko*, who are viewed as morally bankrupt and growing rich at the expense of the *talakawas*. In Hausa morphology, the word *boko* implies "sham, fraud, deceit or lack of authenticity" (P. Newman 2013, 2). According to Murray Last (2012), "The 'boko' in Boko Haram refers not to western education (as all the western media repeat unthinkingly) but to the westernized lifestyles, the materialistic ethics of a governing elite that have for decades systematically 'stolen' the revenues from the nation's oil account, and left the common people despite the nation's huge wealth, persistently poor without proper schools, clinics, jobs. . . . 'Boko' thus comes also to mean sham or fake, standing for all that's pseudo, or simply lies, in a westernized 'modernity.'" The term *yan boko* means "child of the book" and is used to describe the elite class created by the British colonial policy of indirect rule in Nigeria. Andrew Walker uses the term to describe "the people who have their heads turned away from Allah by easy money and corrupting Western values" (2012, 7). To be *yan boko* is to be spiritually and morally corrupt, lacking in religious piety, and guilty of enriching oneself rather than dedicating oneself to the Muslim *umma* (community). Not only are the *yan boko* seen as the root of Nigeria's problem, but their Western education is troubled. According to a statement by the Boko Haram leadership, the sect is against not only Western education but also Western culture and civilization, as the latter is encompassing of the former.

Boko Haram does not in any way mean "Western Education is a sin" as the infidel media continue to portray us. Boko Haram actually means "Western Civilization" is forbidden. The difference is that while the first gives the impression that we are opposed to formal education that gives the impression that we are opposed to formal education coming from the West, that is Europe, which is not true, the second affirms our believe [*sic*] in the supremacy of Islamic culture (not Education), for culture is broader, it includes education but not determined by Western Education. In this case we are talking of Western ways of life which include: constitutional provision as it relates to, for instance the rights and privileges of women, the idea of homosexualism, lesbianism, sanctions in cases of terrible crimes like drug trafficking, rape of infants, multi-party democracy in an overwhelmingly Islamic country like Nigeria, blue films, prostitution, drinking beer and alcohol and many others that are opposed to Islamic civilization. (*Vanguard* 2009)

Between 1804 and 1808, Sheikh Usman Dan Fodio waged the Sokoto (Fulani) Jihad[5] across a series of emirates, against what he perceived as the corrupt and apostate Hausa ruling elite of his time. Dan Fodio decried the prevalence of exploitative taxes and oppressive practices among officials of the *sarkis*—the sovereign authority on which the political, judicial, and military powers of the Hausa were invested—which he perceived as unjust and alien to *da al-Islam*, or "true Islam" (Vaughan 2016, 18). Such practices are described in his *Kitab al-Farq*, in which he accuses the Hausa ruling elites of imposing illegal taxation on the people, including *jangali* (cattle taxes), *gaisuwa* (the giving of bribes to superiors—e.g., judges), *tawasa* (levies on meat in markets), *kamuwa* (illicit appropriation of property), *agama* (all other market levies), and *gargadi* (obligatory military services commutable for cash and inflated titles) (M. Smith 1964, 171; Crowder 1962, 95). Described by Last (2014, 18) as the most successful religious protest movement in northern Nigeria, Dan Fodio's jihad culminated in the Sokoto Caliphate, a confederation of Muslim emirates that became arguably the most powerful economic and political system of the central Sudan during the nineteenth century.

Extending from north of Agades, across from west of Niamey to east of Kano, and south to Ilorin, the Sokoto Caliphate played a central role in the Islamization of northern Nigeria. To this day, the legacy of that caliphate resonates broadly among northern Nigerians, so much so that radical Islamic movements such as Maitatsine, Yan Izala, and Boko Haram exploit its history and memory to legitimize and gain traction for their cause, or "to ground ideology in local context" (Barkindo 2016; Loimeier 1997, 3–4). Mohammed Yusuf and his successor, Abubakar Shekau, have lauded Dan Fodio (a committed Qadiri Sufi) in their preachings, perhaps because "Dan Fodio's support for jihad and his rigid interpretations of Islamic law suited their own understanding of the place of Islam in the region" (MacEachern 2019, 160–61). Boko Haram has mobilized not only local jihad but also global jihad for local and national purposes. Olivier Walther and William Miles observe, "The rise of Boko Haram provides a clear illustration of how an extremist group can exploit local memories and historical narratives related to the Kanem-Borno Empire to ground ideology in a local context, while at the same time claiming allegiance to the Islamic State and its Pan-Islamist vision of a unified Muslim world" (2018, 2).

Mobilization into Boko Haram: Disaffected Youth as a Social Base

In early March 2015, Boko Haram leader Shekau pledged allegiance (*bayat*) to ISIS and its late "caliph" Abu Bakr al-Baghdadi, leading to the creation of Wilayat Gharb Ifriquiya, or the Islamic State West Africa Province (ISWAP). ISWAP would later split with Boko Haram, citing Shekau's "indiscriminate bombings and shootings that took the largest toll on civilians rather than the security forces. ISWAP's propaganda promotes the idea that Muslim civilians are safe with them" (Anyadike 2019). Contra to the cult of Yusuffiya, which enjoyed significant popular support, the targeting of fellow Muslims under Shekau has reduced local support for Boko Haram. Although there are indications that Boko Haram had some connections within the ruling and big-men strata of society comprised of rulers and big men, most Yusuffiya were young men from the grassroots level (Paden 2012, 50), including *achaba* drivers, cobblers, petty traders, security guards (*mai-gadi*), load carriers (*daukan kata*), water hawkers (*mai-ruwa*), the guild of shoe recyclers (*katsa katsa kimaka*), and the *almajirai*. The bulk of those immobilized youth belonged to the Kanuri—the major ethnolinguistic group in Borno State. They were mostly "marginalized people with little education, or lower middle-class elements with some education but with few prospects in the oppressive competition and corruption of Nigerian society" (Mustapha 2012). Boko Haram is not only a religious sect but also a "class-based movement" that largely garners support by pulling at the heartstrings of millions of people who feel marginalized and excluded by the Nigerian state (Hansen 2016, 85–86; Cooke 2016).

Boko Haram's social base also includes Nigerian graduates without gainful jobs. Those graduates openly expressed their anger by tearing up their diplomas and denouncing Western technology while dedicating themselves to Sharia. Regarding Boko Haram's followers, a respondent in one empirical study of Boko Haram noted, "They are frustrated; they . . . have a degree but cannot find jobs. They see the successful and rich people and resent them. They want to kill them" (Botha and Abdile 2017, 501). For those disaffected youth, joining Boko Haram gave them a means of economic survival and a sense of belonging and purpose. The frustration with *boko*, especially its failed promise of gainful work, is a shared experience among youths across the Lake Chad region, who see formal (Western) education as rarely translating into financial protection. While Boko Haram certainly appealed to marginalized and powerless persons in society, its early origins are not to be found among such groups. As MacEachern reminds us,

> The predecessors of Boko Haram, the so-called Nigerian *Taleban*, counted as members a number of young people from wealthy and well-connected Kanuri families from northeast Nigeria. These included the nephew of the governor of the neighboring Yobe state, the son of a high-ranking official in Borno state government, and five sons of Alhaji Kambar Adam, a wealthy contractor in Borno, one of whom ultimately became a high-ranking leader of Boko Haram. These young men were not *achaba*, impoverished motortaxi drivers, or poor farmers . . . , although by the late 2000s [the group] certainly appealed to such people in and around Maiduguri, in large part because of the preaching of Mohammed Yusuf. (2018, 178)

That account supports a 2018 report by the International Crisis Group (ICG), which found that recruits to violent groups generally show enormous diversity, "from *madrasa* students to upper middle-class youth at private universities" (22). Notably, many marginal and idle (Kanuri) men who joined Boko Haram were lured and recruited from the Maiduguri Railway Terminus at the border of the Mafoni District, where Yusuf retreated following his ideological differences and conflict with his teacher Ja'far. Once thriving, that railway terminal lay fallow after years of closure, with some parts occupied by internally displaced persons. A few meters away from the terminal lies the rubble of the birthplace of Boko Haram. Historian Corentin Cohen (2015) contends that "as rural Kanuri migrated to the city in the 1980s and 1990s, informal settlements sprang up along old train tracks. As

Fig. 3. Maiduguri Railway Terminus. (Photograph by Daniel E. Agbiboa.)

the city transformed and densified, these populations could not combine
urban jobs with subsistence farming on the city's outskirts. Furthermore,
they lacked the skills needed to integrate. This acculturation explains the
low social status that Kanuri hold in Maiduguri and their subsequent overrepresentation in Boko Haram's ranks." Maiduguri's Railway Terminus is a
place where "for decades, hordes of young people who have been uprooted
from their homelands deep in the bush have ended up" (Seignobos 2016).

That many Boko Haram members were recruits at a transit space like
the railway station is hardly a coincidence. Under colonial administration
in northern Nigeria, railway stations were seen as primary sites of "sub-
version, labor activism, and crime" (Ochonu 2009, 80), because "colonial
railroads allowed for strikes and the concentration of the working class in
urban centers, where they could disrupt political systems and bring about
revolutions" (Menoret 2019, 140). In the postcolonial era, the train has
become a locus of terror. Marian Aguiar argues that the cultural process
of terror converges on the very image of the train: "The icon of the railway belongs to a collective, transnational cultural consciousness that has
long cast the railway as the scene or agent in nightmarish scenarios" (2011,
153). Across urban Africa, transit spaces are among the most vibrant spaces
of everyday politics and socioeconomic activity. At the same time, transit
spaces are "non-places," spaces characterized by anonymity and deperson-
alization (Auge 2009). Bus and train stations represent "gateways between
urban and rural areas; they are sites of political contestation and popular
mobilization; they serve as nodal points for the circulation of value, knowl-

edge, meaning, and ideology; and they provide large numbers of people with a place to hear news, meet friends, and find shelter. In short, like marketplaces, they are loaded with social, economic, political, and cultural significance" (Stasik and Cissoko 2018, viii).

Boko Haram's pattern of mobilizing a youth underclass reproduces the established practices of marauding gangs and bandits in the Chad Basin (i.e., the *coupeurs de route*, or "road cutters"), who mainly recruit rootless young men from pastoralist communities and urban marginals without prospects (MacEachern 2018, 140). During fieldwork in Yola, I asked Aliyu, leader of the Vigilante Group of Nigeria, why Boko Haram exists. His response was particularly illuminating. He explained,

> My thinking is around three things: economic reasons, social reasons, and religious reasons. The economic reasons have to do with poverty and joblessness, because the majority of Boko Haram members are unemployed local youth. And, as you know, an idle mind is the devil's workshop. Second, it has to do with social issues. A lot of social vices are happening, including drug addiction, criminality, gangsterism, and so on. All this also contributed to the formation of Boko Haram and its ability to recruit. And on the religious aspect, there is this religious intolerance. You will often hear one Muslim calling another Muslim a non-Muslim, thereby making him vulnerable to all sorts of dangers. And it was tolerated. So, the differences that existed within the religious circles are also a key reason why Boko Haram emerged.

Most prominent among the marginal groups to join Boko Haram were *achaba* drivers, described as people who survive at the bottom of society: "They are men (and only men) without much formal education, often without any other marketable skill. Many sleep rough, under bridges or awnings, some sleep on their motorcycles, guarding their source of income" (Walker 2016). In 2012–13, one-third of all motorcycle smugglers operating along the Cameroon-Nigeria borders were Boko Haram (Seignobos 2015, 96). For many youths living from hand to mouth, joining Boko Haram offered one of the few routes out of poverty. Nigeria's case is neither new nor sui generis. On the politics of slums and Islamic militancy in the Middle East, sociologist Asef Bayat argues that "poverty and precarious life, together with anomie and lawlessness, condition the dispossessed to embrace ideologies and movements that offer communities of salvation and support while preaching radical politics." As Bayat summarizes, "The very existential character of the urban dispossessed, their ecological reality, renders them amenable to embrace the extremist ideas of radical Islam" (2007, 579–80).

Combining the call to jihad with practical material benefits, Yusuf invested a great deal of resources in the social advancement and marriage of his followers. He offered them at least one meal a day and organized up to five hundred marriages for unmarried men, which is particularly attractive in a social context where marriage is an essential component of identity. Yusuf was also involved in microfinance schemes that provided young, unmarried members with "credits to open small businesses or buy vehicles, money when combatants enlist, promises of wages and motorcycles" (ICG 2017b, 6). He thus enabled the urban and rural poor to "carve provisional spaces of existential possibility in the face of severely narrowed futures" (Masquelier 2019, 4). A local respondent from Damaturu, who heard Yusuf preach several times, believes that poverty was a central factor in the popularity of Boko Haram: "They [Boko Haram] were meeting with young boys initially and giving them money, like N 10,000 [US$26] per person. There have been preaching sessions in this town when Yusuf used to come and preach in Bindigari in Damaturu. I personally have passed by and saw Yusuf preaching more than five times. I don't stop to listen to them because they say 'Boko Haram' [Western education is evil], and my children go to 'Boko' [Western school]. That time, I don't fancy listening to them or what they are saying."

Yusuf's microfinance schemes were a lifesaver if we consider that, across the Lake Chad region, "many young men invoke a lack of capital as the principal reason why they just sit, waiting for the government to intervene. They speak of wanting to set up a tailor's workshop or earning a living as *kabu-kabu* driver but not having the money to buy the sewing machine or motorbike they would need to set themselves in business" (Masquelier 2019, 17). In one empirically grounded study, "many youths reported that they either accepted loans prior to joining [Boko Haram] or joined with the hope of receiving loans or direct support to their business" (Mercy Corps 2016, 13). Yusuf owned some of the *achabas* that were loaned out, and he collected daily returns from them. Yusuf's investment in unmarried men takes on an added significance if we consider that "married men can draw support from kin and other webs of social connections in ways that single men cannot" (Masquelier 2019, 16). As a respondent in Masquelier's study said, "If you are married and you need money, they will loan it to you because you have responsibilities. But no one helps you if you're wifeless" (2019, 16).

By buying *achabas* for many young men in Borno State to win their "hearts and minds," Yusuf activated the concept of "people as infrastructure," which emphasizes "economic collaboration among residents seemingly marginalized from and immiserated by urban life" (Simone 2004, 407). AbdouMaliq Simone tells us that in a radically uncertain environment where material infrastructures are absent, people themselves become infrastructures. By investing in disaffected urban youth and helping them to get married and gain recognition (i.e., to become somebody), Boko Haram enabled the mobility of locally immobilized youth, thereby transforming the sect into a champion of the possibility of life in the city. In essence, Boko Haram became an infrastructure, "a matter that enables the movement of other matter" (Larkin 2013, 329). By buying *achabas* for youth in exchange for their loyalty, Yusuf performed what had become de rigueur for northern Nigerian politicians, such as Senator Ali Sheriff,[6] seeking electoral victory. In Nigeria, politicians have a habit of distributing *okadas* and/or helmets to young men as an election stratagem (Agbiboa 2017). Furthermore, the popular Alhaji Muhammadu Ndimi Mosque in Maiduguri, which was frequented by Yusuf, became more than just a mosque, helping to feed orphans and street children in Maiduguri. Against a backdrop of fragmented families, failed educational systems, and inflated bride price, Yusuf offered urban marginals "a chance to make their way in the world" (Peters and Richards 1998, 183). A former governor of Borno State, Kashim Shettima, reminds us,

> Over a period of thirty years, the ruling establishment abandoned the common people. . . . Nobody bothered about their education and health, and nobody cared how they made their living. . . . This was the ready-made situation that the Boko Haram leader capitalized on. He started organizing the youth, procuring motorcycles for them for their transport business, assisting them to get married at little cost, and creating . . . an alternative society.

The financial incentive for young men who joined Boko Haram was compelling. A fifty-two-year-old man from rural Borno State observed, "These youth, none of them have ever held N 10,000 [US$27] of his own. These youth move on horses and donkeys but were given new motorcycles. What do you think will happen?" (NSRP 2016, 35). By offering financial support to hundreds of youth in dire financial straits, Yusuf became a man of the people. Maiduguri's Indimi Mosque was often crowded with people of all ages, especially youth, 95 percent of whom lacked even a basic education (*Dan-Borno* 2010). As well as finding support among the urban poor, Yusuf's message resonated among the wealthy. Many young men would join Boko Haram after attending Yusuf's revolutionary orations,[7] which left a significant impression on them (Mercy Corps 2016, 12). That effect is consistent with a study of the vulnerability of Muslim youth on the island of Mindanao in the Philippines, where young respondents generally affirmed that the presence and, perhaps more important, the personality of charismatic recruiters from radical groups left an impression on them and essentially drove them to become radicalized: "Many respondents explained that they knew recruiters and that these were active in local educational institutions (*Madaris*) and in mosques after the Friday prayers. . . . The recruiters were often charming and persuasive. . . . Most individuals gradually adopted radical views through listening to radical preachers, attending prayer groups, and having regular contact with the recruiters" (Institute for Autonomy and Governance 2017, viii, ix).

The next section of this chapter shifts attention from the mobilization of marginal youth into Boko Haram to a social category of mobile yet stuck males that constitute Boko Haram's social base, the *almajirai*, "who follow a peripatetic Islamic scholar (usually in the dry season) as he travels from community to community ministering to their needs" (Swindell et al. 1999, 394). In more ways than one, the *almajirai* have a shared experience with *achaba* drivers: both are young males who feel trapped in a context of poverty, inequality, and social stigmatization. Notable members of the *almajirai* include Boko Haram founder Mohammed Yusuf, who "grew up an *almajiri*, living on the street begging bowl in hand" (Walker 2016, 144). Abubakar Shekau, Yusuf's deputy leader who took over leadership after Yusuf's extrajudicial death in 2009, was also an *almajiri*, who left his village of Shekau as a boy to pursue Islamic studies in Maiduguri under a *mallam* (Islamic teacher) called Baba Fanani (Okere 2014, 17). According to Shekau's mother, Falmata Abubakar, Shekau there met Yusuf, who she says "brainwashed" her son (Odua 2018).

Mobilization into Boko Haram: The *Almajirai*

As was the case with the Maitatsine, Boko Haram's membership comprises the *almajirai*, a group of poor migrant boys who come from mostly rural households and are enrolled in traditional Koranic schools (Lubeck 1981). Christian Seignobos (2016) argues that the *almajirai* "became the recruitment base for more than 50 percent of [Boko Haram] members."[8]

He further states the message that Boko Haram delivered to thousands of *almajirai*: "You have traded your begging bowl for the Kalashnikov that God has given you to rescue you from oblivion." Predominantly used by poor rural families, traditional Koranic schools are widespread throughout West Africa and afford "a privileged perspective on life such that habitual ways of seeing and living in the world can be actively questioned. They allow for possible futures within the ordinary, at times dispiriting, present" (Masquelier 2019, 6).

The word *almajirai* is rooted in the Arabic word *almuhajir*, which describes a person who migrates for the purpose of gaining and propagating Islamic knowledge, under the tutelage of a *mallam*. The *mallam*'s purpose is to stand in loco parentis to the *yan ci rani* (seasonal migrant boys), teaching them the fundamentals of Islam and how to write and recite the Arabic alphabet. During the course of their apprenticeship, the *almajirai* are sent out to the streets to win their daily bread by begging for alms (*bara*). The *almajirai*'s economic marginalization is turned into an "embodied position" through the enforced activity of begging, which "makes visible the damaging impact of social immobility on aspiring selfhoods" (Masquelier 2019, 1). Commonly known as *almajiranchi*, the embodied practice of begging was intended to toughen the migrant boys, since hardship, to a certain degree, was seen as character building. As Last puts it,

> Hausa culture presumes that poverty and hardship are a necessary part of character building and appropriate for the young. Just as there is a hungry season in the annual farming cycle, so too the young are expected to go hungry even when the workload is at the hardest. The harvest and fatness of middle age will come in due time, if the work is done well. (1990, 11–12)

That belief is deeply rooted in popular consciousness in northern Nigeria, as illustrated by such common Hausa sayings as "Karatu sai da bakunta" (One cannot acquire knowledge if one does not leave home) or "Karatu said da karanchi abinchi" (One must experience hunger in order to gain knowledge). The *almajiri* system "empowers young men to create spaces for living that are also testing grounds for how life might be lived" (Masquelier 2019, 6–7). Insecurity is thus not only instilled in mobile bodies but also registered on the senses. Among the Hausa-Fulani of northern Nigeria, for example, a boy's way of demonstrating that he is now a grown-up, an adult in the social sense of the word, is to "allow himself to be flogged in full view of everyone without flinching or betraying any fear. He is proud to do this, for this is not a punishment but a test of his courage and manliness" (Kirk-Greene and Sassoon 1956, 26).

From Alms to Arms?

By law, the *almajirai* are permitted to beg in mosques, streets, and roads, keeping part of the proceeds and surrendering a portion to their *mallams*. *Almajirai* are frequently forced by their *mallams* to hand over the entire day's takings and are punished (even severely tortured) if they refuse. That arrangement is partly responsible for the abuse of the *almajiri* tradition in northern Nigeria under Islamic movements such as Maitatsine. Falola writes,

> Many preachers exploited young children for money. The more *almajiri* one had, the more money could be made. Weekly levies were imposed on children whose parents could pay. Other children, they sent to the street to beg for money, which they would bring back to the preacher. One of Marwa's wives told the Tribunal that her husband made an average of N 200 a day from the panhandling of his *almajiri*. (1998, 148–49)

The abuse of the *almajiri* system in northern Nigeria continues to this day, passing from the alarming stage to the fatal. In the course of writing this chapter, for instance, news broke that Nigeria police rescued more than three hundred men and boys chained and starving in a building run by a traditional Islamic school in the northern city of Kaduna, what a police official graphically called a "house of torture." In a manner reminiscent of human slavery, many of the captives were children who had metal chains around their ankles. The detainees had been tortured, sexually abused, starved, and prevented from leaving—in some cases, for several years. Some of the boys told local authorities that their relatives had taken them to the building because they had believed it was a Koranic school. That news has intensified existing calls to ban the *almajiri* system (*Jones* 2019).

In an environment where insecurity immobilizes people and where the well of conspiracy theories never run dry, it has become trite to identify cohorts of idle *almajirai* with "the material from which violent, vengeful outlaws are made" (Comaroff and Comaroff 2004, 523). As Masquelier (2019, 4) points out with respect to Niger, instead of blame falling on the government that has left them without the prospect of a secure livelihood or the means of becoming fully adult, un(der)employed young men are scapegoated for their "lack of productivity" and criticized for "sitting around." In Nigeria, popular views of the idle *almajiri* as a disaster waiting to happen are shaped by "histories of association" (Ahmed 2004, 32) consistent with Oscar Lewis's (1966) analysis of the "culture of poverty" in Mexico, in which the habits, values, and behaviors of the poor are used to explain their predicament, giving rise to myopic state-instituted solutions that focuses on the effects rather than the root cause of the problem. The popular perceptions and treatment of *almajirai* also echo Kristin O'Brassill-Kulfan's central thesis in *Vagrant and Vagabonds* (2019), which describes how vagrants, poor migrants, beggars, and homeless people were targeted by the complex system of bureaucracy and policing of the poor and transient in the early American republic, "inciting both the pity and scorn of the public" (2019, 2). O'Brasill-Kulfan used the term *indigent transiency* to describe how the potent mix of poverty, immiseration, and mobility featured prominently in determining how the poor lived, interacted with, and were viewed by public officials (including local and state governments) and ordinary citizens, both under the law and by law enforcement: "Despite important differences in their identities and how they worked and moved, these groups [the vagrants, poor migrants, and homeless people] occupied a distinct legal category, sharing a level of poverty and instability that placed them at odds with authorities, under constant scrutiny, and vulnerable to frequent attempts by the state to control their movements" (2019, 2).

Popular perceptions of the *almajirai* in northern Nigeria are clearly exemplified by one concerned citizen's letter to the Nigerian newspaper *The Nation*.

> How can parents who give birth to children throw them to the streets to fend for their selves? Instead of sending them to proper schools, they are enrolled in Arabic teaching centers where they are taught about Islam. Islamic clerics who are supposed to act as mentors use the opportunity to introduce radical beliefs thereby brainwashing these pupils as tools of violence that then go about killing people and being suicidal in nature. . . . For those of us fortunate enough to have lived in the north, we see these *almajirai* in large numbers loitering around the streets wearing tattered clothes with bowls in their hands looking for the next available meal. The question is, if these young kids grow up, what will be their fate? They see the rich getting richer (who send their children to the best schools at home and abroad). The state government and the leaders and

religious leaders of the north are to be held responsible for this der-
eliction of duty where lack of proper enlightenment to the masses
on health and welfare, benefits of family planning, provision of education institutions have been neglected by those entrusted to govern
these regions. Yet, they use government funds meant for the citizens
of the state to enrich themselves and are now wondering how Boko
Haram has become a menace. (*Nation* 2013)

The letter echoes Robert Kaplan's (1994) essay on a "coming anarchy,"
which places West African young men on the Procrustean bed of "out
of school, unemployed, loose molecules in an unstable social fluid that
threatened to ignite." In the letter, the *almajirai*'s plight elevates the concerned citizen into a position of power over the *almajirai*. As Elizabeth
Spelman observes, "compassion, like other forms of caring, may also reinforce the very pattern of economic and political subordination responsible
for such suffering" (1998, 7). Moreover, the letter's overrepresentation of
the *almajirai* crisis fixes the *almajiri* as the one who has the problem and
who can overcome that problem only when the government feels moved
to intervene.

Nigerian politicians also tendentially criticize the *almajirai*, including
those entering Nigeria from neighboring Niger and Chad, as the main
source of terror in northeast Nigeria. Recalling his experience of growing
up in the capital city of Maiduguri, for example, Frank Nweke Jr., Nigeria's
former minister of information, claims that Boko Haram is a product of
state failure to address the perennial crisis of *almajirai* in northern Nigeria.

As a child, I watched as the seeds of Boko Haram were sown in Maiduguri, where I grew up. As we were taken to school everyday, we
saw the kids sitting under trees being indoctrinated. As we returned
from school in the afternoon, we saw the same children at the
roundabouts, begging for alms and as we went to catechism in the
evening, we found them back under the trees receiving their own
religious studies. Many of them did not attend any formal school.
Today, they have become the cause of insurgency to the nation; a
nation that failed them. (*Premium Times* 2014)

The common assumption of a close link between traditional Koranic
schools and the rise of future jihadists reveals "how the emotion of hate
works to animate the ordinary subject, to bring that fantasy to life, by con-
stituting the ordinary as in crisis, and the ordinary person as the real victim.

The ordinary becomes that which is already under threat by the imagined others whose proximity becomes a crime against person as well as place" (Ahmed 2004, 26). A refreshing departure in that regard is the 2005 analysis of Pakistan's *madrassas*[9] by Peter Bergen and Swati Pandey, which questions dominant assumptions that *madrassas* are citadels for the training of future terrorists. Bergen and Pandey found, "While *madrassas* may breed fundamentalists who have learned to recite the Koran in Arabic by rote, such schools do not teach the technical or linguistic skills necessary to be an effective terrorist. Indeed, there is little or no evidence that *madrassas* produce terrorists capable of attacking the West."

Hannah Hoechner (2018) challenges the alleged indoctrination of the *almajirai* by radical Islamist movements (e.g., Boko Haram) and redirects our focus to the abysmal conditions under which children and youth come of age in northern cities. Hoechner's fieldwork in Kano reveals that nothing in the *almajiri*'s core training or limited curriculum suggests a process of systematic radicalization or indoctrination. During her fieldwork in Kano, she encountered neither "gullible children" nor "angry youth" ready to engage in terrorism. A better approach, she writes, would be to ask "why some youth can't pursue the education they would like to pursue, and why there are so few jobs available even for those who manage to acquire modern education. This inevitably leads to questions about poverty and the unequal distribution of wealth" (Hoechner 2018). Hoechner's point of view reinforces the conception of youth precarity as a site-specific phenomenon that is embedded within local histories and social relations yet deeply intertwined with wider processes of material transformations and power relations (Peluso and Watts 2001, 5). Youth mobilization for dangerous work is "an activity characterized by circumstances, goals, expectations, behaviors, and discourses in particular contexts" (Daiute 2006, 9).

If there is a weakness in Hoechner's argument, it is her tendency to gloss over her own important admission that the "*[a]lmajirai* may well be, and probably are, among the followers of Boko Haram" (2015, 61). While existing research on the poverty-conflict nexus has yielded mixed results at best (see Justino 2009; Krueger and Maleckova 2003), it is less ambiguous that circumstances of poverty and local (im)mobility provide a fertile ground for the mobilization of children and youth for dangerous work (Meagher 2014, 2; Agbiboa 2013).[10] In a letter on the *almajiri* crisis in northern Nigeria, a group self-identifying as "concerned mothers" (and including such prominent women as Fatima Akilu and Aisha Mohammed-Oyebode) points out,

During a recent trip to Borno, driving from the airport to town, visiting IDP camps full of Boko Haram returnees and halfway houses for released Boko Haram detainees, it is clear that the most basic needs of food, shelter and education for our children is not a priority. This is the story from Kano to Zamfara, Katsina to Yola: the streets are teeming with destitute children waiting for random morsels of food, including from those whose wealth is ill-gotten, misappropriated from our collective patrimony. Our children have become down-trodden, destitute, and immiserated. A whole generation is locked into a cycle of poverty, having not a day of formal education; be it Western or Islamic, but are instead turned into beggars on the streets, in front of the very homes of those whose residents should hold their future and their hope in trust. The subjugation of and destitution of a generation of Nigerians is largely what has fueled Boko Haram and other militant organizations. (*Newsdiary* 2020)

In search of protection and support, marginal persons are increasingly turning to nonstate armed actors who assume the functions and symbols of the state rather than to politicians and state agencies. A former governor of Kano, Rabiu Kwankwaso, notes of the *almajirai*, "A very poor man who is looking for something to eat can easily be recruited by the insurgents and so can the unemployed and illiterate, and that's exactly what is happening" (Dixon 2014). Poverty levels in the northeast and northwest are 40 percent higher than those in the southwest, and unemployment in the north is three times as high. Barely one in five adults in northern Nigeria is literate, compared to 80 percent in southern Nigeria. Even educated northern youth are unable to find gainful jobs in the struggling northern economy (Meagher 2014, 2). Given the rather restricted nature of the private sector, the vast majority of (un)educated youth are forced into the overloaded informal economy where they face stiff competition, job insecurity, predatory actors, and marginal gains (Masquelier 2019, 9). In turn, youth unemployment has given rise to popular discontent and resentment against the Nigerian government and its failure to deliver on its promise of dignified work and better life. Not surprisingly, a survey by the United Nations Development Programme showed that 13 percent of respondents who had joined an extremist group in Africa reported doing so for employment opportunities (UNDP 2018, 58). In addition, between 2012 and 2014, almost 10 percent of young male fighters who joined ISIS were unemployed when recruited (Foster and Milton 2018, 14). In a rapaciously consumerist culture, where the politics of desire is ultimately measured in the possession of commodities, "those without are constantly confronted with their privation" (Comaroff and Comaroff 2004, 523).

Against that backdrop, it is not surprising that Boko Haram's membership includes Western-schooled graduates, school dropouts, and Koranic students. In a 2015 survey, the Nigerian Stability and Reconciliation Programme found that relative deprivation in the north renders many youths vulnerable to recruitment by Boko Haram (NSRP 2015; Agbiboa 2013). Umar Sani and David Ehrhardt (2014) found that over two-thirds of family members they interviewed noted that a Boko Haram relative had formerly been an *almajiri*. By virtue of their stigmatized identity and social disability, *almajirai* are particularly vulnerable to recruitment by radical Islamist groups that express support for commoners and promise them a better life. The findings of a recent study by Mercy Corps (2016, 13) show that nearly half of former Boko Haram members said they joined the sect because of its promise of financial support.

The *Almajirai*: Marginality as a Resource

It is important for scholars to approach *almajirai* "not so much as the excluded, disadvantaged, and aggrieved members of society but also as the 'included' who are able to take advantage of the perverse incentives" that war economies offer (Iwilade 2014, 592). That approach is particularly important in light of a growing corpus of works that have called for a better understanding of the urban poor as "individual and collective agents who are capable of mobilizing people, resources and representations in various ways, across varying geographical distances" (Jaffe et al. 2012, 645; Vigh 2010, 142; Richards 1996). The poor may be powerless, but they are not passive: "They do not sit around waiting for their fate to determine their lives. Rather they are active in their own way to ensure their survival" (Bayat 2000, 539). That point aligns with studies that have called for more attention to how particular relations of subordination produce a capacity for action (Mahmood 2005, 18), how subjection can constitute a form of action (Bayart and Ellis 2000, 219), and how the lived realities of marginalization, restriction, and social control also constitute political subjectivities (Joe Turner 2016, 143).[11]

A useful example is the agency of marginal young men in Niger. Widely suspected as a fertile recruiting ground for Salafi-jihadi groups such as Boko Haram and Ansaru, Niger is replete with jobless and idle young men who "ironically, often describe themselves as a ticking time bomb to underscore the urgency of addressing unemployment among the young. The state, their choice of language implies, ignores them at its own peril" (Masquelier 2019, 8). In that example, we see how victimized youth use their very marginalized status as a resource by appropriating the alarmist discourses about them to draw attention to their crippling condition of joblessness produced by government failure. Writing about the civil wars in Liberia and Sierra Leone, William Murphy describes how, in a restive environment—one where kinship ties no longer guarantee social security or personal advancement—patronage provided child soldiers with "a response to the political marginalization and economic destitution enforced by the corrupt regimes of the nation-state" (Murphy 2003, 62). In other words, youths in Sierra Leone and Liberia increasingly relied on the patronage of military commanders as a way to address their local immobility and economic desperation. A similar thing can be said of the many young people who saw in Boko Haram a path to economic survival and social recognition. In northeast Nigeria, testimonies of children rescued from Boko Haram camps demonstrate that they joined not only because of financial incentives (Mercy Corps 2016) but also due to peer pressures and familial ties, including cases of parents offering their children to insurgents for economic gain or to obtain security guarantees (UN Security Council 2017, 7; Nagarajan 2017, 7). A male youth in Borno joined Boko Haram to protect himself and his family and to safeguard his livelihood.

> I officially joined them when they started killing indiscriminately in Bama. Because I needed an identity to remain safe, I decided to pledge my allegiance to them. At that time, I needed protection and immunity from persecution by them so I could continue with my business. When they attacked Bama and took over the military barracks and burned all the houses in our community, my family's house was spared. (Mercy Corps 2016, 12)

The foregoing examples show that the aspirations of the poor to "move on" are often shaped by the spaces of openings and closures in their localities and supralocal networks (Jaffe et al. 2012, 645). Referring to young men who formerly identified as *almajirai*, a Muslim cleric in Adamawa State commented, "They have no job opportunities after graduating from *almajiri* school. You are unemployed, you are poor and you have no means of survival. This makes them easy targets of Boko Haram. . . . When they [Boko Haram] came to Mubi they (the young men) would be given money; N 5,000, N 10,000. The moment they see money they get interested.

They join" (cited in Hansen 2016, 87). In a northern Nigerian context, where success and failure ultimately depend on connections, or "whom you know," the poor and vulnerable are in constant need of a guardian or protector who can safeguard their spiritual and material well-being. As Olivier de Sardan (1999, 41) puts it, "Woe betides the man who knows no one, either directly or indirectly." The need for protection is particularly strong for marginalized groups such as the *almajirai*, who are habitually mocked and bullied with impunity (Hoechner 2015, 68).

Against that backdrop, it comes as no surprise that the *almajirai* have been strongly linked to the social bases of Maitatsine and Boko Haram, both of which draw the majority of their members from the poor and destitute. Many radical Islamic teachers (*mallams*) and preachers in northern Nigeria exploit the *almajiri* system for their narrow interests. Regarding Marwa, the notorious leader of Maitatsine, Falola writes, "He had many such boys, ranging in age from 10 to 14, who had been brought to him by elderly people or even by their parents. The system allowed for indoctrination into particular beliefs and loyalty to a leader, who became a father figure" (1998, 159). Of the *almajirai*, human rights activist Shehu Sani said, "These are . . . vulnerable children. They have in many cases turned to extremism and crime because they were sent away by their parents at a tender age and they grow up under the care of teachers who use them" (Dixon 2014). It is also instructive that the tribunal of inquiry into the Maitatsine uprisings, led by Justice Aniagolu, advised the Nigerian government to check the recruitment of the "horde of unemployed, gullible and idle citizens in our cities" (Falola 1998, 159). The tribunal warned, "The traditional practice of teaching children the Holy Quran popularly known as the *almajiri* system, whereby an Islamic teacher collects young boys from their parents to elsewhere other than their home villages for the purpose of teaching them Islam, was a major remote cause of the [Maitatsine] disturbances in Kano" (AFP 2010b).

Hannah Hoechner (2015, 64) is correct in her call for more attention to the structural causes of the *almajiri* predicament, including the ways in which children and youth negotiate the constraints under which they live. In that call, she reinforces the main policy question in northern Nigeria today, which is "how to fund the English-speaking Western (i.e., *boko*) schools in the north and how to link them with the Islamic primary and secondary schools. Funding tends to come from the center and percolate down to the state and local levels, constraining the capacity of local school systems to experiment and adjust to local realities" (Paden 2012, 60). That policy question is especially important in light of the root causes of the *almajiri* crisis. As Idris Abdul-Qadir tells us, "With the disposal of many Emirs and the defunding of religious schools by the British [during the colonial era], formal control over the *almajiri* system was lost. This is certainly the genesis of the predicament of the *almajiri* system today" (*Newsdiary* 2020).

It seems likely that the content of the *almajiri*'s rote learning system may render Koranic students susceptible to desperate politicians and conflict entrepreneurs (Aghedo and Eke 2013, 105). That the *almajirai* are often made to recite songs that express contempt for their peers receiving Western-style (*boko*) education is well documented: "In town, the funny spectacle of the school children walking in military-like rows, with their curious uniforms and an abecedary under the arm would always be accompanied by the mocking songs of their peers, sitting on the mat of a qur'anic school with their *allo* (wooden qur'anic slate) and pen-stalk: *'yan makarantar bokoko, ba karatu ba salla, sai yawan zagin malam* (children of the modern school, they do not pray nor recite the Qur'an: they only learn to disrespect our scholars)" (Brigaglia and Fiji 2008/9). Such songs play directly into the hands of Salafi-jihadists, such as Boko Haram, that not only openly express disdain for *boko* but seek to carve out a "pure" Islamic caliphate. From Somalia to Afghanistan, radical Islamist movements have used the lure of fighting against un-Islamic practices (*bida*) and elements as a recruitment tool. Boko Haram has often singled out Western schools (*boko*) and all those trained in it (*yan boko*), attacking them with lethal regularity. The attacks are guided by Yusuf's belief that *boko* is innately corrupt and heretical.

Yusuf argued that Islam is at odds with *boko*: "These foreign, global, colonialist schools have embraced matters that violate Islamic law, and it is forbidden to operate them, support them, study and teach in them" (2009, 84). Ironically, Yusuf's children attended a Lebanese-Nigerian school with Western curricula (Public Library of US Diplomacy 2009c). Between July 2013 and February 2014 alone, two high schools in Yobe State were attacked by Boko Haram, resulting in the death of one hundred children (Kyari 2014). The most notorious of those violent attacks was the group's abduction in April 2014 of 276 school-aged girls from a government secondary school in the town of Chibok, sparking the global hashtag campaign "Bring Back Our Girls." Many of the girls were moved into Cameroon, where "at least some were made available to insurgents as 'wives'—in essentially the same status as enslaved young girls in the early twentieth century and beforehand" (MacEachern 2018, 169). In an earlier incident, in September 2014, 145 women and girls (between eight and twenty-three years old) were abducted from villages in Adamawa during several coordinated attacks (UN Security Council 2017, 13). On February 19, 2018, Boko Haram fighters again kidnapped an estimated 105 girls from the Government Girls Science and Technical College in Dapchi in Yobe State. In December 2020, Boko Haram abducted hundreds of schoolboys in the northwestern Nigerian state of Katsina (BBC 2020b). In Borno State, Boko Haram's heinous school kidnappings have forced authorities to close all schools indefinitely, setting back education in a northern region already posting some of the lowest levels of education and human development in the world.

This chapter has explored the nexus between local immobility and mobilization into Boko Haram of youth who are "stuck" or "not moving well enough." In a northern Nigerian environment characterized by desert encroachment, a youth bulge,[12] and un(der)employment, Boko Haram has found fertile ground for recruiting people seeking better lives. For their part, marginalized and stigmatized youth (e.g., *achaba* drivers and *almajirai*) often choose to join armed opposition groups as a way of achieving economic survival and social recognition.

THREE

The Motorcycle Helmet Law and the July 2009 Violence

Research overwhelmingly shows that use of crash helmets by motorcycle drivers significantly reduces overall death rates and lethal head injuries. A study by the United Nations shows that motorcyclists are twenty-six times more likely to die in a traffic accident than are drivers of passenger cars. Wearing an appropriate helmet improves chances of survival by 42 percent and helps riders avoid 69 percent of injuries (United Nations 2016, xi). In developed countries such as the United States and England, available empirical data indicate that states without helmet laws generally see a significant increase in traumatic brain injury (TBI) and death resulting from motorcycle accidents. Statistics demonstrate that motorcyclists without helmets are three times more likely to suffer a TBI in a crash than are those wearing a helmet. The fatality rate per thousand is 6.2 percent for non-helmeted drivers and 1.6 percent for motorcyclists who wear helmets (Walter 2012). Also significant are the economic costs of motorcycle accidents to the public.

Yet, in many parts of the world, mandatory helmet laws raise serious ethical and philosophical questions about autonomy, that is, the freedom or ability to be self-governing or to make personal decisions without undue influence or interference from others. A case in point is the United States, where opponents of helmet laws claim that such legislation encroaches on their right to choose; they argue that individuals should decide what level of risk they are willing to expose themselves to while on a motorcycle (M. Jones and Bayer 2007). Such "my body, my choice" claims run counter to the pro-helmet argument based on paternalism, that is, the "intentional limitation of the autonomy of one person by another, where the person who limits autonomy justifies the action exclusively by the goal of helping the person whose autonomy is limited" (Beauchamp 2010, 104). In his classic work *On Liberty*, nineteenth-century philosopher John Stuart Mill argued against that type of state encroachment on personal decision-making.

> The only purpose for which power can be rightfully exercised over any member of a civilized community, against his will, is to prevent harm to others. His own good, either physical or moral, is not a sufficient warrant. He cannot rightfully be compelled to do or forebear because it will be better for him to do so, because it will make him happier, because in the opinion of others, to do so would be wise, or even right. These are good reasons for remonstrating with him. Or reasoning with him, or persuading him, or entreating him, but not for compelling him. With regard to his independence, he has absolute right. (Mill 1989: 13)

Autonomy aside, other opponents claim that motorcycle helmets actually pose a safety risk by impairing the driver's hearing and peripheral vision. In Vietnam's Ho Chi Minh City, for instance, commercial motorcyclists have argued that inability to see the faces of other drivers was a main reason they resisted using safety helmets. Others maintain that accidents are a matter of fate and ineluctable (Truitt 2008, 13, 15). The reasons that people in developed countries give for rejecting crash helmets or even for using motorcycles are not necessarily the same as the reasons adduced by motorcyclists in the developing world. In much of Europe and North America, for example, motorcycles are generally used for recreation; they make up approximately 2 percent of registered motor vehicles (Yu et al. 2011, 794). But in countries in sub-Saharan Africa, South Asia, and the Middle East, motorcycles represent a primary means of transportation, economic survival, and social becoming (Truitt 2008; Agbiboa 2018a). In those countries, motorcycles are "part of life"; without them, "you are like a prisoner" (Mashal and Shah 2017). In fact, research demonstrates that the poorer a country is, the higher its motorcycle fleet growth rate will be. With more motorcycles on the road, there certainly will be an increased risk of accidents causing injury or death, especially if appropriate helmets are not used (United Nations 2016, xi).

In developing countries such as Nigeria and Taiwan, motorcycle drivers and their passengers account for over 80 percent of head injuries (Yu et al.

2011, 794). Challenges to the use of crash helmets in emerging countries are complex, including peer pressure among young riders (e.g., ridiculing helmet wearers); the claim that helmets are only needed for long trips (even though most accidents occur close to home); the contention that helmets are considered hot and uncomfortable (e.g., in regions with tropical climates); the damaging effect on women's hairstyles (whether traditional style or simply fashion); the issue of special headgear (e.g., turbans); the practical issue of what to do with the helmet when it is not being worn (preventing theft, damage, or sheer inconvenience when, e.g., shopping); and issues of hygiene, if the helmet is not owned by the rider (United Nations 2016, 11). Beyond that list is the cost of a crash helmet, which is usually beyond the financial reach of both drivers and their passengers.

This chapter revisits the controversy surrounding the enforcement of a new bicycle helmet law in Borno State, with special attention to the central role it played in transforming Boko Haram from a group of disaffected youth in 2009 into a full-blown insurgency that has raged on since 2010, with no end in sight. The manner in which the helmet law was enforced by the Borno State government (through its security agencies) sheds important light on why government friction with Boko Haram transformed from a nonviolent conflict into a violent insurgency. This analysis of the helmet dispute between Boko Haram and formal authorities in Borno State builds on the insight by John Comaroff and Simon Roberts (1981) that the "dispute process may provide an essential key to the disclosure of the sociocultural order at large." It also draws on the argument that "if terrorists perceive the state as unjust, morally corrupt, and violent, terrorism may seem legitimate and justified. . . . Evidence also indicates that many terrorists are activists with prior political experience in nonviolent opposition to the state" (Crenshaw 1981, 390; see also Botha and Abdile 2019, 506).

Theoretically, this chapter is directed by the "conflict spiral" model, which posits that escalation results from a vicious circle of action-reaction (Pruitt and Kim 2004, 94–96). The spiral model is essentially a bilateral reaction model, because each party is—or, more accurately, claims to be—reacting to the other party's prior actions. Once started, conflict spirals are hard to stop, because each party feels that failing to retaliate will be perceived as a sign of weakness, inviting further annoying behavior from the other side. The contentious manner in which the Borno State government enforced the helmet law in Maiduguri may be said to have triggered a contentious retaliatory or defensive reaction from Boko Haram, which provoked further contentious behavior from the state, completing one circle of the conflict spiral and starting it on its next iteration. The logic of the conflict spiral is evident in the claim that "government use of unexpected and unusual force in response to protestors . . . often compels terrorists' retaliation. The development of such an action-reaction syndrome then establishes the structure of the conflict between the regime and its challengers" (Crenshaw 1981, 384–85).

War Machines: Boko Haram Youth and Political Instrumentality

The involvement of African youth, especially young men, in electoral politics must be understood in light of the way in which electoral violence is instrumentalized by and for political elites. Since Nigeria's return to civilian rule in 1999, politicians have competed for the services of marginal men as political thugs, to silence their rivals, win elections, and maintain their grip on power. In the buildup to the 2003 elections in southern Nigeria, a local editorial described how jobless and disaffected youth were mobilized and secretly armed by politicians to disrupt and manipulate the electoral process. The editorial further noted, "In this contestation and competitive arming of young groups, the party, which controlled the state government, got the upper hand. These political rivalries, coupled with a struggle for turf, contributed immensely to the rise of armed militancy and inter-militant armed violence, which preceded the 2003 elections and became consolidated in the period between 2003 and 2007 general elections" (Aniekwe and Agbiboa 2015, 12–13). After employing marginalized and disaffected young men for their political objectives, politicians in Nigeria generally make little to no effort to improve the men's state of uneasy stasis, proceeding to dump them in a fashion similar to the Islamic teachers criticized by Shehu Usman Dan Fodio for treating their wives like "tools to work with. When they are spoiled, they are thrown on the rubbish-heap" (Shagari and Boyd 1978, 39). The situation brings to mind Niccoló Machiavelli's infamous counsel to new princes to beware of those friends who helped them to power, for "you cannot keep as friends those who have put you there because you cannot satisfy them in the mode they had presumed" (Spikerman 2001, 79–80).

In northern Nigeria, the arming of youths as political thugs has been a leitmotif of its electoral history since 1999.[1] As one scholar explains, "The 2003 gubernatorial election in Borno State . . . was part of a larger trend where godfathers recruited unsavory actors to help them take power, and then later turned on these allies" (Thurston 2018, 28). The social structures in northern Nigeria make it "easy for the young of a locality to act collectively—even to disarm or kill a dangerously violent madman or to beat to death a thief caught red-handed in the marketplace. Nor is it difficult, if you have the right connections, to raise a crowd of youth from villages in the area, a crowd who could act as 'party supporters' and demonstrate, or even riot and loot (their 'fee' being the loot they can gather, but they risk being wounded or even dying in the conflict)" (Last 2003, 3–4). In the Lake Chad region, space, sociality, and daily life are organized around making existentially immobile but able-bodied young men available for all manner of dangerous work, effectively turning them into "war machines" (D. Hoffman 2011). The case of Boko Haram is instructive.

In 2012, the white paper of the Ambassador Usman Galtimari Presidential Committee on the Security Challenges in the Northeast traced the region's youth militias, of which Boko Haram is an offshoot, to politicians who set them up in the run-up to the 2003 and 2007 gubernatorial elections: "The militias were allegedly armed and used extensively as political thugs. After the elections and having achieved their primary purpose, the politicians left the militias to their fate since they could not continue funding and keeping them employed. With no visible means of sustenance, some of the militias gravitated towards religious extremism, the type offered by Mohammed Yusuf" (Abbah 2012). Paragraph 40(b) of the committee's report traces the roots of terrorism in northeast Nigeria, especially in the worst affected states of Borno, Yobe and Adamawa, to militia groups such as "ECOMOG" (which by design or somewhat confusing coincidence shares the same acronym as the West African multilateral armed force known as Economic Community of West African States Monitoring Group), *yan kalare* and *sara suka* which are linked to prominent politicians and political godfathers in these states. During electoral cycles, these groups are used to harass and assassinate political rivals. When election is over, they usually get out of hands and become a threat to their political supporters and financiers, or become involved in organized crime and communal wars. In its recommendations, the committee urged the Nigerian government to identify and bring to justice politicians who sponsor and weaponize militia groups like Boko Haram (Abbah 2012). The following section of this chapter examines how the checkered relationship between Boko Haram founder Mohammed Yusuf and Ali Modu Sheriff—the former governor of Borno State (2003–11) and a wealthy Kanuri politician—shaped Boko Haram as we know it today.

Yusuf and Shettima: How Things Fell Apart

One important factor in Boko Haram's transformation into an ultraradical group was its political utility for the 2003 gubernatorial candidate for Borno State, Ali Modu Sheriff, who belonged to the All Nigeria Peoples Party. Sheriff enlisted the support of Yusuf and his *achaba*-driving youth to secure the 2003 election, under the promise that, in the event of electoral victory, he would implement true, full Sharia law in Borno[2] and put Yusuf's followers in official state positions (ICG 2014, 4). Sheriff also promised cash (N 50 million) and motorcycles, as well as a position in the Commission for Religious Affairs, as compensation for support (Monguno 2013). In preparation for the 2003 and 2007 gubernatorial elections, Sheriff armed and financed Boko Haram to support his candidacy and intimidate his rivals (Cooke and Sanderson 2016, 19). Yusuf is said to have sent Boko Haram members into the streets in support of Sheriff (MacEachern 2018, 178). In fact, foreign commentators, such as Steven Davis, have claimed that Boko Haram started out as Sheriff's "ECOMOG" thugs who targeted his political rivals in the 2003 and 2007 elections. That group, they argue, later morphed into the deadly Boko Haram we see targeting civilians today, although the core of the old Yusuffiya is no longer part of Boko Haram (*Daily Trust* 2014).

Sheriff won the 2003 elections and became governor of Borno. In return for their help, he placed Yusuf's supporters in government positions. For example, in 2005, he made Buji Foi, a close disciple and financier of Yusuf, commissioner of the newly created Ministry of Religious Affairs and Special Education. Through that channel, Sheriff, who has a reputation for being "thoroughly corrupt and kleptocratic" (MacEachern 2018, 179), funneled large sums of money to Yusuf, which the latter used to organize the microcredit scheme that provided his growing followers with capital to establish their own businesses, ranging from commercial driving to car washing and selling clean water. In turn, those followers provided financial support to Yusuf, who then traded in arms from Chad with the help of his father-in-law, Baba Fugu Muhammed. Sheriff's government also gave Yusuf fifty motorcycles, which he used to set up *achaba* businesses for his followers. The International Crisis Group reported, "The motorcycles were parked at the Boko Haram headquarters, in [a compound named the] *Markaz*, at the close of day by the operators, who would hand over the N 100 (US$1) fee" (ICG 2014, 12). Scores of those motorcycles were burned by the army when they invaded the Markaz during the July 2009 crackdown. Finally, Sheriff released prominent Boko Haram leaders from prison.

Things fell apart between Yusuf and Sheriff after the 2007 elections, in which Sheriff was reelected with the support of the Yusuffiya. Sheriff "felt threatened by Yusuf's expanding influence and reneged on a pre-election promise to make him Chief Imam of Maiduguri" (Cooke and Sanderson 2016, 19). Lamenting Sheriff's failure to keep his pre-election promise of implementing Sharia law throughout Borno State, Yusuf openly condemned Sheriff as *taghut* (an illegitimate ruler authority associated with an intrinsically evil system) and preached against his administration, which he branded as hopelessly corrupt and apostate. The resulting fallout between Sheriff and Yusuf marked the beginning of Boko Haram's radically anti-government ideology (Ehrhardt 2019, 119). Yusuf's ideology and preaching revolved around three major ideas: accusations against an oppressive, secular government; exploitation of Muslims and people's sense of injustice or victimization; and promotion of jihad and glorification of martyrdom (Apard 2015, 45; see also Kassim and Nwankpa 2018). In a sermon delivered in 2006, Yusuf told his followers, "The infidels must be killed. They're not worthy of trust. Most of them are people who can't keep their word. They're sinners, they don't know the truth" (Sesay 2019, 73). In 2007, Buji Foi resigned from his role as commissioner of religious affairs, in protest against Sheriff's administration (Brigaglia 2012b, 35).[3]

The police frequently harassed Yusuf because of his radical ideas, and he was arrested several times. In November 2008, for example, he was arrested by state security services on grounds of public incitement to violence. However, at a January 2009 hearing that took place in the Nigerian capital city of Abuja, he was released on bail. In April 2009, the case against him was dismissed, with the federal court citing lack of sufficient evidence. According to the report of the Galtimari Presidential Committee, Yusuf's release amounted to a serious mistake, because it "made a hero out of him, as the reception accorded him upon his return to Maiduguri attracted a mammoth crowd that temporarily undermined state authority and served as an avenue for him to attract additional membership into the sect" (Abbah 2012). Sheriff has always maintained his own innocence and denied facilitating Boko Haram's rise, claiming that "people make comments on what they don't know and in life, you don't speak on matters that you are not very competent on. Who said that I am a mentor of Boko Haram? There is no truth in the statement" (Ogbu et al. 2011).

Against that backdrop of strained relations between Sheriff and Yusuf, the Borno State government made every effort to "criminalize Boko Haram members by imposing motorbike laws" (Cooke and Sanderson 2016, 19). Sheriff's government sought to exercise its power over Boko Haram, with power understood here as "a way of acting upon an acting subject or acting subjects by virtue of their acting or being capable of action" (Foucault 1980, 220). In summary, then, Boko Haram's desire to reinstate Sharia and its critique of the *yan boko* is inextricably linked to the state. Michael Watts explains,

> First, [Yusuf's] critique of the state and its apparatuses—during the 2011 elections they assassinated politicians and destroyed public schools, military installations, and police stations—was propelled by the violence meted out by the army and police, and what they took to be the moral, religious, and ethical bankruptcy of the state. Second, Yusuf's own involvement with the sharia implementation process exposed the corruption and duplicity of the government in regard to Islam. Third, Yusuf and his movement were deployed (and in some respects empowered, and probably armed) by the state in the 2003 Borno elections, but were promptly abandoned and betrayed by the same political classes after the electoral victory. And, not least, Boko Haram was clearly supported by powerful actors within the state apparatuses and the political classes, largely during the years of Goodluck Jonathan, as a means to destabilize the administration. (2018, 42)

The Helmet Law and Operation Flush II

In postcolonial Africa, "every law enacted is submerged by an ensemble of techniques of avoidance, circumvention and envelopment which, in the end, neutralize and invert the legislation" (Mbembe and Roitman 1995, 340). Those techniques suggest that the law is a primary site of political struggle, both in its suspension and in how it is formulated, interpreted, and applied (Gregory 2007, 211). Nowhere is that political struggle more apparent than in the road transport sector and its associated regulations and enforcements. On July 25, 2009, Maiduguri, the capital of Borno State, saw a violent uprising that resulted in the extrajudicial killing of Mohammed Yusuf and up to eight hundred of his followers. The catalyst for the uprising was the enforcement of a helmet law in Borno State in January 2009, mandating that all motorcyclists and their passengers must wear crash helmets. Ostensibly, the law was a government response to a nationwide public health crisis: Nigeria's roads are among the most accident-prone in the world—with four thousand people dying and some twenty thousand injured on the road yearly—and *achaba* crashes accounted for most traffic injuries by 2009 (Friedman 2014). However, "the mandatory use of crash helmets by motorcycle riders, although a national policy, was not enforced in other places with the same zeal (as obtained in Borno state under Sheriff). In fact, the enforcement policy stopped once the [Boko Haram] movement was crushed in July 2009" (Kyari 2014, 24).

Whatever its merits (and there are many), the helmet law inspired a biopolitics of dispossession that imposed "diverse spaces of exception: spaces where people can be controlled, coerced, tortured, or even killed with impunity because their geographical location [and practical occupation] is imagined and administered as somehow beyond the reach of justice" (Sparke 2007, 339). A special joint antirobbery patrol team, locally known as Operation Flush II (OF II)—comprised of the army and mobile police—was charged by Sheriff with enforcing the helmet law, as well as an existing law that forbade *achaba* drivers from operating after 6:00 p.m. and taking more than one passenger at a time. Police checkpoints were used to enforce the traffic laws. Established in November 2008 under Sheriff's government, OF II was ostensibly designed to protect lives and property in Maiduguri (Haruna 2008; Gusau and Kwara 2009). At the time, the city was plagued by various security threats: "armed robbery, house burglary, intimidation, abduction of young girls and ritual killings, [and especially] the daily highway robbery experienced along major highways, from Maiduguri to Damaturu, Maiduguri to Biu, Maiduguri to Gwoza, and Maiduguri road linking it to the northern part of the state" (*Dan-Borno* 2008). Many blamed those threats on the rise of *achabas* in Maiduguri.

As part of the government's security architecture, OF II members were generally caught between two roles: "the stated public-service role of providing effective security to persons and property, and the obverse, a postcolonial force for internal repression, applying force to keep the populace subjugated to the interests of a surplus-extracting elite" (Owen 2012, 3). Its success in decreasing banditry notwithstanding, OF II escalated tensions on the roads of Borno by dispossessing and brutalizing mobile people (*Daily Trust* 2009; Thurston 2018, 133), plunging many drivers into a constant state of anxiety and perplexity. For example, *achaba* drivers caught without helmets were subjected to a range of degrading punishments: "frog jump, rolling in culvert, carrying your motorcycle on your head, sweeping the tarmac, and in a very special case, a notorious rider was caught putting on calabash [a dried pumpkin shell] but painted to look like a helmet, he was later asked to chew the whole calabash or else" (*Dan-Borno* 2010). The OF II's crackdown on and dispossession of helmetless drivers resulted in several protests by *achaba* operators. OF II men often used excessive and sometimes deadly force against the protesters. For example, in an incident that occurred in Biu in Borno State in October 2009, two out of a hundred *achaba* drivers protesting the enforcement of the helmet law were shot dead in a violent clash with OF II members. Several other drivers were injured in the process. In retaliation, an angry *achaba* mob burned down Biu government offices, including the residential quarters of the Federal Road Safety Commission (Idris 2009). In short, with the emergence of OF II as official enforcers of the helmet law in Maiduguri, the capital city became less a place where the cry and demand for the right to the city is heard over and over again—and more an arena for the attempted legitimation of a brutal political economy and landscape" (Mitchell 2003, 190). OF II resorted to "lawfare"—that is, the inherent violence in the law—to discriminate, coerce, and erase people's livelihoods (Comaroff and Comaroff 2006, 30). In that respect, OF II mirrors the Nigerian state, which, time after time, adopts violence as a central tenet of state doctrine and law, reinforcing the view that "law and violence are not opposed but hold each other in a deadly embrace" (Gregory 2007, 211).

Crash Helmets and the Right to Difference

The helmet law and restriction of *achaba* mobility was particularly designed to target Yusuf's followers, many of whom earned a living as *achaba* drivers; they complained that the crash helmet would not fit over their turbans. The creation of OF II was a deliberate attempt by Sheriff's government "to draw Boko Haram out for a fight by harassing members going to or returning from *dawah*, as they called their preaching activities. Restriction of movement of motorcycles at night and the attempt to enforce the use of crash helmets were all aimed at achieving this" (Egbewole and Hammed 2018, 12). Sheriff himself relished his central role in establishing OF II following his political fallout with Yusuf. "As a governor," Sheriff said, "I had to take charge and restore some measure of order to my domain. I started creating laws. I first started by making a law regulating motorcycles, because at night, you find over one thousand motorcycles in the city. They would move from one end of the town to the other with different kinds of weapons: cutlasses, swords, etc. . . . And because they don't wear helmets, I insisted that they begin to do so. I asked that their members be arrested and tried" (Bello and Sabo 2009, 11). The helmet law provided an opportunity for Boko Haram to mobilize against the government, which Yusuf castigated as oppressive and "un-Islamic."

By rejecting crash helmets, the *achaba* drivers of Boko Haram were engaging in what social theorist Michel Foucault called "counter conduct," or expressions of "the will not to be governed, like that, by these people at this price" (1997b, 72). Perhaps more important, they were asserting their "right to difference," which, according to Henri Lefebvre (1976, 35), is essentially the right to differ from pre-established groups and pre-determined categories. Far from a mere "celebration of diversity in urban space for the sake of difference," the right to difference ensures that all urban residents, without exception, possess "the capacity and will to differ and that a commitment to 'living together in difference' actually exists" (Öz and Eder 2018, 1035). Government failure both to extend to motorcycle drivers a fundamental right to the city and to recognize the drivers' right to difference played an important role in the escalation of tensions between Boko Haram members and state security forces. That impact makes sense in light of studies showing that "perceptions of a threat to one's normative and cultural values" may "trigger violence and lead to a privatized sense of justice" (Öz and Eder 2018, 1039).

The right to difference aside, the required bicycle helmets were pricey, costing around US$29 in a city where an estimated 80 percent of residents survived on less than US$1 a day (BBC 2009). The expense of the helmets forced many *achaba* drivers to improvise with calabashes or pots tied to their heads with string, in a bid to avoid the helmet law and perhaps mocking law enforcers. That improvisation demonstrates the capacity of the poor and marginalized to "turn violence, the absurd and even terror itself into a source of derision" (Mbembe and Roitman 1995, 351). *Achaba* drivers caught defying the law were arrested and had their *achabas* impounded by the state (BBC 2009). Construction workers cashed in on the helmet law, renting out their safety helmets for N 500 (US$3.60) a day. While some passengers feared that helmets could be laced with magic spells to make the wearer easier to rob or kidnap for ritual purposes, others worried they might pick up an infection from strangers. The enforcement of the helmet law and the subsequent ban of *achabas* forced many *achaba* drivers to relocate from Maiduguri to nearby states where *achabas* were still permitted. Some who had purchased *achabas* a few days before the ban at the cost of N 120,000 (US$315) were forced to sell them after it for N 30,000 (US$78), as the new law had rendered motorcycles useless. But many *achaba* drivers associated with Boko Haram stayed, determined to assert their right to the city.

The July 2009 Violence

Given Yusuf's growing agitation for an Islamic caliphate and open condemnation of Sheriff's administration, security personnel enforcing the law believed that the *achaba* drivers of Boko Haram refused to wear helmets because they did not recognize the legitimacy of the Borno State's government under Sheriff (Gusau 2009). Consequently, OF II members unleashed a crackdown targeted at helmetless *achaba* followers of Yusuf, beating and imposing fines on them. Yusuf's critique of the state and its *yan boko* became "inseparable from the violence of the army and the police, confirming for the insurgents the utter decay of the state" (Watts 2014, 120). His agitations ultimately put him and his *achaba* followers at loggerheads with the state. The tensions came to a head on June 11, 2009, when some Yusuffiya were pulled over by OF II agents. The Yusuffiya were driving their *achabas* in a funeral procession to bury four of their members who had died in a car accident along Biu–Maiduguri Road the previous day. Some of the Boko Haram mourners were intercepted by OF II personnel and asked why they were not wearing crash helmets. The followers of Yusuf saw the inquiry as a provocation, given that they were in a funeral procession. The ensuing altercation quickly escalated into a deadly shooting by the OF II men, in which seventeen Yusuffiya were injured and taken to University of Maiduguri Teaching Hospital for treatment (Kwaru and Salkida 2009).

The violence between Boko Haram and OF II escalated, with each side blaming the other for starting the conflict. Yusuf was not happy that "the government neither sympathized with the victims nor paid for their medication while there was no apology from police or any investigation" (Gusau 2009). Interpreting that maltreatment as a deliberate attempt by the state and its security forces to humiliate his group, he linked the shooting of his followers to what he saw as "a pattern of anti-Muslim violence in Nigeria" (Thurston 2019, 133–34) and around the world. He claimed, "The government of Nigeria has not been built to do justice. . . . It has been built to attack Islam and kill Muslims" (Kassim and Nwankpa 2018: 181). Yusuf saw OF II as the embodiment of a state-sponsored anti-Muslim campaign. In his view, "the true Muslims would now confront the *taghut*: the idolatrous, tyrannical secular state" (Thurston 2019, 134). Nowhere is Yusuf's grievance toward the state better articulated than in his *Open Letter to the Federal Government of Nigeria*, delivered in a video that circulated a day after the June 11 clash and showed Yusuf preaching in Hausa, accompanied by high-quality graphics of weapons. The *Open Letter* marked "the start of Boko Haram in Maiduguri," according to one of my interviewees, Ibrahim, who listened to Yusuf preach many times in a ward at the railway quarters called

Gwaidangari. Yusuf condemned the oppression of his group by the state and called for an aggressive defense of Islam against the Khawarij (those who seceded).

> In Islam, when we have a truce with someone not to harm, and he turns his back against our agreement, God has stated "Once they turn their back on their promises after the agreement and they accuse your religion, fight them for they don't keep their promises, perhaps war will stop them." Their utterances are common, you will hear them say: "I am a soldier," "I am not a politician," and "we don't negotiate with people," Alas! It is all falsehood unless if they have not been oppressed.
>
> And we thank Allah that our members have stood their ground on that day without fear. Our ability to stand their oppression was a special gift from Allah who removed fear out of the minds of the believers. This is something to celebrate by thanking God. We give Glory to Allah for our ability to withstand oppression despite the variety of weapons they carried and the pool of blood we saw, yet we did not retreat. This is not the matter of saying that it was Allah who destined that such will happen! Yes, Allah has destined that right from the beginning, just like the way he destined a thief to steal and face amputation, and the way he destined a drunkard who drinks and gets lashed eighty times. I hope it is well understood. (Yusuf 2009)

Following a local intelligence report on July 23, 2009, nine Yusuf-fiya in possession of improvised explosive devices, including seventy-four empty bombshells and several bags of gunpowder, were arrested in Biu. The Yusuffiya claimed that they were no longer safe and were preparing to protect themselves from state security forces (Gusau 2009). One of those arrested, Abu Hapsa, explained, "We have not used the explosives yet. We were carrying out religious activities in peace. It was the police who shot our men some months ago for no just cause and since that incident, we made up our minds to arm ourselves to resist any future attack on us by anyone" (Gusau 2009). Another member of the Yusuffiya claimed, "We thank Allah for bringing us into this condition [arrest]. We were arrested because we made and kept these weapons in our abode to defend ourselves against the enemies of the religion. We want to ensure that Islam is the only religion from here to Spain. We believe in our leader [Yusuf] when he told us to prepare all these things [weapons] as tools for defense because some people were coming to attack us. We believe our leader will lead us to heaven" (Ola 2009). Those comments represented Boko Haram as the victim of state violence, rather than as the aggressor. On the day of the arrest, another set of Yusuffiya executed an attack on the residence of a deputy commandant of the Nigerian Mobile Police (MOPOL) in Maiduguri's GRA area, killing his guards and burning down his house. The insurgents then proceeded to the police headquarters in Maiduguri and killed several officers on duty (Omonobi et al. 2013). On July 25, Yusuffiya also attacked police stations in Bauchi and killed dozens of officers. In a local newspaper, Yusuf lamented what had happened in Bauchi.

> What I said previously that we are going to be attacked by the authorities has manifested in Bauchi, where about 40 of our brothers were killed, their mosque and homes burnt down completely, and several others were injured and about a hundred are presently in detention. Therefore, we will not agree with this kind of humiliation. We are ready to die together with our brothers and we would never concede to non-belief in Allah. I will not give myself up. If Allah wishes, they will arrest me; if Allah does not wish, they will never arrest me. But I will never give myself, not after my followers were killed in Bauchi. Is it right to kill them? Is it right to shoot human beings? To surrender myself means that what [the police] did is right. Therefore, we are ready to fight to die. Democracy and the current system of education must be changed, otherwise this war that is yet to start would continue for long. (Gusau 2009)

On July 26, Yusuf launched five days of violent attacks against the police in the states of Borno, Bauchi, Yobe, Gombe, Kano, and Katsina. "I will remember that very Sunday, 26th of July, but I will not remember the exact time," said Salihu, a taxi driver who drove me from the airport in Maiduguri to my hotel in Wulari. He continued, "It was on a Sunday night when those followers of Yusuf, those Yusuffiya, come and attack police headquarters in this our area. They killed many police officers, and their attacks lasted until Friday, 31 July." After five days of mayhem, an operation by the Third Armored Division of the Nigerian Army brutally suppressed the Boko Haram uprising and killed roughly eight hundred Yusuffiya. On July 28 and 29, the army shelled Yusuf's compound, flushing out more of his followers and killing several dozen of them. After just four days of fighting, Nigeria's National Emergency Management Agency estimated that four thousand people were internally displaced. During that period, state security services made widespread arrests of suspected Boko Haram members.

Speaking to US Embassy officials at the time, a Sufi activist in Maiduguri described the arbitrary, scorched-earth tactics of Nigerian security forces who "shot motorists and pedestrians just because they have a beard." "As a result," he said, "residents are shaving their beards and changing the style of their dress to avoid being targeted" (Public Library of US Diplomacy 2009c).

The Extrajudicial Killing of Mohammed Yusuf

The July 2009 search for Yusuf came to a head on its fifth day, when army officials captured him, hiding in his father-in-law's goat pen (Houreld 2009). Video clips and images uploaded online show a handcuffed and half-naked Yusuf with a bandaged arm being interrogated in Hausa by the police, who recorded the scene with their mobile phones (Duodu 2009). At the start of the decisive week, Yusuf had predicted, "If we give ourselves up or they get us or me, . . . they will kill me" (Gusau 2009). He was right. The army handed Yusuf over to the police after a brief interrogation at Maiduguri's Giwa barracks. The interrogators mainly focused on the contradictions between Yusuf's lifestyle and his public sermons (for excerpts from Yusuf's interrogation in police custody, see Duodu 2009).

Yusuf was extrajudicially killed in police custody on July 30, 2009. While the police alleged that he was killed while trying to escape (BBC 2009), an eyewitness recalls how "three MOPOL started shooting him. They first shot him in the chest and stomach, and another came and shot him in the back of his head. I was afraid and started running. When I came back, he was dead. There were a lot of people taking pictures [of his body]" (HRW 2012, 53). That eyewitness report is entirely plausible, given that the Nigeria Police Force has a history of corruption, arbitrariness, use of excessive force, extrajudicial killings, and forced disappearances (Agbiboa 2015; Owen 2012). Across Nigeria, police officers are ordinarily seen as "alien to the regions they monitor" and more as "occupying troops than as helpful civil servants" (McCall 2004, 14). *Achaba* drivers regularly bemoan the extortionate power and delay tactics of the police on the road, as having "rendered the state less a public good than a social relation of domination founded essentially on coercive exchange, plunder and consumption" (Mbembe and Roitman 1995, 335). Militarily, the July 2009 violence "foreshadowed the harsh tactics Nigerian security forces would use in attempting to crush the sect, including extrajudicial executions and mass arrests" (Thurston 2018, 140). Historian Elodie Apard argues that the humiliation of Yusuf and his followers and the desecration of his body illustrated "the injustices [Yusuf] had never stopped denouncing. His body provided his followers with proof of government brutality; it also gave them a good reason to mobilize. His extrajudicial execution and the violent attacks that accompanied it triggered the transformation of Yusuffiyya into a violent, and, henceforth, clandestine activist group" (2015, 53). Put simply, the Nigerian security forces that were supposed to quash the sect ensured its rise instead.

The circumstances surrounding the extrajudicial death of Yusuf attracted worldwide publicity and condemnation, with a Maiduguri-based *mallam*, Sheikh Yakubu Musa, claiming that Yusuf was executed at the behest of Sheriff to prevent the former from revealing the latter's scandalous connections to others in the government.[4] By Musa's account, Yusuf's death was a deliberate attempt by Sheriff's government to "silence that which is unspeakable" (Steedly 1993, 238). Musa also accused security forces of shooting indiscriminately at innocent people during the Friday clash (Public Library of US Diplomacy 2009b). "Why was Yusuf summarily executed without any trial?" asked another Islamic cleric, who went on to explain, "I want to say point blank that if Yusuf was allowed to talk, many people in high positions in the government would be indicted, including people in the security forces. Had he not been arrested before? He was arrested before and taken to Abuja, but was released. Who are the people who worked for his release?" (AFP 2010b). Those allegations prompted the federal government to establish a "high-powered Post-Mortem Committee," charged with investigating the matter (*Vanguard* 2014b).[5] However, Sheriff, who described Yusuf as a "lunatic," dismissed public concerns over his death.

> You know, I can't understand this kind of law, or even this type of emotions. Why should a man kill several people and when he dies, you want to make him a hero of sorts? Why should people be sympathetic to a hardened criminal who died, or begin to question how he died? I'm baffled by that type of reasoning because it is counter to common sense. (Mustapha 2014, 150)

Sheriff's depiction of Yusuf as a "lunatic" reinforces the point that social science "has not prepared society to view terrorists as rational, reasonable, relatively ordinary individuals. They are instead portrayed as bizarre, sick and crazy" (Silke 2006, 36). Like Sheriff, Alhaji Adamu Yuguda Dibal, the deputy governor of Borno State from 2003 to 2011, criticized the "mystification" of Yusuf as a "messiah" after his arrest, then went on to question Yusuf's character by recalling how Al Qaeda severed its early ties to the Yusufiya after reaching the conclusion that Yusuf was "an unreliable person" (Public Library of US Diplomacy 2009a). According to Dibal, Mohammed Yusuf's death was hardly extrajudicial and was necessary in light of the state of emergency that existed in Borno State. His view is echoed by a professor of Islamic studies at the University of Maiduguri, who claims, "Everyone knew the [Boko Haram] conflict was a time bomb waiting to explode, as Mohammed Yusuf and his followers threatened the peace of the state long before the conflict broke out."

Following Yusuf's death, a twelve-member Islamic Preaching Board, meant to regulate preachers' conduct, was inaugurated in Borno State as a bulwark against extremism, with Dibal claiming that "unless the government is in touch with the clerics, there will always be a problem" (Public Library of US Diplomacy 2009a). Sheriff, who noted that only scholars duly licensed by that board would be allowed to preach, urged its members to use their in-depth knowledge of the Koran and Islamic texts to "checkmate bad preachers" (BBC 2010). On May 5, 2010, Sheriff signed an executive order that declared Boko Haram a society dangerous to government and that prohibited anyone from identifying with the sect (*Daily Trust* 2010). Despite relaxed security presence in Maiduguri following the July 2009 crisis, rumors persisted that Yusuf's deputy, Abubakar Shekau, remained alive, with audiotapes in circulation threatening revenge.

FOUR

Mobile Warfare, Abuses by Security Forces, and Civilian Resistance

The terrorist campaign is like a shark in the water: it must keep moving forward—no matter how slowly or incrementally—or die.

B. Hoffman 2006, 234

People who move and act faster, who come nearest to the momentariness of movement, are now the people who rule. And it is the people who cannot move as quickly, and more conspicuously yet the category of people who cannot at will leave their place at all, who are ruled.

Bauman 2000, 120

The extrajudicial killing of Boko Haram founder Mohammed Yusuf in the July 2009 violence transformed what began as a religious protest movement among a group of disaffected youth into a full-blown, armed insurgency that has killed thousands and displaced millions in northeast Nigeria and across the Lake Chad region. A key defining feature of Boko Haram's emergence in 2010 under Yusuf's second-in-command, Abubakar Shekau, is its violent sectarianism and mobile warfare driven by a deep "psychology of vengeance" (Silke 2008). I use the term *emergence* here to denote "a means to identify, hold open and analyze processes of social change without losing sight of the pre-existing practices and generative conditions that provide its contextually specific shapes" (Rubin et al. 2019, 432). Shekau's Boko Haram may be said to have emerged from the vestiges of Yusuf's

Boko Haram, although the former is not coterminous with the latter. As Katrin Pahl puts it, "In the transition from one subject to the next, the former subject does not simply disappear. The new self encompasses and is forced to relate to the remains of its former manifestations" (2013, 6).

Under Shekau's hawkish leadership, violence became "the only theologically legitimate option left for Boko Haram" (Thurston 2018, 32). Boko Haram vowed to avenge the state's brutal crackdown. The group made several demands, including severe punishment for those who had killed its leader and other members of the sect, reconstruction of its places of worship destroyed by security forces in Maiduguri and other states, and immediate release of detained members (*Nation* 2011, 1–2). A captured Boko Haram member warned, "The gruesome killings of our brothers . . . has not in any way dampened our spirit. In fact, it has made us more steadfast and determined in our holy struggle to oust the secular regime and entrench a just Islamic government" (*Guardian* 2010). That effect supports the point that "catalyst events (i.e., violent acts that are perceived to be unjust) provide a strong sense of outrage and a powerful psychological desire for revenge and retribution" (Browne and Silke 2011, 99). Recalling the resurgence of Boko Haram, a resident of Maiduguri recounted,

> After Mohammed Yusuf's death in 2009, everything calmed down around Maiduguri, and we stayed a year without any problem of those Yusuffiya people. And then one day, we woke up to the news that those people of Yusuf are returning to our city and writing everywhere *La ilaha ila'allah* [There is no god but God]. You're seating at your house and you suddenly see two boys on *achabas* will drive pass you with long cloaks. They will raise it up and bring out guns and start shooting. Pow! Pow! [mimicking the sound of guns]. If you run to soldier and report that Boko Haram is killing, they will say, "It is not our business. You didn't alert us." So, you just start running for your dear life.

Ideologically, the Boko Haram that emerged under Shekau adopted a far more austere and orthodox line of Salafism than Yusuf had espoused. Under Shekau, Boko Haram became obsessed with the use of the doctrine of *takfir*, a religious concept that signifies the act of excommunication—declaring another Muslim an "infidel" (Akhlaq 2015, 1). At the tactical level, Boko Haram became "undisputed masters of mobile warfare" (Seignobos 2015), corroborating the argument that "transportation technologies and systems are now a major theater in the terror war" (Packer 2006,

Fig. 4. Three Boko Haram men on a Chinese motorcycle. (Photograph by Christian Seignobos.)

380). In routine ambushes at checkpoints and major transit routes across northeast Nigeria, Boko Haram fighters increasingly deployed speed and mobility as potent weapons. The poor condition of road infrastructures in the region impinges on travel speed, making it easier for Boko Haram to attack motorists and itinerant traders.

In mobile warfare, the superiority of armed insurgents over the regular army and the settled population rests squarely on "the speed of their own movement; their own ability to descend from nowhere without notice and vanish again without warning, their ability to travel light and not to bother with the kind of belongings which confine the mobility and the maneuvering potential of the sedentary people" (Bauman 2001, 15). Boko Haram's reemergence was announced in June 2010 with a video declaring war on the infidel Nigerian state. A regular trademark of the revived Boko Haram was the use of gunmen on motorcycles to eliminate security personnel, politicians, and religious leaders recalcitrant to back its cause.

Boko Haram's mobile terrorism soon extended to civilians (especially communities seen as state informants) at markets, bus stations, and places of worship. On July 28, 2019, sixty-five villagers walking home from a funeral ceremony in Budu near Maiduguri were killed by Boko Haram's motorcycle-riding gunmen (Paquette and Alfa 2019). Boko Haram's weaponization of motorcycles is hardly surprising, since, as previously argued, many followers of Yusuf were *achaba* drivers and, therefore, *au fait* with the streets, highways, and border communities around the Mandara Mountains and the shorelines of Lake Chad. For years, Boko Haram's *achaba* drivers "honed their skills of mobility, evasion, and violence in contact with state power and state elites" (MacEachern 2018, 175). That honing made motorcycles central to the group's operational tactics and made their drivers its invaluable allies. As "owners of the map" (Sopranzetti 2014), *achaba* drivers used their unmatched knowledge of Maiduguri's urban terrains, especially its shortcuts and backdoors, to decamp after drive-by shootings, leaving the Nigerian military in confusion. Boko Haram fighters "most probably leave the region they have attacked immediately and plan another attack from a different location" (Curiel et al. 2020, 14). Unlike Boko Haram, Nigerian security forces have a poor knowledge of the physical and social terrains. Buba Zabu, driver of a tricycle taxi in Yobe, recounted,

> One thing about *achaba* is that it is a business mostly done by youth, and Boko Haram is equally populated by these local youth who have the knowledge of nooks and corners of our neighborhoods and how to access all areas in the town and surroundings. When the trouble started getting worse, if they commit anything, they have the knowledge of escape routes that the security operatives do not know, and they cannot reach them.

The utility of motorcycles for Boko Haram is obvious, allowing its young and agile fighters to quickly assemble on congested and unpaved roads and disperse into the surrounding bush along narrow trails. On September 28, 2013, for example, an estimated one hundred armed insurgents drove motorcycles into the Yobe State College of Agriculture in Gujba. They escaped hours later with the help of their motorcycles, but not before killing forty-two male students and one lecturer. A staff member recalls what he saw from hiding: "Each of the about twenty motorbikes I saw had at least three armed fighters. They were dressed in black t-shirts, with their heads and half of their faces covered in checkered scarves" (HRW 2016, 35).

Boko Haram's mobilization of automobility in its "holy war" mirrors the manner in which motorcycles remain fundamental to the illegal activities of smugglers and road bandits (*coupers de route*) across the Chad Basin, allowing them to carry out their operations farther from their frontier sanctuaries, since they can return to them relatively quickly and effortlessly. Another advantage that a motorcycle has over other means of transport is that it can be concealed easily. Muhammed, a former *achaba* driver (now a driver of a tricycle taxi) in Maiduguri, told me, "On a motorcycle, one can kill more than ten people at a go, quickly escape through rough routes, and even enter a house and keep it in a room for more than one year, and no one will know the vehicle used in carrying out the job. If you don't enter the house, you won't know there is a motorcycle in the house, and tomorrow they can assemble at a given point and go to commit the same thing and disperse to go and park the motorcycles in their rooms." It is no wonder, then, that *achabas* have been the vehicle of choice in numerous rebellions, from Syria and Iraq to Southern Thailand and Afghanistan (Abuza 2011; HRW 2007; Mashal and Shah 2017).

Between 2013 and 2015, when Boko Haram under Shekau began to violently take over Nigerian territories, the sect intensified its recruitment through scorched-earth tactics. Boko Haram "offered civilians a stark choice: embrace Boko Haram's brand of Islam, or face violence" (Thurston 2018, 2). In rural and peri-urban zones in the states of Borno, Adamawa, and Yobe, the group would typically invite men and boys to join them in *aikin Allah*, "the work of Allah." Those who refused to join were killed, their bodies often left to rot in the streets. Alhaji Bulama Kawu, a veteran hunter helping the Nigerian military to repel Boko Haram in the Sambisa Forest, described Boko Haram's brutal mobilization regime in his native Gubja.

> They asked us to join them or they kill us. They started killing people by beheading innocent souls and planting their heads on the chests of the deceased. We all left the community and ran away for safety. When they first came, they issued a strong decree that those in the community and those in the farms must either join their sect or move elsewhere from wherever one is without taking anything along. Those that went back to the community were killed while most of us fled. At a stage, we made up our minds to go back to our community. We teamed up with the soldiers, fought them, and succeeded in pushing them back and returning to our community.

Prison Raids: Mobilizing the Immobilized

Prison represents "the carceral landscapes of our world, precisely as the antithesis of movement, of freedom of movement. There is not a more dramatic opposition to the idea of movement than the prison" (Mbembe 2018). Since the resurgence of Boko Haram in 2010, "the prison rather than the Mosque has in effect become [Boko Haram's] place of recruitment, not so much because it allowed for the indoctrination of jihadists but because individuals arbitrarily arrested were likely to join the combatants who would free them" (Pérouse de Montclos 2016, 881). Boko Haram swelled its ranks through regular prison raids, freeing captives indefinitely detained by the military on "suspicion of being Islamic militants or for simply provoking soldiers during their crackdown on the insurgency" (Hinshaw 2013a). Between 2013 and 2019, over thirty-six hundred children (as young as five) were detained by the Nigerian military (*Guardian* 2019). In the first half of 2013 alone, 950 Boko Haram suspects died in custody under absolute *conditio inhumana* (Hinshaw 2013a). In 2015, Amnesty International reported that about seven thousand people had died in military detention in the northeast(Amnesty International 2015). A review of morgue records from University of Maiduguri Teaching Hospital, dating from October 2012 through July 2013, shows that "hundreds of bodies left the Giwa Barracks on some days. On June 3, for example, the record shows soldiers brought 350 bodies from the jail. On June 24, there were 115 bodies. On June 29, another 263. Most days listed, the morgue received over 30 bodies" (Hinshaw 2013a). Those often tortured, suffocated, anonymous, and disposable bodies are a stark illustration of the intersection of sovereignty (imperium) and biopower (Mbembe 2003, 12; Agamben 1998), where the bodies of prisoners become "pure vessels of violence" (Butler 2004, 18) and where "war, at the microlevel of the imprisoned body, means torture" (Hannah 2006, 634). A detailed report by the Nigeria Stability and Reconciliation Programme found that "corpses of civilians killed by the military were not released until family members [were compelled to] sign forms stating that their relatives were Boko Haram fighters" (NSRP 2016, 3).

Isa Gusau (2010), a respected journalist in Maiduguri, has argued that Boko Haram insurgents attacked prisons because of their conviction that convicts were unjustly convicted through Western laws. In other words, one of the group's goals is to free inmates from Western-imposed stasis and inability to move at will. Boko Haram's power is thus set in motion by its capacity to make mobile those immobilized by a securitarian and westernized Nigerian state. Official calculations for 2010–15 show that Boko Haram destroyed fifteen out of eighteen prisons in northeast Nigeria alone (Pérouse de Montclos 2016, 881). On September 8, 2010, for example, two hundred insurgents on motorcycles, armed with machine guns and improvised explosive devices, raided a prison in Bauchi where many of Boko Haram fighters awaiting trial were incarcerated. They freed 732 out of 762 inmates, including 150 of their members (AFP 2010c), turning Bauchi into "a key node in the larger northern network" (Paden 2012, 50). The insurgents were formidably armed. A state official recalled, "Due to the overwhelming firepower which the attackers deployed on their mission, they were easily able to overcome the stiff resistance which was put up by the gallant prison officers who attempted to block the progress of the assault on the prison" (AFP 2010b). Boko Haram attacks also leveraged the element of surprise. Isa Yuguda, then governor of Bauchi, said, "It came at the time nobody was expecting, considering that we are in the holy month of Ramadan, when all true Muslims are expected to be fasting and not engage in anything that could lead to the shedding of blood" (AFP 2010b).[1] That surprise tactic, common to guerrilla warfare, is one that Boko Haram would employ again and again. In November 2012, forty armed insurgents stormed the Special Anti-Robbery Squad's prison in Abuja and freed a number of the sect's senior members in state custody. In May 2013, two hundred insurgents stormed a jail in northeast Nigeria, setting 105 prisoners loose and burning down the complex. After another attack by the sect that freed 60 prisoners in Kano in 2012, a message found on one of the cell walls was telling: "What we want is justice in Nigeria" (Hinshaw 2013a).

Body-Vehicle Hybrid: Boko Haram's Drive-by Shootings and Combat Suicide

Between July and September 2010, the states of Borno and Yobe witnessed a spate of hit-and-run killings by motorcycle-riding gunmen believed to be Yusufiya, leaving several police officers dead and creating an ecology of fear across Maiduguri. In those attacks, Boko Haram's insurgents, with AK47s concealed under their long robes, quickly identified their targets and gunned down victims, sometimes inside mosques or private homes. In an incident on the night of August 25, 2010, four Boko Haram gunmen on *achabas* ambushed and killed three police officers in the cities of Maiduguri and Damaturu, the epicenters of the July 2009 violence. In the Maiduguri incident, "The inspector was riding, and the corporal was backed on the motorbike. As they were moving, unknown to them, two motorcyclists were trailing them from behind. They came very close to them, opened fire and killed them. They shot them from behind at the back of their neck"; in Damaturu, "the attackers were two in number and they went to the house on a motorcycle. Immediately they arrived, they used gun and killed the police constable who was guarding the house before they fled away on motorcycles" (Idris and Dauda 2010). Between January and September 2012, an estimated 119 police officers were killed by Boko Haram gunmen, more than in 2010 and 2011 combined. Between 2010 and 2012, twelve Borno-based Islamic clerics and eight traditional leaders accused by Boko Haram of disclosing personal information of sect members to state security forces were shot and killed in their homes and mosques by armed insurgents on motorcycles (HRW 2012).

In light of Boko Haram's rapid hit-and-run tactics, including drive-by killings on motorcycles, security forces in Borno believed that the insurgents had "infiltrated the commercial motorcycle [sector] in the state, pretending to be motorcycle operators while targeting their unsuspected passengers, who may not share their extreme religious ideology. As such, many have restrained from patronizing the commercial cyclists at dusk, while residents often scurry home early from their various engagements" (AFP 2010a). Boko Haram's drive-by shootings went beyond Borno. In Kano, for example, the police commissioner noted that between February 13 and May 14, 2012, Boko Haram gunmen on motorcycles killed eighteen police officers and injured six others (HRW 2012). In an effort to immobilize Boko Haram insurgents, the Borno State government banned the nightly use of *achabas* and forced drivers to dismount at checkpoints. In that way, the state followed the example of Afghanistan, which banned motorcycles and riding double following their frequent usage by Taliban members in hit-and-run assassinations (Mashal and Shah 2017). At the time, the commissioner of police in Borno State warned, "This is only the start. . . . If this strategy doesn't work, we will call for a total ban on motorcycles in the state" (AFP 2010b).

After 2009, Boko Haram became adept in combat suicide (including bombing motor parks), inspired by the organizing logic of martyrdom in which "the will to die is fused with the willingness to take the enemy with you, that is, with closing the door on the possibility of life for everyone" (Mbembe 2003, 37). The group increasingly diffused its terrorist violence through a range of improvised explosive devices (IEDs)—vehicle-borne (VBIEDs), body-borne (BBIEDs), motorcycle-borne (MBIEDs), and tricycle-borne (TBIEDs)—aiming to "kill and to be killed and to spread the fear of killing throughout the society" (Urry 2002, 62). Boko Haram has continued to show interest in soft targets within the transport infrastructure, such as security checkpoints, bus stations and terminals, and other transit areas vulnerable to suicide attacks due to their public accessibility and the ease with which armed insurgents can reach large crowds.[2] As a respondent in Yobe State told me, Boko Haram targets the transport system mainly because "transport business is something that brings many different people from different walks of life together. It is in this business you see people arriving or departing, and these [Boko Haram] boys like to see where people gather together, such as motor park, markets, or on the roads. If you stop a vehicle for two minutes on a major highway, you will create a holdup of vehicles in the neighborhood of one hundred depending on the time of the day." In April 2014, a Boko Haram VBIED exploded at Abuja's crowded Nyanya bus station, a major terminus for commuters in the capital city, killing one hundred people. Two weeks later, Boko Haram carried out another VBIED attack at Wazobia Park in Nyanya (opposite where the last attack occurred), leaving scores dead (*Vanguard* 2014).

Like the Taliban in Afghanistan, Boko Haram regularly abducts children for use in planting IEDs and carrying out suicide bombings (Darden 2019, 6). The group's IEDs range from simple improvised grenades (i.e., emptied soda cans packed with explosives), which can be thrown from *achabas*, to more skillfully built explosives that can be left at target spots. Boko Haram's use of IEDs extends to animals. Insurgents sometimes strap bombs around cows and push them into informal settlements or camps for the internally displaced (Onani and Ngwakwe 2014, 5). On the modern warfare of "body on body" that suicide bombing represents, Achille Mbembe writes,

> The candidate for martyrdom transforms his or her body into a mask that hides the soon-to-be detonated weapon. Unlike the tank or the missile that is clearly visible, the weapon carried in the shape of the body is invisible. Thus concealed, it forms part of the body. It is so intimately part of the body that at the time of detonation it annihilates the body of its bearer, who carries with it the bodies of others when it does not reduce them to pieces. The body does not simply conceal a weapon. The body is transformed into a weapon, not in a metaphorical sense but in the truly ballistic sense. In this instance, my death goes hand in hand with the death of the Other. Homicide and suicide are accomplished in the same act. (2003, 36–37)

Boko Haram's lethal combination of IEDs with automobiles (e.g., VBIEDs and MBIEDs) reclaims the ways in which Tuareg rebels in Mali and Niger during the 1990s converted four-wheel-drive Toyota pickup trucks into "modern chariots," wielding the existing techniques of cars and weapons into a "new technology of war" (Klute 2009, 194).[3] During combat, the Tuareg rebels made clever use of their driving skills and the prevailing dust-laden winds of the Sahara to create dust storms offering cover to fighters as they attacked and retreated. Victims were left in a "haze of dust" (Lecocq and Schrijver 2007, 141). Boko Haram's growing sophistication at weaponizing automobility is perhaps exemplified best by its twin suicide car bombing[4] of the police headquarters and UN building in Abuja in June and August 2011, emulating examples from elsewhere of violent groups (e.g., the Irish Republican Army and liberation forces in Palestine) that have used the car bomb as a weapon of choice. At the police headquarters, an insurgent driver joined the convoy of former police chief General Hafiz Ringim, before the driver rammed his car into the police compounds and detonated his IED, killing eight. In the incident at the UN building, which killed twenty-three people, an insurgent drove a car through two security barriers—which indicates that the car was carefully reinforced to withstand the impact—before detonating his IED as he crashed into the UN reception area (BBC 2011).

Mike Davis outlines seven fundamental reasons why car bombing is a classic "weapon of the weak" and a major attraction to jihadist groups. First, car bombs are stealth weapons of surprising power and destructive efficiency. Trucks and vans, he argues, can easily deliver the explosive equivalent of the bomb load of a B-24 (the workhouse heavy bomber of the United States Army Air Forces in World War II) to the doorstep of a prime target. Second, car bombs are loud in every sense. In addition to their specific operational functions (killing enemies, disrupting daily life, generating unsustainable economic costs), such explosions are usually advertisements for a cause, leader, or abstract principle (including terror itself). Third, car bombs are extremely cheap: forty or fifty people can be massacred with a stolen car and approximately US$500 of fertilizer and bootlegged electronics. Fourth, car bombings are operationally simple to organize. Fifth, akin to "collateral damage," car bombs are inherently indiscriminate: "If the logic of an attack is to slaughter civilians and sow panic in the widest circle, to operate a 'strategy of tension' or just demoralize a society, car bombs are ideal" (Davis 2007, 10). Sixth, car bombs are highly anonymous and leave minimal forensic evidence. Seventh, the most dramatic impact of the car bomb has been precisely its enfranchisement of marginal actors in modern history: "No other weapon in the history of warfare has proven to be such a promiscuous equalizer of combat between elephant and fleas" (Davis 2007, 11).

On February 10, 2020, armed opposition groups (Boko Haram / ISWAP) attacked the village of Auno, located on a major highway connecting Maiduguri to Damaturu. The insurgents arrived on trucks mounted with heavy weapons, killing an estimated thirty people, burning at least eighteen vehicles, and looting, before kidnapping the remaining women and children. Most of the victims burned alive were truck drivers and their conductors who had stopped overnight to sleep on their way to Maiduguri (Al Jazeera 2020). Boko Haram's attacks on road users, including its mounting of fake checkpoints and kidnapping for ransom on major highways, has made it difficult for humanitarian aid workers to do their jobs, giving rise to criticisms of the Nigerian state by civil society organizations and motorists. A commercial trucker in Borno State said, "Despite these daily insurgent attacks, the roads are left without adequate security personnel; one will travel up to fifty kilometers without any manned security post. We really do not understand what is happening with the soldiers." In January 2020, Nigeria's UN humanitarian coordinator, Edward Kallon, bemoaned worsening insecurity on major highways across Borno State, especially the brutal killings of aid workers.

> I am extremely worried by the increasingly insecure environment that humanitarians are working in to provide urgent and vital assistance to civilians affected by the crisis. The humanitarian community is troubled by the increasing trend in vehicular checkpoints set up by non-state armed groups along main supply routes in the states of Borno and Yobe. These checkpoints expose civilians and humanitarians to heightened risks of being killed or abducted. I urge all parties to the conflict to protect the civilian population, including aid workers, from such grave violations of international laws, especially women and children who are among the most vulnerable and are caught up in the violence. (Haruna 2020)

The Nigerian Union of Journalists (NUJ) has also criticized the absence of protection on the highway between the states of Borno and Yobe. It has called on journalists to do more to report mobile attacks. Alhassan Haruna, the northeast zonal vice president of the NUJ, commented,

> We are calling on President Muhammadu Buhari to cut short his stay in the UK and return home and address the pathetic situation in the Northeast. A responsible government should not wait and fold its arms, watching citizens being killed and abducted on a daily basis on a highway that is said to be guarded by armed soldiers and police. It is unacceptable in this advance era for government to leave its citizens at the mercy of terrorists. It is unheard of that the only road to a state as big as Borno cannot be protected for the ordinary populace who have never asked for anything more than the freedom to move and right to be protected. (Haruna 2020)

Danger Zones: Transit and Cross-Border Trading Routes

Boko Haram's mobile attacks have targeted strategic roads and bridges, including the route that connects Maiduguri to Gamboru on the border with Cameroon, as well as the bridge at Gamboru-Ngala, which links the states of Borno and Adamawa to Cameroon and Chad (Faul and Abdulaziz 2014). The attacks have reversed the steady increase occurring in recent decades in cross-border trade in the Lake Chad region (Magrin and Pérouse de Montclos 2018, 53).[5] By targeting those strategic transit and trading circuits, Boko Haram not only disrupted the free flow of goods and services[6] but also isolated people from proximate communities. A former inhabitant of the town of Gwoza in Borno said, "I have not gone to my hometown for a year now. At first, Boko Haram were always attacking villages and towns around Gwoza. These attacks forced many to flee the area, and since then, many of us aren't willing to take the risk of going home. But the worst thing now is that roads to our towns have been destroyed. We can't even go to Gwoza now, and people there can't come out. We're completely cut off from the rest of Nigeria" (Iweze 2014, 6).

In 2014, a major bridge connecting Nigeria and border communities near Cameroon and another bridge linking Maiduguri and Damaturu were blown up by Boko Haram (Pérouse de Montclos 2014, 13), impinging on movement and restricting food supply. Severe food crises in parts of northeast Nigeria have arisen because months of fighting have destroyed access to roads and bridges (Kah 2017), isolating rural areas in the states of Borno, Yobe, and Adamawa from food aid, while hindering farmers' production and sales opportunities (Mercy Corps 2017). In some communities, such as those in and around the northwestern Mandara Mountains, local inhabitants face acute famine because crops have not been planted or harvested effectively in the last three years (MacEachern 2019, 156). Today, roughly eight hundred thousand people are trapped in areas in northern Borno that are beyond the reach of humanitarian assistance. A UNDP official charged with implementing an integrated community stabilization program in the northern region commented, "Everything hinges on security, as all of our work requires access. Our first question is: is the community accessible?" (Brechenmacher 2019, 14).

Emergency blockades, curfews, land mines laid by Boko Haram, and fuel restrictions have further hampered efforts to deliver food aid to more than 1.5 million people on the brink of famine (*Reuters* 2017). The situation is so dire that internally displaced persons (IDPs) that I visited in the town of Abadam, an area of Borno State freed from the control of Boko

Haram in 2015, told me that they were more concerned about food than they were about Boko Haram's return attacks. Looking to return to their communities to pick up the pieces of their lives after Boko Haram's attack, IDPs lamented the paltry support received from soldiers. Girbua, a farmer from the town of Goneri in Yobe State, recounted,

> They [Boko Haram] came to this community and drove us away for a good three years. The community was completely deserted for these three years, without even seeing a single dog on the streets. There was a time when the Nigerian Army had a meeting to support Goneri people to go back to their community. We asked the army commander for his men to provide security for us to return to our community, but they denied us and asked us to come back and guard ourselves, which we agreed to. This is a rural community; we don't have anything to boast of. I sold some of the food crops I could salvage and animals remaining to arm the youths who were helping us ward off thieves even before the Boko Haram invasion. We are now seventeen months since we returned to our community after three years. No one has ever supported us with anything since our return.

"The Terrorists Rule the Road": The Mobilization of Automobile Deception

In the vast majority of Boko Haram's automobile attacks, its fighters have disguised themselves in army uniforms and mounted fake blockades on highways, where they have kidnapped, raped, maimed, and killed using land mines, ancillary to holdups on the road. A study by the Mines Advisory Group, a landmine clearance charity, shows that mines laid by Boko Haram killed at least 162 people in two years. Casualties rose from twelve per month in 2016 to nineteen per month in 2017–18, making Nigeria's casualty rate from mines the eighth highest in the world (*Guardian* 2018). The presence of mines on roads has profoundly impacted the ability of local populations to move around freely, especially farmers and road transport workers. One respondent told me, "Everyone I have met in Borno State has been affected in one way or the other, whether losing a family member, a friend, or a house. People can't move around freely in most of the region, and much of the land can't be used to farm or collect firewood, so the impact on communities is huge."

Umar, a taxi driver from Mubi in Adamawa State, told me, "Boko

Haram insurgents take advantage of roads that are not in good shape by pretending to be working on bad roads with potholes and [in the process] bury some improvised explosives to harm road users. You know we have people who volunteer to be repairing roads. Boko Haram seizes the opportunity and plant land mines. They can also mount roadblocks in the morning, afternoon, and night to kill and injure unsuspecting road users." Boko Haram's mobile deceptions allow its fighters to gain closer proximity to unwary travelers. A major problem for drivers in the region is the problem of distinction, that is, determining whether a checkpoint or blockade has been mounted officially, by the Nigerian military; semiofficially, by progovernment militias (i.e., vigilantes and hunters); or unofficially, by Boko Haram insurgents. In this light, roads and checkpoints in northeast Nigeria mirror a postcolonial Nigerian society where signs and their referents have become virtually detached from each other and where "there is hardly a reality without its double" (Mbembe and Roitman 1995, 340). At the same time, roads and checkpoints reproduce the Nigerian state, which is simultaneously present and absent in people's day-to-day lives.

As a result of Boko Haram's deadly and deceptive attacks on travelers, local residents have generally abandoned some roads out of fear, especially Maiduguri–Mafa–Dikwa Road, Damaturu–Buni Yadi–Biu Road, and Maiduguri–Bama–Gwoza Road. In July 2014, fifteen travelers were killed when armed insurgents ambushed them along Maiduguri–Mafa–Dikwa Road (Marama 2014). In February 2019, Boko Haram's ambushes and abductions of road users along Damaturu–Buni Yadi–Biu Road caused widespread disruption (Marama 2019). "Whenever we leave the road from Maiduguri, we just say our final goodbyes to our family in case we don't return," said Shehu, who heads Borno's Civil Society Forum. He added, "The terrorists rule the road" (Parkinson and Akingbule 2020).

Boko Haram's deceptive automobile warfare is perhaps illustrated best by two coordinated attacks, the Benisheik massacre of 2013 and the Baga massacre of 2015. In the former, insurgents disguised in army uniforms stopped traffic on a major highway between Damaturu, Benisheik, and Maiduguri, proceeding to kill 159 travelers caught in the holdup (Al Jazeera 2013). Some Benisheik survivors recalled how insufficiently armed Nigerian soldiers fled their checkpoints at the approach of the armed insurgents. Others spoke of gunmen on *achabas* and dressed as soldiers, who shot victims after pulling them from their cars and forcing them to the ground (Hinshaw 2013b). A man who went to Benisheik the following morning in search of a colleague graphically described what he saw at the fake checkpoint mounted by Boko Haram men: "There were bodies all over . . . three here, two there, four near the next—all lying face down, dead near to their vehicle. Then I saw a long line of bodies . . . about 30 of them. But weirdly, one of the trucks was carrying cows, which were still alive. Who are these people who kill the humans, yet leave the cows standing?" (HRW 2013). Describing his ordeal, a Benisheik survivor who was shot in the leg by the insurgents recalls, "We were asked to get out of our cars and lie face down by nine men dressed as soldiers who blocked the road. They shot dead five people and went about slaughtering fourteen others before someone called them on the phone that soldiers were heading their way. They abandoned the rest of us and sped into the bush on their motor-cycles" (Alexander 2013).

The Baga massacre is possibly the deadliest single massacre perpe-trated by Boko Haram since 2009. The insurgents attacked in approxi-mately twenty vehicles, with ten to fifteen armed men to a vehicle; they killed probably as many as two thousand civilians, razed homes and mar-kets to the ground, and kidnapped hundreds of residents of fighting age (Fessy 2015). Fatima, a resident of Baga and an eyewitness to the carnage, described how dozens of men dressed in army fatigues and black head wraps ran riot on the fishing town: "I saw them on motorbikes and cars, and I could hear them shouting *Allahu akhbar!* [God is great!]. . . . I entered our house and told everyone to run . . . Boko Haram is coming." A Baga resident who barely escaped death said, "I got on a motorbike and saw people fleeing until I reached the water." The resident continued, "The water and roads were full of bodies. They even killed my own brother. [Boko Haram] told people to leave Baga and then they fired on them as they fled" (Muscati and Hassan 2015). For many people fleeing Baga, Lake Chad—bordering Nigeria, Cameroon, Chad, and Niger—was simultane-ously a main escape route and a soft underbelly. Samer Muscati and Tirana Hassan (2015) relate,

> At the shore, terrified civilians desperately tried to get on boats, to hide in the water, or find other ways to flee. Some managed to escape by boat, yet most weren't so lucky. Boko Haram fighters patrolling the perimeter of the lake in vehicles fired on them, killing many. Witnesses described the bodies of women, children, mothers with babies on their backs' floating in the lake as far as the eye could see.

One "silent victim" of Boko Haram's deadly road ambushes and vehicle burnings since 2009 is the National Union of Road Transport Workers (Audu 2013). At a presentation of 450 vehicles to the NURTW's Borno chapter as a compensation for over 750 of its vehicles lost to Boko Haram attacks, Governor Kashim Shettima lauded the courage of the NURTW to keep moving people and goods in the face of senseless killings and marginal gains. The NURTW's efforts bring to mind Joshua Grace's (2013) description of drivers as "heroes of the road."

Boko Haram's automobile warfare has forced many local politicians and traditional monarchs to travel by air. In May 2014, Boko Haram snipers shot and killed the emir of Gwoza, Alhaji Idrissa Timta, along Biu–Garkida Road, while he was on the way to attend the funeral of the emir of Gombe, Alhaji Shehu Abubakar. The emirs of Uba and Askira, traveling in the same convoy with Timta, narrowly escaped (Marama and Mosadomi 2014). Following the attack, a visibly shaken Governor Shettima (who also traveled by road for the funeral) admitted that "traveling to Gwoza takes more than courage." He added, "If I say I was not petrified traveling through that 135 kilometers of road to Gwoza I would be lying, because that road had been designated a no-go area for about two months now due to incessant attacks and killings that occur there" (CBS News 2014). It is not hard to see why Gwoza is considered a notorious haven for Boko Haram. The terrain is rocky and hilly, with heights of about thirteen hundred meters above sea level. In 2014, Gwoza saw an influx of insurgents fleeing the Sambisa Forest (United Nations 2017, 14). Today, roads out of Gwoza remain very dangerous, and phone networks are poor to nonexistent. To ensure safe passage, therefore, Shettima needed the protection of 150 soldiers of the Seventh Infantry Division's Operation "Lafiya Dole," police special squads, and members of the Civilian Joint Task Force. In addition, a Nigerian fighter jet provided air cover as the governor's convoy traveled the dangerous Maiduguri–Bama Road to get to his destination (Associated Press 2014). In September 2020, a Boko Haram attack on the convoy of Borno State governor Babagana Zulum, along Cross Kauwa–Baga Road in Borno, killed over thirty people (Marama 2020).

As mobility scholars have argued, "Travel can be a positive experience; we need not consider it pure cost. . . . Travel can be a pleasure, if we pay attention to the human experience: the visual sequences, the opportunities to learn or to meet other people" (Lynch 1981, 274). In the context of northeast Nigeria, travel is the exact opposite: it is experienced as pure danger rather than pleasure; travelers are increasingly confronted with the temporality and fragility of their petrified lives. The roads in particular have become "a locale for the catastrophic and tragic, the venue in which life plans and purposes are brought to an abrupt end, a final marking of a life with its ultimate fare" (Rosin 2000, 390). In Borno State, for example, drivers often shared stories of how insurgents buried land mines on roads more traveled and how "snipers wait in trees to fire at passing cars, which are then attacked by gunmen hiding in bushes by the side of the road" (VOA 2014). Abubakar, who drives tanker trucks carrying gasoline along the Lagos–Maiduguri route, describes how ten of his colleagues plying that route were killed within a period of three weeks: "The [Boko Haram] militants stopped them and cut off their heads with an electric chainsaw and burned the trucks" (Fleming 2015). Inusa, a thirty-three-year-old truck driver who travels the four-hundred-mile highway between Kano and Maiduguri, recalls a day when five of the truck drivers who worked his route did not come back; one of them was found with his head severed by a chain saw. In a video message on September 26, 2013, Boko Haram claimed to have killed up to two hundred people on the roads of northern Nigeria in 2013 alone (Hinshaw 2013b).

Boko Haram's automobile attacks have shown no signs of abating. Between June and November 2020, for example, more than two hundred people were murdered or kidnapped on the four main highways leading into Maiduguri (Parkinson and Akingbule 2020). On May 26, 2019, up to twenty people were slaughtered when Boko Haram gunmen ambushed a convoy transporting civilians from Sabon Gari to displacement camps in Damboa in Borno State (F. Kelly 2019). Boko Haram has also launched several successful road ambushes against soldiers. In an attack in September 2020, eighteen people (four soldiers, ten police officers, and four civilians) were killed when the Boko Haram splinter group ISWAP ambushed a government convoy on the road between the town of Monguno and the fishing town of Baga (BBC 2020a). In July 2019, six soldiers were killed when Boko Haram gunmen shot at their gasoline truck near Jakana, thirty kilometers from Maiduguri. A similar attack was conducted in December 2018, when thirteen soldiers died after a deadly Boko Haram / ISWAP ambush along the highway near the village of Kareto (Al Jazeera 2019). Boko Haram's near-daily attacks on lives and properties in transit "reduces people to a precarious condition that affects the very way in which they define themselves" (Mbembe and Roitman 1995, 330). One vehicle bumper in Maiduguri framed that existential reality with a sticker that read "Dead Man Walking."

Boko Haram typically intensifies its road ambushes during Nigeria's rainy season, between June and September. Trucks and four-wheel-drive vehicles cannot navigate northern Nigeria's unpaved roads during that "wintering period" (as the colonial army once called it). Waterlogged roads replete with potholes make it extremely difficult for soldiers to patrol, forcing them into a "wintering truce" (Seignobos 2015, 93). Even Boko Haram's motorcycles often run into snags in the lowlands, forcing its fighters to use horses in their operations—to transform themselves into "devils on horseback" (*janjaweed*).[7] By cutting off Boko Haram's principal supply lines, particularly for fuel, soldiers force the insurgents to swap their unfueled vehicles for horses, which they use to carry out attacks in remote villages (Press TV 2015). On August 31, 2015, for example, Boko Haram insurgents on horseback reportedly killed eighty people in attacks on three villages in Borno State (Al Jazeera 2015). In fresh attacks on September 2, 2015, horse-riding insurgents killed twenty-six people in Borno (H. Umar 2015). In June 2018, the Nigerian military killed ten horse-riding Boko Haram insurgents during an operation at Ngelkona in the Ngala area of Borno State (*Premium Times* 2018). Those terrorist attacks by horseback prompted the Seventh Division of the Nigerian Army in Maiduguri to prohibit Borno residents, particularly traditional rulers, from riding horses, beginning in September 2015. In an effort to distinguish local populations from terrorists, the military warned that anyone found riding a horse would be treated as an insurgent (*Daily Post* 2015).

Zones of Ambiguity: Boko Haram and Cross-Border Smuggling

At the heart of Boko Haram's violent insurgency are the "frontier spaces" of the Lake Chad region, "a unique territorial ecosystem in which various other zones . . . of political piracy, . . . barbaric violence, . . . weak citizenship . . . exist adjacent to, within or over each other" (Weizman 2007, 7). The term *frontier spaces* is used here to denote social spaces where "what is and is not legitimate authority, and who authorizes such legitimate power, is often an open question and an object of deep contention. The disorderly and often violent forms of rule associated with unreliable and partisan legal orders, unaccountable forms of state governance, and ineffective forms of public authority, typically coexist with the questionable legitimacy of most *other* forms of authority—civic, customary, corporate, religious" (Watts 2018, 478). So how do the frontier spaces of the Lake Chad region matter for Boko Haram?

Much like the civil wars in Sierra Leone and Liberia, Boko Haram highlights the porosity of African borders haphazardly drawn by European colonialists and "the need to reflect on the state at its territorial margins" (Ferme 2004, 81). "Practices and politics of life" in marginal areas (e.g., borders) have "shaped the political, regulatory, and disciplinary practices that constitute, somehow, that thing we call 'the state'" (Das and Poole 2004, 3). The Lake Chad region, the hub of Boko Haram, is located in the Sahelian zone of West and Central Africa. The region's fluid boundaries and spatial dynamics have been the subject of a welter of studies focusing on cross-border dynamics and security cooperation (Walther and Retaille 2017; Choplin and Lombard 2014; Klute 2009), smuggling and semiofficial trade networks crisscrossing the Sahara (Scheele 2012; MacEachern 2018; Debos 2011; Roitman 2004b), and trans-Saharan migration and trade (Marfaings and Wippel 2004; Gregoire and Labazee 1993; Magrin and Pérouse de Montclos 2018). Paul Nugent engages the border as a primary site of power that enables and constrains, making border zones sites of ambivalence and ambiguity (2002, 8). With its strategic location as a crossroads in West Africa, a key feature of the Lake Chad region is not only its porous borders but also their illegal activities (Onuoha 2013; Roitman 2006). Most people pay little attention to the nominal borders, taking advantage of their porosity for various illicit enterprises (van Dijk et al. 2001, 23). From the ambiguous zones of the Lake Chad Basin, it is clear that borders do not necessarily work in the service of the state, nor are they simply constituted or enforced through the regulation of state laws and policies (cf. Christensen and Albrecht 2020, 390).

"Terrorists work in a deterritorialized way," argues Cindi Katz (2007, 356). That is especially true of Boko Haram. Since 2015, the group has increasingly relocated its activities and attacks to nearby Cameroon, Niger, and Chad, following its failure to retain operational capacity in many of its former strongholds in northeast Nigeria (e.g., Maiduguri), as a result of civil-military pressures and mobility constraints. Available figures show at least 1,499 illegal and 84 regular (legal) entry points into northeast Nigeria from Cameroon, Niger, and Chad. In Adamawa State alone, there are an estimated 25 illegal routes into Nigeria from neighboring countries (Onuoha 2013). Boko Haram has exploited the northern basin of Lake Chad, trading routes, and the religious and cultural affinities that Borno shares with riparian states in Lake Chad (Cameroon, Niger, and Chad) to smuggle arms and "sell" abducted women (e.g., the girls kidnapped from the town of Chibok), recruit foot soldiers,[8] mount food raids, and evade government surveillance (Seignobos 2016; Agbiboa 2017; Kah 2017). Cameroonian historian Saibou Issa argues, "Smuggling is at the heart of the war. . . . Boko Haram is also a for-profit criminal enterprise that incorporates many smugglers, and which depends on crime and violence that generate significant income in an environment of socio-economic distress" (cited in MacEachern 2018, 172). That some people with almost identical language and descendants are found across the border makes it difficult to identify strangers, increasing the likelihood of local collaboration (Cyffer 2006, 34). The situation is complicated by the ECOWAS (Economic Community of West African States) Protocol on the Free Movement of People and Goods, which has inadvertently supported Boko Haram's cross-border smuggling (Onuoha 2013, 5).

Boko Haram's smuggling business is buttressed by its "mobility capital" (Ciavolella 2011), that is, its inheritance and appropriation of decades, if not centuries, old networks of illegal activities and moneymaking in the Lake Chad region (MacEachern 2018, 172). That situation reinforces the close connections between the social networks underlying insurgent organizations and the spatial patterns of their attacks (Walther and Miles 2018). It also explains why, regarding Boko Haram and events in the Lake Chad Basin, "history often seems to be replaying itself" (Seignobos 2016). A case in point is Cameroon's Far North Region. Now used by Boko Haram to smuggle firearms, fuel, illegal drugs, basic food staples, and stolen vehicles into Nigeria, the extreme north region has been a space of banditry and robbery for centuries, entrenching a political economy of chaos, ambush, and plunder (Münkler 2005, 14). As a result, traders and drivers are wary of traveling long distances, for fear of being killed or robbed.

In recent decades, Lake Chad's porous border has been used to smuggle *zoua-zoua* (illegally imported Nigerian gasoline) into Cameroon, by local youth riding Japanese or Chinese motorcycles. Relying on their strength and courage and their knowledge of back trails to do their dirty work, young men smuggling *zoua-zoua* have seen themselves as "both operating outside the law and sustaining the economy of the region, in circumstances where they had no other way of making a living" (MacEachern 2018, 128–29; see also Roitman 2006). Their perception reinforces the argument that smuggling and other forms of informal economic livelihoods are widely seen as legitimate in the face of government failure and socioeconomic necessity (Raeymaekers 2010, 575). Boko Haram's operations of arms smuggling thrive on "the use of specially crafted skin or thatched bags attached to camels, donkeys and cows where arms are concealed and moved across the borders with the aid of nomadic pastoralists or herders" (Onuoha 2013, 5). The jihadists often connive with corrupt cross-border traders and custom officials to conceal arms, weapons, and drugs with goods that are smuggled into Nigeria via heavy trucks, trailers, and lorries (Onuoha 2013, 5). Given the sheer volume of goods overloaded on the large trucks, and the widespread nature of security force extortion on Nigerian highways, little or no inspection is conducted on them by security agents, whose priority is what they can purloin or set aside for themselves. Sometimes, Boko Haram insurgents bypasses the roads by making use of traditional long canoes to smuggle hundreds of fighters and dozens of motorcycles from the Lake Chad region into Nigeria (Seignobos 2015, 105). A significant portion of Boko Haram's finances comes from cross-border fish trades (such as in nearby Niger), and from levying taxes on goods transported via the check-points it controls (O'Grady 2015). In Borno State, the group's checkpoints are strategically positioned along main supply arteries of limited statehood, such as Maiduguri-Monguno, Monguno-Gajiram, Maiduguri-Damboa, Magumeri-Gubio, Chabbal-Magumeri, Gubio-Kareto, Kareto-Damasak, and Damboa-Biu. Extortion at such checkpoints make up the bulk of Boko Haram's $5–10 million annual income, the other sources being donations, kidnapping for ransom, and bank robberies (Nellemann et al. 2018, 137).

The Boko Haram insurgency is complicated by the highly variable rainfall and climate change in the Lake Chad region, which has severely impinged on the livelihoods of roughly thirty million people, many of whom are fishermen, crop farmers, and nomadic herdsmen (Cyffer 2006; Sparkman 2019). The climate and security risks have drastically affected fishing livelihoods and irrigation farming (UNFAO 2009), forcing farm-ers and fishermen ("lake nomads") to migrate. Drought-induced transhu-mance has intensified communal conflicts over the use of scarce common resources (e.g., land and water), resulting in bloody clashes between farm-ers and nomadic herdsmen and between upstream and downstream users (Bolori 2005, 35).

Zones of Indistinction: "Shoot First and Ask Questions Later"

[Boko Haram] are like normal people like us. You will pray with them in the mosques, go to same markets and transact assorted business, do lots of social engagements like weddings, naming ceremony but you won't know who they are. And just like everyone travels freely, so do they: they go buy stuff and sell. It is only if one exposes himself that you will recognize who he really is. There are boys that were born here, they school here and some are hustling like all of us here. If they join this thing called Boko Haram you won't know until when they show their true colors or if one of them get arrested and he mention names then people begin to wonder. These are boys you don't see them abusing substances or fomenting trouble anywhere. People relate with them freely without knowing their [extremist] orientation until when something happens.

Branch secretary of keke napep in Bedde, Yobe State

In June 2011, at the height of the Boko Haram insurgency, the Nigerian government deployed a special joint task force (JTF), codenamed Operation Restore Order (ORO), to Borno and other affected parts of northeast Nigeria, to "crush" Boko Haram. But JTF ORO troops were unfamiliar with the terrain, languages, and locally known Boko Haram members, making it difficult for the troops to build the networks of trust and reciprocity that are key to overcoming an enemy within. Bunu Bukar, secretary of the Borno Hunters Association, explains, "You cannot be brought from another part of Nigeria to Borno to fight insurgents without knowledge of the local terrain," especially when the insurgents behave like "normal people." "Look at it this way," said a vigilante man in Maiduguri, "you bring in an officer who doesn't know the language and culture of the people, [and] he must become suspicious of any youth he sees, because he doesn't know the Boko Haram elements who even the people staying with them do not know."

Far from improvising clever ways of winning the "hearts and minds" of the population, a fundamental rule of counterinsurgency that allows state security forces to overcome the problem of knowledge (Kilcullen 2006, 30), JTF ORO proceeded to lump locals into a "suspect community," defined as "a community created in and by the securitized imagination and enacted in processes of 'othering' through a range of security practices of counter-terrorism" (Breen-Smyth 2014, 223). As one respondent lucidly put it, "Suspicion is all the greater because we do not know who is Boko Haram and who is not. . . . To the military, the locals are 'Boko Haram,' and to Boko Haram, the locals are traitors." Another respondent remarked, "The army came with the mindset that everyone in Maiduguri was Boko Haram." Yet another local resident recounts that Nigerian soldiers were "abusive and intolerant. Soldiers could mishandle you, they crashed into cars, used bayonets to puncture people's tyres" (Healy 2018). In short, under JTF ORO, notions of civilians and insurgents collapsed into what Giorgio Agamben (1998) calls a "zone of indistinction," thereby damaging the affective terrain of counterinsurgency (Khalili 2014, 38).

Absent an efficient registering machine that made society knowable (Gopfert 2016), which is a key function of governmentality, suspicion became sufficient grounds for indefinite detention, random killings, and forced disappearances. Abdul Raufu Mustapha observes, "Facing unidentified enemies in the northeast, initially getting little cooperation from a population terrorized by insurgents, and poorly provisioned, the tendency for some in the military was to shoot first and ask questions later" (2014, 14). A security officer put it bluntly: "When we can't see the enemy, civilians become the enemy" (Dietrich 2015, 6). It is no wonder, then, that at the peak of the violent insurgency, from 2010 through 2013, JTF ORO is estimated to have killed three times more civilians than did Boko Haram insurgents (NSRP 2016, 12). As a consequence, during the course of my fieldwork in the affected parts of northeast Nigeria, simply mentioning the name of Boko Haram in public conversations was anathema among fearful locals. The scorched-earth tactics of JTF ORO alienated civilians and hurt any chances of local cooperation: "The rounding up by the federal authorities of young men in the proximity of each bomb attack or drive-by shooting in Borno and the burning of houses regarded as [insurgent] hideouts have alienated many innocent citizens. The community, it would appear, has closed its ears to pleas by the authorities for information as to who is (or who is not) a member of Boko Haram" (Paden 2012, 50–51).

The war on Boko Haram and the problem of knowledge is compounded by the group's guerrilla-style tactics in built-up areas, which gives its fighters "the profits of visibility," that is, "the arrangement of space to either encourage or prevent the visibility of places, of paths, or of people" (Fogle 2011, 93). The conflation of civilians and insurgents in the war against Boko Haram reflects a crisis of knowledge in counterinsurgency doctrines and practices, caused by a flawed epistemology and ignorance (Zulaika 2012). Labels often have a lethal quality (Abrahams 1987). With the label of "suspect community" stamped on them by the JTF ORO deployed to restore order, civilians, especially young men, were rendered disposable, and their spaces of sociality and maneuver morphed into a "happy hunting ground" (Breen-Smyth 2014).

In May 2012, the Ambassador Usman Galtimari Presidential Committee on the Security Challenges in the Northeast concluded that JTF ORO cannot win the hearts and minds of the people under the "present poisonous atmosphere." The committee further called for the immediate replacement of JTF ORO with a new cohort familiar with the local terrain, speaking the main languages, and having "a human touch, care and concern by avoiding unnecessary brutality and ruthlessness" (Abbah 2012). In mid-2015, following the election of President Muhammadu Buhari, a cross-border security strategy in form of the Multinational Joint Task Force (MNJTF), the regional offensive involving troops from Chad, Cameroon, Nigeria, Niger, and Benin, was revived. The MNJTF was originally established in 1994 as an instrument for cross-border control of organized criminal activities in the Lake Chad region. Despite the expectations that greeted the disbandment of JTF ORO in August 2013 and its replacement in 2015 with the Seventh Infantry Division as the umbrella command for the war against Boko Haram, codenamed Operation "Lafiya Dole" (Peace by Any Means), indiscriminate violence on civilian populations continued to be widespread and extreme in their visibility. "Sometimes, we don't even know who the real enemy is, whether Boko Haram or soldiers," said Hafsa, whose husband was killed by a bomb detonated by armed insurgents.

The indiscriminate violence of the military proved counterproductive and alienated locals, who became reluctant to offer any information that could help the state counterinsurgency campaign. Local frustrations were further deepened by the "state of emergency" in place, which saw phone services cut off, motorcycles banned at night, curfews and roadblocks imposed, and soaring food prices (BBC 2013). A security person from Bama recalls how unnamed policemen from that town burned a popular market to the ground after one of their colleagues was killed in a Boko Haram attack. In revenge, angry Bama traders pooled their resources and offered them to Boko Haram members to "teach the policemen a bitter lesson." That story supports the argument that abuses by security forces may lead a suspect group to perceive that state security forces, rather than armed insurgents, poses the greatest threat to their physical security and social livelihoods (Breen-Smyth 2014, 231). Consequently, bonds may develop on the basis of shared experiences of victimization and a collective desire to avoid being constantly targeted.

Eyes on the Road: The Emergence of the Civilian Joint Task Force

One obvious but frequently overlooked aspect of contemporary wars is their terrible toll on civilian populations. Research shows that as a conflict actor weakens relative to its adversary, it tends to use violence against civilian populations as a means of reshaping the strategic landscape to its benefits (Wood et al. 2012, 647; Wood 2010). To complicate matters, civilian protection strategies launched by states, international organizations, and nongovernmental organizations have been largely ineffective (Jose and Medie 2016). Consequently, local populations are ever more dependent on providing their own security, either independently, in conjunction with the state, or in a negotiated relationship with armed opposition groups (Jentzsch et al. 2015; Bellagamba and Klute 2008; Van Metre 2019). Such local security initiatives are commonly spearheaded by civilian defense groups (CDGs), including vigilante groups and civil militias, that operate alongside the regular army or work independently to protect their communities from rebels and other local security dilemmas (Agbiboa 2020;

Dirkx 2018; Kasfir et al. 2018). Across Africa, CDGs have become a popular survival mechanism for local populations caught between armed insurgents and brutal state security forces and preyed on by both. Examples include the Kamajors in Sierra Leone, which emerged as the symbolic and material center for mobilization of community defense against the rebel forces of the Revolutionary United Front (RUF); the Arrow Boys of Teso, who protected villages against the Lord's Resistance Army (LRA), led by Joseph Kony, in Uganda; and the Zande Arrow Boys, who battled the LRA and later rebelled against South Sudan's Dinka-led regime (ICG 2017; D. Hoffman 2011; R. Jones 2008).

Populated mainly by mobile civilian subjects who assume intelligence responsibilities and limited combat roles, CDGs deliver a range of public goods, including maintaining law and order and providing services of dispute resolution. Through their local connections, self-defense forces are usually more adept in providing timely and actionable local intelligence as well as identifying suspicious behaviors and strangers in their localities (Kafir et al. 2018, 262). At the same time, CDGs can exacerbate conflicts, as polarizers of local communities and instigators of communal wars (ICG 2017; Carey et al. 2013; Rodgers 2007; Anderson 2002). In Nigeria, Cameroon, Niger and Chad, CDGs have long been linked to political reprisals, communal violence, extortion, random killings, and other kinds of criminality (R. Jones 2008), partly because politicians often create, align with, or hijack those nonstate armed actors to deal with various security concerns and to achieve the politicians' own political goals.

On one hand, the rise and growing influence of CDGs in the context of counterinsurgencies calls into question the Weberian assumption on state monopoly of the legitimate use of violence. On the other hand, it challenges the continued treatment of civilians as passive victims of war rather than as active participants. Despite the large corpus of works on intrastate conflicts, we still know very little about how and why CDGs emerge in insurgent zones, how they mobilize popular support and integrate themselves among local communities, and, most important, how they mobilize mobility in the war on terrorism. For all the academic and policy interest in Boko Haram, the voice, experiences, and coping strategies of civilians who carry on amid an often violent everyday existence have received relatively little attention.

From 2013 onward, Boko Haram adopted a strategy of terrorism against local communities suspected of forming a civilian defense group—known as the Civilian Joint Task Force (CJTF), or *kato da gora* ("youth with sticks")—against Boko Haram. As a pro-government vigilante group headquartered in Maiduguri, the CJTF helps to run security checkpoints and provide tips on Boko Haram members in localities, taking advantage of local knowledge and social networks (Agbiboa 2018a). The CJTF is widely credited with forcing Boko Haram out of Maiduguri and into the Sambisa Forest and Mandara Mountains. Ganiyu, the overall chairman of the CJTF, said that the emergence of the CJTF in Maiduguri was "a direct product of harassment by Boko Haram insurgents and harassment by Nigerian security forces." According to Ganiyu, "Because security men don't know who was the real Boko Haram, they will cordon off any area and take every male youth away for 'screening.' Then later on, we, the youth of Maiduguri, we decided that enough is enough. That's why we chose to cooperate with the army, that we are going to fish out those bad apples living among us. That's how we started this group."

Ganiyu's account was reinforced by Sanusi, a taxi driver in Maiduguri. "Let me tell you," Sanusi said, "we have three types of Boko Haram. We have a real Boko Haram. We have a military Boko Haram. And we have a political Boko Haram. You don't know who will save you. Only God. If Boko Haram doesn't kill you, soldiers will kill you. This is why those CJTF boys took up bamboo sticks. Because they say if the Nigerian state cannot protect us, let us protect ourselves." For vigilant citizens like Ganiyu and Sanusi, the Nigerian government, which manifests itself through its brutal security forces (in particular, its army and police), has not only failed in its responsibility to secure lives and properties but constitutes a threat to the survival of ordinary citizens. That threat maps well onto perceptions of the predatory nature of the postcolonial state in Africa (Mbembe 1992; Comaroff and Comaroff 1999; Masquelier 2001).

CJTF members were originally armed with rudimentary weapons such as sticks, swords, machetes, and bows and arrows. "Guns are too expensive," a CJTF leader in Maiduguri said, "costing between N 600 and N 700. We cannot afford that." CJTF weapons and bodies are not infrequently laced with charms of invisibility and immunity. A security man in Maiduguri's airport reported, "Some of them, if you shoot them, the bullet will not penetrate their bodies, because they have taken bulletproof medicine. So, they fear nobody." Bitrus, a CJTF member from Gombi in Adamawa, said, "We have personal protection from our parents that gives us the ability to deflect bullets, such as this one on my head. Some hidden charms have been embedded within my skull to protect me from harm." The belief in magic as a powerful tool of warfare is rooted in Africa's warring tradition (Wlodarczyk 2009). Anthropologist David Pratten has argued that "the remaking of selves out of the secrets of the supernatural are familiar and effective frameworks in the quest for order and certainty" in Nigeria (2008, 46). A prime example from southeast Nigeria is the group known as the Bakassi Boys, who developed a reputation for invincibility by claiming to be able to deflect bullets as a result of particular initiation rites and *jujus* (charms) (R. Jones 2008, 6). The use of magic by the CJTF reclaims the ways in which traditional Muslim youth groups in northern Nigeria, including the *yan faratua* (local hunters) and the *yan tauri* (performers who can't be cut or pierced by any metal), "emphasize bravery and skill with weaponry and forms of magical protection" (Casey 2008, 73).

Many young men joined the CJTF out of a feeling of personal loss that they then channeled toward repelling Boko Haram. A survey by L.Y. Umar (2014, 69) in the local government areas (LGAs) of Maiduguri and Jere in Borno State found that 70 percent of CJTF members had lost a friend or relative to Boko Haram's violence and were driven by the resulting sense of loss. Buylama Musa, a CJTF member from the town of Goneri in Yobe State, told me, "We joined because they killed our parents and relatives so we decided that we have to fight back, because the same lives that they have is what we have and so we decided to also fight back." Ganiyu, who joined the CJTF in 2013 after some of his close friends were killed in a Boko Haram attack on their neighborhood, had worked for sixteen years as a secretary in the Peoples Democratic Party (PDP). In 2013, as the insurgency intensified and his friends were killed, Ganiyu resigned voluntarily from the PDP to help the fight against Boko Haram. "I feel very happy doing this work because I am protecting the lives and properties of my community," Ganiyu said, adding, "For now, I am a respected person in my community. When I talk, people listen. Just the respect we get keeps us moving." A sense of personal loss is also palpable in Bakura Wanzam's journey into the CJTF: "I joined this fight to save my people. I want to inform you that my father was slaughtered like a goat in Yadi Buni, and you can see why I had to join. We saw these insurgents killing our parents and relations, so we sacrificed our lives and said these are people like us and we must fight them to a standstill." For young men like Wanzam, violence has become a lived reality that is embedded in fields of recollection and anticipation.

Although many Boko Haram members were known to local residents like Ganiyu and Wanzam in the "wards" (neighborhoods) where they grew up, "no one could dare identify them," said Bomboy, head of the CJTF sector in Hausari Ward, "because if you do, they will sneak back and warn you and eventually kill you in public." The situation was complicated by the state's coercive counterinsurgency tactics that conflated civilian populations and Boko Haram jihadists. Bakura, a leader of the CJTF in Maiduguri, told me, "When we first thought of joining the CJTF, there was still the fear that if we tell the Nigerian military who Boko Haram really was, they will come around and eliminate us." Caught between militants and military, many youths turned to the pro-government CJTF as a means of survival, partly because "soldiers order villages to form the CJTF and kill them if they refuse, accusing them of being Boko Haram—and if they do, they face Boko Haram reprisals" (IRIN 2013).

The story of Bukar Bama Sheriff is particularly illustrative. He is the chairman of the CJTF in the Borno town of Abadam, which was controlled by Boko Haram until 2015. I met Sheriff at a camp for the internally displaced in Abadam, where his group of *yan gora* were manning the gates and providing security in the absence of the state. Headquartered in Malumfatori, the LGA of Abadam has an estimated population of one hundred thousand and is one of the sixteen LGAs that constitute the Borno Emirate. In October 2014, Boko Haram captured Abadam, killing up to forty people and forcing residents to flee to neighboring Niger. In February 2015, the MNJTF recaptured Abadam, but as early as August 2016, Abadam remained a stronghold of Boko Haram (United Nations 2017, 3). Sheriff, who also holds a political position in the LGA of Abadam, said he first became involved in security surveillance work on behalf of the state in 2011, when the joint task force posted to the town of Abadam sought his help in finding a suitable location to settle down. Sheriff's cooperation with the soldiers soon exposed him to the wrath of Boko Haram. "You know," he told me, "Boko Haram has very strong local intelligence and social network. So, if there is any cooperation between you and the JTF, they will know and they will try to eliminate you." Initially, Sheriff served as the vice chairman of the CJTF in Abadam, reporting to Buba, the overall chairman. Both Sheriff and Buba received death threats from Boko Haram, warning them to cease their support for the CJTF or "prepare to die." Boko Haram made real its threat when it brutally attacked and killed Buba in his house, leaving a warning note for Sheriff.

Following Buba's death, Sheriff assumed control of the CJTF in Abadam and vowed to continue working for the CJTF as an informant. By virtue of Sheriff's presence on Boko Haram's list of "most wanted" in Abadam, his friends and relatives became endangered as well and distanced themselves from him at public events. "People around me reacted in two ways," Sheriff noted, saying, "People in Abadam started hating on me and isolating themselves from me. They don't want to talk or seat next to me at public events out of fear of being linked to me. People always tried to convince me to abandon my support and intelligence work for the JTF to save my head and that of my family. But I tell them that if you join the *yan gora*, Boko Haram will not rest until they finish you. They will target you until the end." For Sheriff, there was no easy way out of his precarious life: "Immediately you identify yourself with the CJTF, even when you leave your work, even when you resign publicly, you have only resigned for yourself in the eyes of Boko Haram. They will still hunt you down and kill you." There was also the small matter of dealing with a brutal Nigerian military. Sheriff explained, "If you begin like me by giving them information about the insurgents hiding in the wards, and then you later decide to stop, they too will start suspecting and targeting you. They will say you have changed your mind and started to work for the insurgents. This is why my situation is extremely difficult."

Sheriff can be thought of as a local "knowledge broker," a person whose intimate knowledge of places and people helps security forces to "see things," and his relationship with the state involves "a balancing act between suspicion and trust" (Gopfert 2012, 44). Local intermediaries are often distrusted because "their ultimate loyalties are ambiguous and they may be double agents. They are powerful in that they have mastered both of the discourses of the interchange, but they are vulnerable to charges of disloyalty or double-dealing" (Merry 2004, 45). Despite his harsh reality, Sheriff insists that "nobody forced me to join this group. I do this work because if I don't, the impact of Boko Haram will still affect me." The emergence and influence of the CJTF challenges us to look beyond the state to "recognize multiple systems of governance, multiple forms of political community, and the less formal, daily interactions and enactments through which governance and political belonging take shape" (Jaffe 2018, 1099).

The Popular Legitimacy of Vigilante Militias

The CJTF's efficiency in identifying and arresting Boko Haram members, aided by the task force's intimate road knowledge and social networks, forced Boko Haram to eventually decamp from Maiduguri to remote parts of Borno State (Gwoza Hills and Mandara Mountains), where hunter militias took up the fight. Since 2014, a local security assemblage of hunters and vigilante militias in the states of Adamawa and Yobe have worked closely with the CJTF and the Nigerian military to flush out armed insurgents seeking cover in the Sambisa Forest. The role of local security providers has become even more critical in light of the Nigerian military's recent strategy of retreating to highly militarized garrison towns—so-called supercamps—leaving over a million people in rural communities to protect themselves (Alfa and Maclean 2020).

A veteran hunter from Yobe State, who described how the Boko Haram insurgents used to plant land mines along the road, explained, "We hunters guide the soldiers to go through the bushes and avoid the roads until we get to the Boko Haram base." Another hunter, from Gombi in Adamawa State, boasted about his power to "tie down the forest and make the insurgents get lost in the bush and become easy targets." Boko Haram's relocation to the countryside and its surrounding forests represents a throwback to the Kanama phase of its formative years (2003–4), when it withdrew from the city, formed a kind of puritanical Islamic community, and attacked state security forces from there. Such a move is not unusual for rebel movements in West Africa, as "the roots of revolt in most African countries lie in the cities, and more specifically, the capital cities. Most guerrillas are merely 'passing through' the countryside on their way to capture power in the city" (Mkandawire 2002, 207).

The status of CJTF members as "sons of the soil" confers them with popular legitimacy, yielding trust and access, which proved key to fishing out Boko Haram members hiding within communities. It is natural that local inhabitants will have more trust for other natives than for outsiders (Peic 2014, 166). In Hausari Ward, where the CJTF began, residents told me that CJTF members are more effective than soldiers because the former are "natives like us" and "know the bad eggs in our midst." One CJTF man said, "You know we are indigenes, and people either have our mobile numbers or those of our relatives, and they feel free to report anything unusual around them. The moment they notice any suspicious movement, they contact us on phone, or if there is no network, they can use their bicycles to connect with one of us." The bravery of CJTF members has endeared them to local populations, setting them apart from Nigerian soldiers, who were often viewed as deserters and strangers. "Our success hinges on patriotism and bravery," said a CJTF leader, explaining, "The military were not patriotic initially, as they were urging their colleagues to abandon the war since it was not their homeland that was at stake, and many of them either deserted or withdrew. For us, there is no going back." A sixty-eight-year-old man in the Wulari area of Maiduguri noted, "Without the CJTF, the army and police will not go anywhere. Because where these boys will enter, a police or army officer will be afraid to enter. They have courage and want to give everything in defense of their land and people. That is why we proudly call them 'our boys.'"

For Usman, a resident of Maiduguri, the difference between the CJTF and soldiers comes down to trust: "We are with the army, but we know not to trust them to defend us. We have already had two situations [of Boko Haram attacks] in Gwoza and Bama where soldiers ran away from their security posts. So how can you depend on them to protect you? In Bama, I was an eyewitness. I saw them mingle with civilians to escape to Maiduguri. So how can you imagine they would protect you?" Usman's claim is not unsubstantiated. In January 2019, for example, Boko Haram fighters attacked Rann, a town in Borno State with thirty thousand displaced people, and killed sixty. A report by Amnesty International on the attack offers a damning portrait of military unpreparedness—or outright fear of Boko Haram.

> Disturbingly, witnesses told us that Nigerian soldiers abandoned their posts the day before the attack, demonstrating the authorities' utter failure to protect civilians. Alleged withdrawal of troops triggered a massive exodus of civilians to Cameroon, as fear spread that Boko Haram would take advantage and attack the town. At around 9 am on 28 January, a group of Boko Haram fighters arrived on motorcycles. They set houses ablaze and killed those left behind. They also chased after those who attempted to escape and killed some people outside the town. Eleven bodies were found within Rann town, and 49 bodies were found outside. (Amnesty International 2019)

In a country where bribery and corruption are widespread and systemic, funds earmarked for military hardware and equipment often bleed into private pockets. In 2015, for example, Nigeria's former national security adviser, Sambo Dansuki, reportedly stole US$2 billion allocated for weapons to fight Boko Haram. He was also accused of awarding phantom contracts to buy twelve helicopters, four fighter jets, and ammunition (*Premium Times* 2017). In May 2014, twelve soldiers at the Brigadier Maimalari Barracks in Maiduguri, angry following Boko Haram's ambush and killing of their comrades, opened fire on a vehicle conveying their commanding officer; the soldiers said their comrades were sent to the battlefield without proper weapons (BBC 2014). The twelve soldiers were sentenced to death in September 2014 after being found guilty of mutiny. The first quarter of 2015 alone saw sixty-six soldiers sentenced to death by general court-martials for mutiny and other charges (*Punch* 2016). In January 2015, the army sacked 277 soldiers over their refusal to confront Boko Haram when the jihadist group attacked and overran the town of Mubi in Adamawa State in October 2014. In their defense, some of the convicted soldiers argued that far from the popular view that they deserted their duty post, the truth was that their numbers and weapons were far inferior to those of the Boko Haram fighters. Such claims recurred ad nauseam during informal conversations with the CJTF. A leader of the vigilante militia told me, "When you get to [Boko Haram] camps, you find they have artillery pieces, antiaircraft guns mounted on vehicles, and Ak-47s, while all we have are hunter guns that you load and shoot only once before you load and fire again. This sometimes takes five minutes." A driver from Gombi in Adamawa State recalled a situation when he sheltered twenty soldiers who were too scared to face Boko Haram in battle due to the group's superior weaponry.

> The soldiers told me they were only armed with AK-47, while the insurgents were armed with "AA" anti-aircraft guns with big and deadly ammunitions which, if fired, will reach like "Welcome to Yola" (a signboard about seven kilometers from Yola), while the rifle of the soldiers, if fired, will reach, like, the market from here (less than two kilometers). You can't fight these people, so the soldiers retreated and claimed that government has a hand in this insurgency. I gave some of the soldiers that slept in my house mufti, and they tore their uniforms, disassembled their rifles, packed them in sacks, and ran back to Yola through Gire, using commercial vehicles after coming out of the bush paths I showed them. Some of them deserted the army from there.

The above remarkable claim by escapee soldiers, implicating the Nigerian government in insurgency, is not unrelated to widespread suspicion that links the ineffectiveness of the military, particularly between 2010 and 2015, to the movement of intelligence and direct assistance from soldiers to insurgents, possibly for political ends (MacEachern 2018, 181). In September 2019, an investigative report by the *New York Times* claimed that Boko Haram "fighters now have more sophisticated drones than the military and are well armed after successful raids on military brigades." The report noted that the jihadists control four of the ten zones in northern Borno State, near Lake Chad, adding, "They are pulling off almost-daily attacks." Drawing on many accounts, the report concluded that "the Nigerian military is demoralized and on the defensive. Some soldiers have complained they haven't had a home leave in three years. Their weapons and vehicles have fallen into despair" (*New York Times* 2019).

Female Vigilantes and the Mobilization of Intimate Knowledge

Today, the CJTF has an estimated membership strength of thirty thousand. A "small but mighty" portion of that number are women and wives, who not only play a fundamental role in the gathering of local intelligence but also help in conducting stop-and-search activities on fellow women, at homes, market spaces, mosques and churches, and commercial transit stations. The emergence of female CJTF members became vital in light of Boko Haram's alarming usage of women and girls as suicide bombers. In April 2015, the Nigerian military rescued 293 abducted women and children from Boko Haram's stronghold in the Sambisa Forest. The army reported having rescued over six hundred women and children since the counterinsurgency began (United Nations 2015, 8). Women are ideal stealth weapons for Islamist groups conducting suicide operations, because they are less likely to be suspected or searched and can easily hide suicide vests in their loose, billowy clothing. Moreover, the Center for International Security and Cooperation reported that "as a result of media attention and global prominence, Boko Haram realized after the Chibok girls kidnapping that female participation in terrorist violence could stimulate additional shock, horror, and thus media value" (CISAC 2018). Boko Haram has taken advantage of "positive security bias" (Gaub and Lisiecka 2016)—that is, the (un)conscious notion that women are inherently less threatening or capable of violence compared to men—as its fighters often disguise themselves in female dress to escape notice. Even Boko Haram leader Abubakar Shekau has been spotted several times disguised as a woman, "alternating between blue and black colored hijabs" (*Punch* 2018).

Thirty-five-year-old Zainab said she joined the CJTF after her brother was blown up in a suicide attack in Dala, Maiduguri: "The personal loss made me vow to expose them so that peace can be restored." A CJTF sector commander from Yola in Adamawa State noted, "Women play an invaluable role in our vigilante work, because Islamic religion doesn't allow men to enter houses, and we make use of the women to go into these houses for either surveillance or arrests." That unique role of women reinforces the argument that "counterinsurgency practice makes men and women legible and assigns them to different categories of various utility for combat and pacification" (Khalili 2011, 1479). "Through their daily work as household organizers, traders, mothers, stepmothers and co-wives," Insa Nolte explains, "women are often the holders of intimate knowledge about changes and news in their compounds as well as in markets, shops and schools" (2008, 96). In an interview with *Daily Trust*, a CJTF man praised the rigorous efforts of the women and wives who support their vigilante work.

> Our wives know how to subject them [suspects] to rigorous stop-and-search. Pedestrians, motorists, *achabas* and their passengers, nobody is exempted from such searches. When the soldiers were conducting the search, it generated a lot of controversy as married women protested against it. . . . This is why we introduced female CJTF to search women's handbags, veils, stomachs, backs, and even their thighs. Sometimes women who appear very dangerous are ordered to kneel down and our wives often found rifles on their backs. Some are even asked to put down their babies for proper search and they do so without any resistance. (Odunsi 2013)

Crossroads: Civil-Military Relations

In dire need of local collaboration, the overstretched Nigerian Army was quick to see the potential of the CJTF as a "force multiplier" and, crucially, "a feasible and effective means of counterinsurgency, providing valuable local knowledge and efficient means to collect intelligence" (Jentzsch et al. 2015, 759). "When we came out, the Nigerian army welcomed us 100 percent," said Abba Aji Kalli, a CJTF spokesperson in Maiduguri. The army helped to reorganize the CJTF along its own lines of command. Maiduguri, for instance, was divided into ten "sectors," each led by a chairman and a secretary nominated by senior military commanders to whom they reported. Each CJTF sector was generally equipped with vehicles and charged with identifying and arresting Boko Haram suspects, manning checkpoints, and guiding soldiers on patrols. Highly mobile, each CJTF sector could be deployed easily wherever needed. Though CJTF members participated in combat, their main role was to ensure peace and stability in recaptured towns or villages through daily patrols and stop-and-search operations. In light of Boko Haram's suicide attacks, many CJTF members also provide security at the entrances to IDP camps, markets, and buildings (Center for Civilians in Conflict 2018,

13). A CJTF member in Maiduguri stated, "Soldiers have the upper hand, but they cannot differentiate between an insurgent and non-insurgent, and they do not know the terrain. When they ask us to lead, we always do. We know the routes and the boys that joined the sect all along. Soldiers are our strength, and we are their eyes."

Most visitors to Maiduguri today will notice the sky-blue or white Toyota Hilux trucks used by CJTF sectors to do their counterinsurgency work. During fieldwork at checkpoints leading into and out of Maiduguri and in nearby towns and villages, I encountered and spoke to small groups of machete-wielding CJTF youth working with five to seven uniformed security personnel carrying AK-47s. The vigilantes, in plain clothes, searched vehicles, while the uniformed security personnel kept an eye on them from behind sandbags, indexing "the terrain of anticipated violence" (Jeganathan 2004, 72). One officer said, "Forget what you read in the newspapers that all is well. We are on a serious alert here." CJTF boys often peer into vehicles as drivers move slowly past. Cars deemed "suspicious" are pulled over for inspection, which usually involves frisking drivers and asking them to open the trunks of their vehicles. In an interview at a checkpoint in Gujba, along the Damaturu–Biu Road, a CJTF member said, "We try to search vehicles to see if they carry arms or food stuff to Boko Haram terrorists." Another claimed that "body language" is key to singling out or, in some cases, arresting (perhaps even killing?) passengers when their vehicles are stopped, reinforcing studies that have demonstrated that the calculated presentation of self in everyday transit spaces (e.g., checkpoints) can be key to one's survival (Hyndman and de Alwis 2004, 552).

Many of the CJTF boys manning the checkpoints work part-time. One youth vigilante told me, "This is rainy season. Every day we go to farms, and when we are back, we help mount the checkpoints on the road to check what vehicles are carrying, to ensure that no one is passing through with arms or armaments that could harm others." "We normally come out in the morning," said another CJTF member, who went on to explain, "If there is anything new, the soldiers will alert us, and we go out with them. If nothing new, we get to the community entrance on the major road from Damaturu to Biu and mount the checkpoint, to keep an eye on anyone that goes in or out of the community. We have been arresting insurgents on the road. We once arrested someone that drove the car of Boko Haram that launched an attack on the state capital last December, and he confessed that himself." That CJTF member's point of view is consistent with a recent report showing that CJTF-controlled checkpoints and patrols have "stopped many people before detonation, had people who had been forced to carry IED vests surrender to them, or enabled detonation in such a way that minimized civilian casualties" (Center for Civilians in Conflict 2018, 14). For many CJTF members, the ability to anticipate danger is vital, since checkpoints delineate and focus attention on the target.

The courage and sacrifices of CJTF members have earned them high praise from civilians and politicians alike, with the federal government hailing them as "new national heroes" (Idris and Sawab 2013). "If not for the CJTF, Maiduguri would have long fallen into the hands of Boko Haram," said Abubakar, a community leader in Maiduguri. He identified its members as "a fearless band of committed youth who know Boko Haram members and the terrain very well." Following a Boko Haram attack on Dalwa and Mafa areas of Borno in February 2015, the former state governor Kashim Shettima praised the CJTF, who quickly rallied in support of the Nigerian military, "in a patriotic battle to defend the soul of Borno state and its people from being seized by determined insurgents" (Odunsi 2015). The contributions of the CJTF underscores the need for a better understanding of the role of "governance without government" (Menkhaus 2006) in counterinsurgency. The state does not have a legitimate monopoly over the use of violence.

The Danger of Civilian Resistance

The emergence of the CJTF and its effectiveness in identifying and arresting Boko Haram fighters played a fundamental role in the transformation of the conflict from an "anti-state insurgency" into a full-blown terrorism (ICG 2017a, 13), putting local populations in direct conflict with Boko Haram terrorists. One captured Boko Haram member commented in 2013, "Our original target was security operatives and politicians. But since the formation of the CJTF, who now reveal our identities and even arrest us, we decided to kill anyone that is from Maiduguri because we believe every person there and some other towns of Borno state are members of the CJTF" (Strochlic 2014). By forcing Boko Haram to relocate from Maiduguri to the countryside, says Mohammed Kyari, the "CJTF and soldiers made life precarious to villagers" (IRIN 2013). In the first half of 2014 alone, Boko Haram launched an estimated ninety-five attacks that killed no less than 2,053 civilians: 1,446 in Borno State, 151 in Adamawa State, and 143 in Yobe State (HRW 2014). The system of automobility has been used in such organized attacks on local populations, particularly communities that formed a joint task force, as evidenced by the presence of convoys of trucks, motorcycles, and armored personnel carriers with armed insurgents, and the planning required to infiltrate the cities in which the violent attacks took place (HRW 2014).

On May 6, 2014, for example, Boko Haram fighters killed 336 villagers in the twin towns of Gamboru and Ngala, before burning down the villages. During fieldwork, a respondent recalled how "they [Boko Haram jihadists] killed over thirty people in this community, especially elderly and sick people. People were asked to leave the village with the only clothes they had on their bodies, and that's how we vacated our homes." Notably, the brutal attack was facilitated by two armored personnel carriers the group had stolen from a Nigerian military base several months earlier (HRW 2014). In February 2015, two suicide bombers rammed their tricycle into a CJTF checkpoint along Miringa–Biu Road before detonating their IEDs, killing two vigilantes and injuring fourteen others (Marama 2015). In June 2015, facts emerged on how hundreds of CJTF members at a checkpoint in Borno were killed trying to prevent bomb-strapped terrorists from detonating their bombs in large crowds. The victims used their bodies as "a sort of boundary between safety and danger, life and death" (Jeganathan 2018, 407). On June 17, 2019, a triple suicide bombing by Boko Haram killed thirty people in Konduga in Borno State (*Defence Post* 2019). In the past, Boko Haram leader Abubakar Shekau has cloaked his suicide bombers in the armor of martyrdom, calling on his followers to embrace it.

In January 2017, during a meeting at the village of Tse-Igber in Abaji in Benue State, ten CJTF members were shot and killed by Boko Haram gunmen on motorcycles, in a trademark drive-by shooting (Okoh 2017). Locals often describe with great pain how insurgents at false checkpoints regularly execute male travelers from Maiduguri as a punishment for the city's cooperation with the military. Anecdotes abound of how insurgents screen passengers based on where they are from, proceeding to kill those from communities suspected of acting as informers for the army. Those freed are then warned not to return to Maiduguri, as it has become the home of *kafir* (Dietrich 2015). In Boko Haram's usage, the term *kafir* extends broadly to all who work with the Nigerian state and its security forces against the group. A resident of Borno described how, on April 25, 2014, Boko Haram laid siege to the Bulabulin Gaura community in Konduga in Borno State, warning those left behind, "You have heard of us, you have seen our guns, if you try to tell someone or tell the soldiers what is happening or where we are, we will come and burn you and kill you" (Amnesty International 2015, 31).

Ibrahim Muktar, a resident of Gwoza, described how he, along with other members of his community fleeing to Maiduguri, encountered the insurgents just outside Gwoza, on the road to Kirawa. The insurgents stopped them and said they were looking for CJTF members running from Gwoza. Muktar claims he saw thirty young men slaughtered on that day: "They told us that . . . when they catch people from Maiduguri, Gwoza, and Bama, any person from these towns, they will kill. They were preaching to the women. They said we are not working for the state, we are working for Islam. We are not touching women and children. But these people in the CJTF, we are going to kill them" (Amnesty International 2015, 41).

In June 2013, Boko Haram released an audio clip declaring an "all-out war" on youth from Maiduguri, "because you have formed an alliance with the military and police to fight our brethren. We call on parent that values the life of his son to stop him from exposing our members. Otherwise he is dead" (IRIN 2013). In September 2013, following the Benisheik massacre, Shekau labeled members of the CJTF "infidels" for supporting the military and threatened to avenge the death of his members. "We warn the CJTF to back out," said Shekau, continuing, "If not, there will be no place for them to hide. We have evidences of how you killed some of our brethren whom you asked if they are Boko Haram before you killed them. . . . We will get to you. . . . We will smash your heads and kill you all. Even if you don't do anything to us we will kill you. . . . You killed our brethren in large numbers" (Odunsi 2014). His statements are consistent with studies demonstrating that "because civilian collaboration with the state is rightfully seen as a grave threat to rebel aims, insurgent organizations often attempt to discourage further collaboration by orchestrating reprisals against communities which join a CDF [Civilian Defense Force] program" (Peic 2014, 167). Ironically, many local residents believe that the Boko Haram insurgents fit the label "infidels." Kawu, a hunter militiaman from Gujba, told me, "Boko Haram thinks they are a religious sect, but this has gone beyond religion. They are the real infidels. They kill their Muslim brothers." In light of Boko Haram's rage against communities that formed a joint task force, many civilians have become increasingly fearful of identifying with the CJTF.

Challenges Facing the CJTF

Members of the CJTF, along with vigilantes and hunters, often complain about lack of adequate financial support from the state and federal government to fight the insurgents. Kawu noted, "We don't have sophisticated guns, only locally made and double-barrel guns, no salary or allowance, no one to give you bullets or any form of support. Even the guns you see with us are bought with our meager resources." During an interview along Damaturu–Biu Road, at the entrance of the Gubja community in Yobe State, a vigilante man lamented the state's lack of (adequate) compensation for the injured and the families of vigilante members killed in the theater of war.

> Our first commander, Ali Dallatu, was killed by the insurgents, and we found his dead body in the bush. He left behind a pregnant wife, and all of us had to contribute money for her upkeep and naming ceremony of the baby she delivered after his death. But government did not do anything. And another member, called Abacha, was missing in action, and we have not heard from him up 'til today. His wife is still around and was not given anything. There is also Bakura Wanzam [mentioned earlier in this chapter] among us here. When he got injured in Shangamari forest, nothing was done to him. We have pictures of his injured face and knee.

Those challenges notwithstanding, CJTF leaders say that they have crossed the Rubicon in their pledge to "fight terror and keep the peace." One member of the group in Maiduguri commented, "There is no going back. Boko Haram have declared war on us, and even if we stop hunting them, they still will come after us, so we have to fight them to the finish" (IRIN 2013). The CJTF members' determination in the face of real danger to their lives reclaims the way in which the rallying slogan among the civil militias of the Kamajors in Sierra Leone, "Kamajor baa woteh" (Do not turn back), served as an injunction against retreating from the battlefield and betraying the community one had sworn to protect (D. Hoffman 2007, 647).

The resilience of the CJTF has come at a huge cost. "We have created a lot of enemies in this work. There are people that are still after us," a CJTF leader said. In Borno State alone, the official death toll for the CJTF between 2013 and 2017 is estimated at seven hundred (Agbiboa 2020). CJTF leaders believe that the fatalities are actually much higher, since there has hardly been a military operation against Boko Haram since 2013 without the loss of at least one CJTF member. Most reports on the CJTF focus only on members killed by insurgent violence and ignore the injured or disabled. Yet the majority of people in violent clashes are not killed but just injured. That fact applies to CJTF members, the vast majority of whom have been critically disabled but not killed. For example, Bakura, a hunter militiaman in Yobe, was injured in the process of helping the military to extirpate Boko Haram fighters in Gujba and felt neglected by the state. He recalls how he sustained his injuries: "There was a Fulani man among the insurgents who wounded me with a machete. One of my colleagues fought and killed him at last, and the second incident was also in Shangamari Forest, when my local rifle got exploded and injured my kneecap. My colleagues contributed money for my treatment, which was not enough, but my family sold my foodstuff and that of my brother to treat me."

The experience of Ali, a CJTF driver, offers another example. "As drivers," says Ali, "We are always on standby, either seated in the vehicle or nearby, so that whenever there is a job to do, one will not be found wanting. Our personal items are always in the vehicles. The army will normally call out to inform us of the location of the insurgents, and we move there until we finish them before we come back to base." In the course of his surveillance work, Ali sustained a major injury that rendered him medically and socially disabled: "I drove my vehicle on IEDs twice since I started this work. We lost our commander in the second incident before the present one was appointed. I was taken to the Dala Orthopedic hospital in Kano State for my treatment, and N 350,000 was paid for my treatment by our leader. I have an iron bar in my leg now as part of the treatment. I can no longer drive."

National Heroes or Coming Anarchy?
The Double Movement to Security

Ray Abrahams argued that the boundary between vigilante and criminal is both fluid and manipulable (1987, 180). The experience of CDGs in Africa—from the Kamajors of Sierra Leone to the Dozos of Cote d'Ivoire and the Koglweogos in Burkina Faso—suggests that they undermine their original role as local security providers when they morph into self-seeking or politically motivated civil militias (Van Metre 2019; R. Jones 2008; ICG 2017). A salutary reminder is the Bakassi Boys. Originating from southeast Nigeria's commercial city of Aba, that vigilante militia group initially enjoyed popular legitimacy as it sought to restore community security and local order. The group experienced a crisis of legitimacy when it was politically hijacked (Meagher 2007), provoking fears that they were "becoming political and therefore corrupt" (D. Smith 2004, 128). The manipulability and political instrumentality of CDGs explains why Meagher (2012, 1097) has criticized the revalorization of nonstate forms of order in the context of hybrid governance in Africa. Meagher argues that the collaboration between state and nonstate security forces may turn out to be a "Faustian bargain" that reproduces, rather than addresses, state excesses. The case of the CJTF is particularly revealing.

Despite its early heroic status, the CJTF's lack of accountability, its vulnerability to state capture, and its afterlife remain a concern for Nigerians and the international community. The CJTF has engaged in extrajudicial killings and other atrocities against civilians, frequently in the presence of the "official" military. In August 2014, Amnesty International released a gruesome video of detainees having their throats slit one by one and dumped into mass graves by the CJTF and military personnel. Included in the list of atrocities carried out by CJTF members are assaulting and killing Boko Haram suspects; facilitating the detention without trial and other limitations on the basic human rights of suspects; recruiting and using children for intelligence gathering and security surveillance; harming civilian populations during military operations against Boko Haram; coercing local communities to form vigilante groups; engaging in forms of sexual harassment and exploitation (e.g., in IDP camps); abusing their power for local score-settling; perpetrating physical violence and intimidating civilians; committing extortion and theft (including diversion of humanitarian aid); and trading and using of drugs (Center for Civilians in Conflict 2020). Those atrocities have eroded the popular support initially enjoyed by the CJTF. In June 2019, for example, an estimated two thousand residents gathered in Maiduguri to protest against the brutality and violence of the CJTF, calling on the Nigerian government to ban the vigilante group. The protest erupted hours after a taxi driver was shot and killed at a CJTF-operated checkpoint in Maiduguri, on suspicion of being a Boko Haram member. "We want the CJTF to be banned from the city because of the abuses we suffer in their hands," said Shaleh, who lives in Maiduguri and added, "They have become a law unto themselves and are treating us badly. And now they have started killing us. The victim was a known resident and his name was Modu but the CJTF shot him for no reason" (AFP 2019).

While the CJTF has been relatively successful in shielding local residents from armed insurgents, it has also provoked fears about its vulnerability to political manipulation. A reporter said, "An unregulated, untrained and crudely armed civilian force may prove to be the last thing Maiduguri's imperiled residents need. . . . Apart from risking their lives unnecessarily, a greater danger of exposing civilians to battle situations includes the possibility of some of these civilians turning into warlords. In the North, such warlords inevitably put on the religious garb. Before we know, civilians helping to fight terrorists may fall under the influence of politicians and other foreign sponsors to float their own terror outfits" (*Vanguard* 2013). The Borno State's government has never hidden its admiration for the CJTF, describing the group's rise as a "divine intervention." Yet some politicians concede that, unless deliberate efforts are made to address the CJTF's existential immobility, including unemployment, hunger, and illiteracy, the group's members "may be the Frankenstein monsters that might end up consuming us" (Okeowo 2015). While admitting that CJTF members "go overboard" from time to time during their vigilante work, a senior public official in Borno deflected attention to Boko Haram as a far greater source of worry for ordinary citizens and travelers in Maiduguri. "The simple issue is terrorists," he said, noting that what CJTF members are doing "is not acceptable, but these Boko Haram terrorists, they will not spare you [when they get you], they will kill you." A local leader in Maiduguri similarly noted, "For now, we have to bear with them [CJTF members]. Compared to what Boko Haram are doing, their own [offenses] are insignificant" (AFP 2013). The evolution of the CJTF indicates that vigilante groups may yield short-term counterinsurgency gains but are likely to threaten the security needs and free movement of people in the long term.

FIVE

Subversive Mobilities, State Counterinsurgency, and the Politics of Dispossession

The power of dispossession works by rendering certain subjects, communities, or populations unintelligible, by eviscerating for them the conditions of possibility for life and the "human" itself. . . . But where and how do the lives of those whose "proper place is non-being" take place . . . ? How is the "substance" of these lives produced?

Butler and Athanasiou 2013, 20

Contemporary wars increasingly aim to "force the enemy into submission regardless of the immediate consequences, side effects, and 'collateral damage' of the military actions" (Mbembe 2003, 31). The war on terror in northeast Nigeria is no exception. In fact, the codename of the joint task force fighting Boko Haram since 2015 is Operation "Lafiya Dole" (Peace by Any Means). One understudied dimension of the war against Boko Haram since 2009 is how the state mobilizes mobility in its counterinsurgency campaign, as well as the consequences of that mobilization for the livelihoods of mobile people who are caught between insurgents and state security forces and targeted by both. Yet research demonstrates that the state asserts its power by delimiting and defining space (Rossi 2015, 157). Mobility is always governed, but it is, first and foremost, a way of governing (Bærenholdt 2013).

This chapter is about how the war against Boko Haram is governed through mobilities. Its analysis extends to the visceral indignities and uncertainties imposed, through the state's biopower, on mobile subjects in conflict. Boko Haram's mobile warfare has required the securitarian Nigerian government to rethink and rearrange its systems for transportation security, with serious ramifications for people whose survival depends on movement and access. Specific attention is paid in this chapter to how mobile subjects in northeast Nigeria negotiate a translocal state power that, in the name of overcoming terror, has "taken control of both the body and life or that has, if you like, taken control of life in general" (Foucault 1976, 252–33).

Understanding processes of mobile governance in northeast Nigeria requires a critical focus on the complex arenas within which power dynamics are exercised and contested (Healey 2000, 919). Accordingly, this chapter is located within critical approaches that emphasize the relations between, on one hand, power as activated through the governance of mobility (Bærenholdt 2013; Packer 2006) and, on the other hand, the embodied experiences of mobile people who are caught in conflict and subjected to what Benedetta Rossi (2015, 265) calls "kinetocracy," a form of government whereby power corresponds to control over mobility. Such an approach is used here to counterbalance the predominant "a-mobile" discourses of insurgencies that continue to "privilege state sovereignty and security ahead of more embodied and material understandings of security" (Hyndman and de Alwis 2004, 544).

Foregrounding mobility as a *dispositif*, or central apparatus, of Nigeria's counterinsurgency campaign since 2009, this chapter analyzes how mobile subjects and their spaces of maneuver are constituted, ordered, disciplined, and governed by a securitarian state, as well as the rationale for doing so. Analyzing mobility as a *dispositif* zooms in on how and why specific subjectivities and mobility practices in the context of insurgency are governed. It emphasizes "the constitution of the space of allowed and forbidden movements . . . and of normal, deviant and impossible mobile subjects which are structured and structuring social power struggles at different scales" (Manderscheid 2014, 609).

Road Closures, Transport, and Trade

There is a growing recognition that not only are armed insurgents and civilian populations mobile, but states themselves have become mobile, partly in response to the subversive mobility of the humans and nonhumans they seek to control or govern (Mountz 2014, 18). In other words, far from an independent or autonomous source of power, the state is "a multiple and mobile field of force relations" (Foucault 1978, 102). That definition applies well in considerations of Nigerian state responses to Boko Haram's mobile warfare in northeast Nigeria. In a concerted effort to restrain Boko Haram's mobility and flexibility, official authorities in northeast Nigeria (particularly in the states of Borno, Yobe, and Adamawa) regarded mobility and the mobile subject as "a constant and immanent threat which needs diffusing or extinguishing" (Packer 2006, 381). Consequently, severe restrictions were imposed on the free circulation of goods, people, and information (Seignobos 2016). Road and border closures, curfews, and the shutting down of power supplies and telecommunications often result from any Boko Haram attack or bombing, with disastrous consequences for the local population and regional economy.

A case in point is the historical fishing town of Baga in Borno, on the shores of Lake Chad. Located about 196 kilometers from Maiduguri and 6 kilometers from Baga, the Doron Baga fish market is the biggest market for processed fish (smoked and dried) in the whole of northeast Nigeria (Mukhtar and Gazali 2000, 83). Apart from its benefits to the economy and commercial activities, Doron Baga has also created job opportunities for many people from both far and near. Since 2013, the fish market and its motor park have become "a focal point of violence because traders resisted extortion and informed the police against Boko Haram" (Pérouse de Montclos 2014, 12). In April 2013, 185 people were killed and two hundred homes in Baga were destroyed as a result of fighting between the Nigerian military and Boko Haram. In January 2015, Boko Haram insurgents again attacked the fishing town, seizing it along with a military base established to fight them. The town was burned and the people massacred, with about two hundred deaths, the largest such massacre in Boko Haram's history (United Nations 2017, 21). The attacks culminated in the closure of the main road leading to Baga, with serious consequences for the fish trade, which, until that time, had been "a significant source of income and a principal state commodity, bringing together the remote fishing community of northeast Nigeria with the major urban centers of the southern part of the county" (Mukhta and Gazali 2000, 84).

Bama–Banki Road, which runs through the Sambisa Forest, is another example. It is central to regional trade, as it leads into Cameroon, Chad, and Niger and passes through the two border towns of Bama and Gwoza, which were formerly controlled by Boko Haram. Insurgents attacked

Bama in May 2013 and February 2014, killing thousands and destroying the market and shops along Bama–Banki Road. In September 2013, the military closed Bama–Banki Road "to reduce carnage and allow for unimpeded attack on the terrorist group" (Olugbode 2018). Bama and Gwoza were cut off, with soldiers blocking the roads linking the border towns to Maiduguri. People escaping from Boko Haram's attacks on Bama had no choice but to take precarious bush paths and travel through Dikwa, about 60 kilometers from Bama and 150 kilometers from Maiduguri, to reach the state capital (United Nations 2017).

The closure of strategic roads and bridges across northeast Nigeria has hampered the ability of drivers and traders to ply their trade. Lawan, an interstate driver from Yobe State, recounted, "For sure [road closures] has touched our business the wrong way. One can load his vehicle and is getting ready to travel and will be told that the road is closed. You load and at times even go out of the park ready to leave, and you must come back to the park with your passengers. Sometimes you come from faraway places like Abuja, Kaduna, or Kano and, on arrival, find that the road is closed. Sometimes you spend, like, two days with passengers in the vehicles. All this has dealt a blow to us." Other drivers have complained about the curfews imposed by the military, which, they argue, increase road accidents as drivers try to "beat time." A driver from Gujba said, "We love this Yadin Buni Road to be relaxed a bit because the 5 p.m. curfew is killing us. Even if one is going to his house any time after 4 p.m., one will never be composed but will try overspeeding to meet up with the timing. Sometimes accidents do occur while drivers are trying to beat the timing. This is what happened some days ago when a Sharon bus collided with a pickup truck. The bus driver was rushing to beat the time for the restriction of movement."

Farmers and fishermen have been severely hampered by closures and curfews that prevent them from getting their goods to the market in an efficient manner, thus weakening the distribution network for agricultural goods (Mercy Corps 2016). A fish seller in Maiduguri lamented the drastic impact of the Boko Haram insurgency on the road transportation of food from northern to southern Nigeria: "Before this Boko Haram insurgency, we use to load forty trucks with fish to the south every week on market days but now it has reduced to five trucks and a maximum of seven trucks a week" (Muhammad 2015). In 2015, the production of corn, cowpeas, rice, sorghum, and millet in northeast Nigeria plunged by 76 percent compared to the four years prior to 2009. In addition, many farmers have deserted their farms for fear of Boko Haram attacks. "No one can move a kilometer due to fear," said a lecturer in Maiduguri, adding, "Most [locals] have fled their homes" (Kah 2017, 183). In November 2020, farmers harvesting crops in Borno State were attacked by Boko Haram gunmen on motorcycles, who killed sixty-five farmers (Alfa and Maclean 2020). Lamenting the disruptive effects of road closures on everyday business, a trader in Yola North said,

> By God, road closures and curfews have brought almost everything to a standstill; it has affected food vendors in the night, and it has affected people going to buy essential commodities or traveling to other places. Assuming you want to go to Ngurore to buy something cheap in the morning, slow-moving traffic due to road closure will not allow you reach in good time, and you will prefer to buy whatever you want at a much expensive price near where you live, and the aim of trading for profit is defeated. In this market, there are lines of shops, as long as from here to the roundabout, that have practically shut down all their shops because of the slowing of business as a result of closure of roads. People were forced to stop trading.

For their part, commercial transport workers across the region are under immense pressure to find alternative, less dangerous routes, which tends to double the distance and cost of transportation. A truck driver from Gujba in Yobe State noted, "The security concerns we face have caused the distance we travel to double as we use other routes. This makes the journey longer and requires more fuel and manpower, so it's more expensive. . . . These are the kind of challenges we face every day." "If you leave Yola at 6 a.m. for Abuja," said a tanker driver in Damaturu, "you can spend the entire night on the road instead of arriving at 3 or 4 p.m. There are about eight hundred checkpoints between Yola and Abuja, and this is not good for business."

Boko Haram's growing attacks on drivers, passengers, and humanitarian aid workers has forced the National Union of Road Transport Workers to tighten measures of security surveillance inside and around motor parks and bus stops. The NURTW's chapter in Borno State now forbids its workers from picking up passengers along major highways; they can take on passengers only at designated motor parks. Emphasizing the need for drivers to remain vigilant, Malam Bellow Maduganari, the NURTW chairman in Maiduguri, announced,

> Henceforth, members from the 87 units in the state capital must always check the identification cards of passengers before conveying

them. Some of the members of our union had fallen as victims of the unfortunate circumstances while others had been killed because of the lackadaisical attitudes of some drivers. Drivers must also be cautious in accepting any messages that look suspicious; motor park authorities should also be cautious of allowing people to sleep in motor parks. Boko Haram mostly target gathering of persons to cause havoc; so motor park operators should not allow anyone to sleep in their parks. If any member of the public wants to embark on any trip, he must wait till daybreak before coming to the park to board vehicles. (*Punch* 2016)

A taxi driver in Yola North told me that the main security threat comes from picking up "isolated passengers" along the way, rather than at designated bus terminals, where passengers generally undergo security screening and have their personal information recorded.

Everything passing through the motor parks is subjected to thorough search by security men, and there is a list that records passenger names, with points where they entered from, their destination, the address of next of kin and phone number. Any time there is a problem, the passenger could be easily traced. Where we do have a problem is when passengers are picked up along the road outside the motor park. I once witnessed this episode when I left Yola in Adamawa State for Maiduguri in Borno State. A vehicle overtook me on the road. The driver stopped and picked up a passenger on the road with some portable load in his hand which turned out to be IED [improvised explosive device]. About a kilometer after, the vehicle exploded, and no one survived in the vehicle in front of us. To me, it is not the people one picks up at the motor park, because they have been thoroughly checked by security personnel and NURTW officials that ensure the safety of everyone. The danger is the isolated passengers picked up on the roadside.

To further decrease the possibility of Boko Haram's deadly ambushes along major roads and highways, passenger transports and goods-laden trucks in Borno State are increasingly traveling in convoys escorted by heavily armed soldiers (Haruna 2020), which may draw unnecessary attention. To assist its armed forces in repelling Boko Haram and extending their "eyes and ears on the roads," the Nigerian government has contracted the services of vigilante and hunter militias who "act as trackers and scouts, gather information about the communities that they know so well, and sometimes fight the insurgents directly" (MacEachern 2018, 176). That surveillance of mobility became necessary in the face of Boko Haram's mobile terrorism, which instills in travelers a fear of moving. Idris Garba, a tanker driver from Damaturu, noted, "For us, there is no rest of mind when we are driving. Some drivers had to abandon their job because of this, especially those that are not northerners. A journey of one week can take you four weeks, because anywhere you go, you have to stop and find out the situation on the ground and ahead of you. Sometimes you have to be attached with armed escorts."

There are widespread fears that Borno State may soon be cut off from the rest of Nigeria, on account of Boko Haram's almost daily fatal ambushes on drivers and passengers along Kano–Maiduguri Highway. Connecting Borno State with Damaturu, the capital of Yobe State, that highway currently remains the only safe route into the state, and members of military security refer to it as the "Golden Gate" (Haruna 2020). Also, since 2014, Nigerian soldiers have battled to prevent insurgents from taking over the Benishek Bridge, the only bridge on the 135-kilometer road linking Maiduguri and Damaturu. Kashim Shettima, former governor of Borno State, noted,

> Nobody could venture out maybe for thirty kilometers beyond Maiduguri. Along Maiduguri–Dikwa Road, once you pass Ngwom you are already in Boko Haram territory. Along Maiduguri-Biu Road, the end of Nigeria was Delia. Along Maiduguri–Mongunu–Baga Road, our territory stopped in Tungushe. The only accessible road to Maiduguri was the Maiduguri–Kano Road that was itself subjected to numerous attacks. Maiduguri was effectively encircled by Boko Haram. In fact, and I am not exaggerating, Maiduguri was on the path of falling into the hands of Boko Haram because they had effectively encircled it. Boko Haram were in control—partial or total control—of nearly 22 local government areas of Borno. (Senema Productions 2017)

Boko Haram's attacks on Kano–Maiduguri Highway have dealt a serious blow to the local economy in Maiduguri, leaving many traders "stuck" and forced to "wait out" the crisis (Hage 2009). Kyari, a textile merchant who is based in Maiduguri and makes large purchases from Kano, complained that "the insecurity on the Kano-Maiduguri Highway, especially between Damaturu and Maiduguri, has already undercut my business. I had the intention of traveling to Kano since December last year, but here I am stranded because there is no guarantee of security on the way in or out of Maiduguri. I'm very worried because very soon I will run out of stock." Automobile dealers in Maiduguri have also experienced a serious nose-dive in the face of Boko Haram attacks, with their business plummeting by about 90 percent. Jidda, a major car dealer in the state capital, lamented, "We are in a dicey situation economically in Borno State. What do you make of a situation where out of one hundred businessmen that go out to bring cars for sales, only about ten now have the courage to do so due to insecurity [on the roads]? Our kind of business is 100 percent dependent on the road. But now the only road available for us to transit our business is being taken over. Everyone fears for his or her life." Jidda noted that the rapid descent of the automobile business has dealt a blow to the survival of a vast network of workers who keep the wheels of industry rolling: "A well-established car sales garage has at least fifty persons dependent on it for their daily bread. We have people who wash and polish cars; we have mechanics, receptionists, automobile electricians, spare parts vendors; we have all tribes depending on the business to survive. But it now means nothing for this multitude of beneficiaries if we can no longer bring into Maiduguri cars for sale."

Soldiering On: The Motorcycle Ban and the Biopolitics of Dispossession

Tim Cresswell argues, "An emphasis on the production of mobilities forces us to consider how particular modes of mobility are enabled, given license, encouraged and facilitated while others are, conversely, forbidden, regulated, policed and prevented" (2006, 735). That argument is true of the official ban on motorcycles (*achabas*) by local authorities across northern Nigeria because of the nefarious activities they facilitate. Giorgio Agamben writes that the term *ban* refers both to exclusion and to the sovereign's power to suspend the law: "The relation of exception is a relation of the ban. He who has been banned is not, in fact, simply set outside the law and made indifferent to it but rather abandoned by it, that is, exposed and threatened on the threshold in which life and law, outside and inside, become indistinguishable" (1998, 28).

Beginning in 2010, the states of Borno, Yobe, and Adamawa banned the operation of commercial and private motorcycles, in the name of preventing Boko Haram's drive-by shootings and securing lives and properties.

The official justification for the ban adds weight to Jeremy Packer's point that "safety as a set of practices and a legitimating discourse has been a goal of biopolitics and a means of ensuring discipline and implementing a control society" (2006, 379), or what Gilles Deleuze (1992) calls "societies of control." Central to the control society is the management of access to space, through which "the ability to be mobile, to move from one place to another, can be governed at the level of the individual" (Packer 2006, 383). At the same time, the *achaba* ban spotlights the concept of "subversive mobilities," which argues that, beyond motifs of profit and power, the reasons why certain modes of transportation become dominant while others fade away (along with the "social worlds" that they made possible) are rooted in politics, fear, and government efforts to control a suspect group (Shell 2015).

The motorcycle ban sent shockwaves throughout the *achaba* community, especially in the adversely affected states of Borno, Yobe, and Adamawa. Umar from Damaturu used to own four *achabas* before the motorcycle ban in 2009: "I was riding one and other boys riding the other three for me. We heard of the news in the evening around 4 to 6 p.m. that motorcycles will be banned, and we were wondering how this will happen until it was explained to us that the ban was to put a halt to the use of motorcycles by Boko Haram insurgents and thieves that commit atrocities and easily escape arrest or identification. The ban took us by surprise, and we were left with nothing to do, as we did not even think tricycles will later be introduced. We suffered a lot, especially those of us with families." Abdullahi, chairman of the Keke Napep Owners and Riders Association in Yola, said, "When it was announced on radio that all motorcycles have been banned throughout Adamawa State, we were completely lost and confused." The state government presented the ban to *achaba* drivers and owners as a fait accompli, thereby denying them of their right to the city. As a collective rather than an individual right, the right to the city is first and foremost about the right not to be excluded from decision-making processes that impinge on one's life and source of survival (Harvey 2003; Lefebvre 1991).

The ban on motorcycles empowered state security agencies to dispossess offenders of their *achabas* by force. The term *dispossession* describes the processes and ideologies by which the bodies of laboring subjects are "disowned and abjected" by a biopolitical and securitarian governmentality (Butler and Athanasiou 2013, 2, 10). Following the motorcycle ban, thousands of dispossessed young men became involuntarily immobilized, reduced to a condition of "bare life," in which any rights they may have had are rendered null by sovereignty in form of the state, allowing their lives to be taken with impunity (Parfitt 2009, 42). The *achaba* ban also affected the livelihoods of pastoralists in northeast Nigeria, many of whom use their low-cost motorcycles to take advantage of domestic and cross-border market opportunities. In short, *achaba* mobilities became a site for the exercise of biopower, which is characterized by the capacity "to make live and to let die" (Foucault 1976, 241; Humphrey 2004, 420).

Michel Foucault recognized the interconnectedness of power, the body, and mobility when he argued that "the individual, with his identity and characteristics, is the product of a relation of power exercised over bodies, multiplicities, movements, desires, forces" (1980, 74). Hard on the heels of the motorcycle ban, anything and anyone not traveling by bush taxi, truck, or protected convoy became suspect in the eyes of security agents. In Nigeria and Cameroon, "innumerable tragic mistakes involve people shot as they rode motorcycles to remote fields. Someone carrying a sack of rice may be accused of being on their way to replenish a Boko Haram faction in the bush" (Seignobos 2015, 94). The allocation of suspicion on the basis of that "faulty epistemology" (Zulaika 2012) further marginalized and oppressed road tranport workers.

In lieu of *achabas*, authorities sanctioned tricycle taxis, or *keke napeps*, as a safer option for travelers. *Keke napeps* were originally introduced in Nigeria in the year 2000, as an intervention tool for job creation and poverty alleviation. However, the yellowish three-wheelers proved wholly inadequate. In Borno State, only five hundred *keke napeps* were purchased by the government and distributed, on loan, to select former *achaba* drivers (Mustapha 2014, 10–11). In Damaturu, 250 out of 8,000 *achaba* drivers who were registered with the Amalgamated Commercial Motorcycle and Tricycle Owners and Riders Association of Nigeria (ACOMOTRAN) were allocated tricycles after the ban in January 2012, while some 7,750 others were left with no source of income (Haruna 2015, 154). A commuter in Yola lamented, "Four hundred tricycles are grossly inadequate for Yola town alone, talk less of the whole state. As you know, the state capital alone deserves no less than one thousand tricycles to address this hardship." The shortages in the state provision of tricycles paved the way for private investors to cash in on desperate commercial drivers looking to acquire *keke napeps* through installment purchase. According to Abdullahi, the chairman of Yola's Keke Napep Owners and Riders Association and founder of the Union of Achaba Riders in Adamawa State,

> The *achaba* ban left us in the hands of the private sector, who suck us dry. A new *keke napep* is N 670,000, but the private sector is giv-

ing them to our boys at the rate of N 1.1 million.[1] The profit they get from the boys is about N 500,000. These private investors are dealing with us mercilessly. Sometimes there is a sickness or some unforeseen situation that prevents us from completing the full payment of the N 1.1 million after twelve months; maybe we are short of only N 100,000 by year end. In this case, the investor will insist on collecting back his *keke* and then sell it at any price to recover his balance. Our boys have been cheated this way by many ruthless businessmen.

The pressure to pay up successfully and claim ownership of their installment-purchased vehicles pushed many drivers into criminal activities, including armed robbery. That situation points to how hardship, including dispossession and duress, forces people to make decisions they would ordinarily not make (de Bruijn and Both 2018, 187). As a coping mechanism in the face of both shortages of *keke napeps* and exploitation by private investors, the few *achaba* drivers who were lucky to receive *keke napeps* from the state resorted to a survival tactic known as "soldiering," to help their colleagues without *keke napeps*. According to Ibrahim, a member of the National Commercial Tricycle and Motorcycle Owners and Riders Association (NACTOMORA) in Yobe State, "When a driver works and gets tired, he gives his machine to someone else to also work with the machine while the owner is resting. The person helped to work the machine instead of staying idle is the 'soldier.'" Referring to after the *achaba* ban, Ibrahim said, "We started taking turns to drive *keke napeps* and get something to feed our immediate and extended families. At times, four people will work with a single *keke napep* for a day just to keep body and soul together. A rider will typically start work at 6 a.m. and give the *keke napep* to someone else to continue from 12 pm to 8 p.m. since most people don't work in the night." Umar Barau, state chairman of the Keke Napep Association in Yobe, states, "What we did is if your brother or friend did not get a machine, then you work today, and tomorrow you allow him to use the machine and get something to buy food for his family, which is what we call 'Mercenary' or 'Soldier.'"

A Mixed Bag: From Motorcycles to Tricycles

The motorcycle ban took away the means of livelihood from over eighty thousand youths without providing a viable alternative, thereby rendering many mobile bodies "disposable," as that notion is defined by Khanna: "To dispose is an exertion of power by the disposer in the utterance of a disposition made explicit, or, indeed, in a decision to exercise control over or a discarding of bodies" (2009, 185). In states such as Kano, where *achabas* were estimated at two million in 2011, their ban amounted to a severe loss of income and livelihood opportunities among the very groups most vulnerable to Boko Haram mobilization (Meagher 2013, 172). *Achabas* were banned in Kano shortly after gun-wielding insurgents on motorcycles attacked the convoy of the emir of Kano, Alhaji Ado Bayero, at Hausawa Quarters in Kano in January 2013. Many commuters have condemned the *achaba* ban, blaming the rise of motorcycles on state failure to guarantee adequate and efficient mobility for its citizens. A commuter noted, "*Achaba* came due to the state's inability to provide adequate mass transport. The question is, Has the state provided an alternative that can level up to the *achaba* drivers? One of the justifications often given by the state is security concerns, but I feel that since the role of *achaba* to the economy is vital, what the state should have done is to place regulations rather than an outright ban." Alhaji Abdullahi German, chairman for good governance in Adamawa State, argues that the motorcycle ban punishes the many for the sins of the few, adding, "This is not the way of tackling insecurity in the state, as this action will, rather, wreak more havoc." A respondent in Yobe State said, "It is a pity and shame, for a government that was elected by poor men will now turn to bite the hands that feed it."

The *achaba* ban affected the movement of up to 80 percent of the residents in northeast Nigeria who rely on motorcycles for their survival and daily commute. In fact, many locals have seen the cost and distance of transportation double as a result of the motorcycle ban. Research shows that higher transportation costs have "a significantly negative impact on wealth and a significantly positive impact on the probability of being multi-dimensionally poor" (Ali et al. 2015, 4). Following the ban, said Umar, a transport union leader in Yobe State, "there was shortage of means of transportation for those going to work, market, schools, and so on, especially those going to remote areas of the city that are not close to a main road. The only means of transportation was *jega* or *tabari* (a tricycle meant for transportation of goods and farm produce), but wooden seats were provided to carry women and children as passengers. Passengers used to be dropped off on major roads, unlike motorcycles that could enter nooks and corners of our informal settlements, and you waste time waiting for an available means of transportation."

Farmers, in particular, have had to walk long distances to get to their farms in the wake of the ban, making them more vulnerable to Boko Haram's deadly attacks. The situation of farmers is not helped by the presence of dangerous military trenches on their paths, constraining their mobility. A local respondent from Damaturu explained, "Soldiers dig trenches around cities to prevent insurgents from gaining access into communities, but these trenches prevent people of the community from their farming activities. A poor man will take his bicycle to go to farm and will meet a very wide trench that he cannot cross but must come back, but when these insurgents come to attack, they can access the town through the main routes and no one can stop them."

Stories abound of people who are kidnapped on the road by armed insurgents, of farmers attacked when they go to fetch firewood or to farm, and of their crops being destroyed or harvested by Boko Haram (Center for Civilians in Conflict 2018, 6). A farmer from Adamawa complained, "We are suffering because you can trek about fifty kilometers into the bush to gain access to our farms. As you know, no taxi can take you there, because there is no road; therefore we rely on our motorcycles to get to farms. I want to plead with the governor to see reasons and ignore this bad advice of banning motorcycles, because the consequences not only render thousands of youths jobless; it also impinges on farmers, students, workers, and other small-scale and petty business men and women in the society, and it is those people that constitute the majority." Some *achaba* drivers and their commuters believe that the ban will force good citizens into "choiceless decisions" (Coulter 2008) out of desperation to survive. Usman, who used to operate *achabas* before their ban in Kaduna, cautions, "Majority of us [*achaba* drivers] don't have any other thing to fall back on, and it is only through this work that we are taking care of ourselves and our families. Now that government has banned our operation, the governor should please provide alternative that will have direct bearing on those of us who are affected, else, the situation will be worse than it is now because a lot of us who have taken *achaba* work as the only means of survival may resort to stealing, armed robbery, kidnapping, and other forms of atrocities" (*Daily Trust* 2012).

Some drivers, however, expressed strong support for the motorcycle ban, which they saw as a necessary evil in the face of Boko Haram's infiltration of the *achaba* business and the group's drive-by killings. According to Umar, chairman of the Keke Napep Association in Yobe, "The *achaba* ban has helped in curtailing the damage done to society by Boko Haram. Before, when Boko attacks with three or more *achabas*, about twenty people could be killed in thirty minutes. But now, with the ban on *achabas*, only about two or three people could be injured when they attack." A passenger transporter from Mubi said, "The ban has affected people in various ways, but we need to consider that it was meant to protect our lives and property." That transporter added, "You cannot use a *keke napep* to escape a hot pursuit. When you reach some places like alleyways, you have to abandon it and escape, unlike *achabas* that can be maneuvered anyhow."

Idris, a former *achaba* driver, noted that driving a *keke napep* is a more lucrative business compared to driving a motorcycle: "I prefer tricycle to motorcycle because you can make more money. With an *achaba*, one can only take one or two passengers at a time and will earn N 50 ($0.13) to N 100 ($0.25). But now, a law-abiding *keke* driver can take three passengers lawfully and you get N 150 ($0.38). If you used to give the *achaba* owner N 500 ($1.26) at the end of the day, now you give him N 1,500 ($3.78). For me, the ban has turned out to be a blessing in disguise. Our people have a saying, '*Kofan Allah ya fi Kofan Chali*' (Allah has more openings than a fishing net)." Buying a *keke napep* is, of course, beyond the reach of the average Nigerian citizen. A new *keke napep* costs N 650,000 ($1,638), which could rise up to N 1 million ($2,520) if purchased in installments. Yet Idris believes that hard work is all it takes to be successful in the business: "Before, I used to make N 4,000 ($10) to 5,000 ($12.60) daily, but today I make up to N 10,000 ($25.21) because of the high demand on tricycle taxis since *achaba* was banned." Idris also cited the added safety benefits of using *keke napeps*, especially for women and children: "I assure you that if the ban on *achaba* is lifted now, many women will not use *achaba*. Women are most comfortable using *keke*. They feel safe using *keke* with their children. If *keke* is involved in an accident, you find that the gravity of injury is less."

Other drivers welcomed the registration of *keke napeps* and the open display of their registration numbers, which they say helps to spot and fight crimes in the sector. Zakari, a former *achaba* driver, told me that the banning of *achabas* and the coming of registered *keke napeps* has reduced the menace of drive-by shootings and bolstered the war against Boko Haram: "In the past, no one has an idea of the number of *achabas* in the state, but with *keke napeps*, we know the number plying the roads in all the states. And if someone does something wrong with a *keke*, the *keke* can be easily tracked, and this has helped us tremendously, and we are in support of the ban." Similarly, a transport union leader noted that "unlike with motorcycles, when a tricycle rider commits a crime, such as hit-and-run, when the code number of the tricycle is brought to us, our register will show the contact details of the owner, and he would be brought to book and disciplined accordingly. Today, anyone that wants to work with tricycle taxis must come and give us his name, phone number, address, and photograph before we give him a tricycle. Anyone working without registration, we report such person to security men. If found guilty, they do the needful to such person."

In Yola, I interviewed thirty-seven-year-old Bakana, a graphic artist contracted by the Union of Keke Napep Operators to aesthetically register the unique code numbers of new drivers. According to him, "We write the code number for every *keke napep*. We write codes so that when you are boarding a *keke*, you read the code, and in case you forget any of your belongings, it can be easily traced. If you are rudely treated by the operator and you lodge a complaint with us, we open the register here in the office and identify the culprit and summon him to resolve the issue. The numbers we give are never the same. They are like a GSM number on our phones, always unique."

The efforts toward greater security notwithstanding, there is growing evidence, since 2015, of Boko Haram's weaponization of *keke napeps* in its terror operations (Marama 2015). In fact, tricycle taxis became the target of security scrutiny after Boko Haram insurgents started using them to launch suicide attacks and drive-by shootings. Tricycle movements in public spaces have been increasingly regulated. A man in Mubi told me that insurgents use *keke napeps* in their attacks because of its capacity to carry more explosives. In December 2019, Borno State governor Babagana Umar Zulum directed a ban on the use of tricycle taxis on highways in Maiduguri, citing growing public safety and security concerns (Jirgi 2019). "We have faced a lot of setbacks," a tricycle driver from the state said, adding, "We don't make as much money as we used to. Before we could make as much as four to five thousand naira ($10 to $12.60). But now, after a hard day's work, we'll be lucky if we make two thousand naira ($5)." Already in November 2019, authorities in Abuja suddenly banned tricycles from the capital city without providing any alternatives, also citing public security threats. In a manner reminiscent of Operation Flush II (discussed in chapter 3), the government's special task force created to enforce the ban on tricycle taxis "operates like terrorists" (*Punch* 2019), seizing *keke napeps* and arresting operators who fail to comply with the ban.

The ban has plunged many young men in the capital into joblessness and idleness. An operator in Abuja lamented, "I don't know what to do right now. Should I start crying in public or just go home and lock myself up? This is my only means of survival. I have two wives and six children depending solely on me for daily bread. What do I tell them? I used to drive *okada* here in Abuja before the government completely barred it. Now they've ended up killing me and my family." Another operator noted, "I woke up this morning, washed my *keke*, and entered the road to do my work, only to see policemen and other security agencies chasing and impounding our tricycles. Seriously, I don't know what to do. I don't even know whom to run to. My life depends on this work. I'm calling on the government to rethink this decision. You people should help us tell the government that we don't have anything to do again" (Nwosu 2019). Those voices provide a window into the sufferings of mobile workers in the face of state counterinsurgency.

Dispossession, Social Death, and Mobilization into Boko Haram

In the extant literature, there is a growing recognition that mobility problems can be a significant barrier to social inclusion (Cass et al. 2005, 540; SEU 2003, 6). Scholars argue that mobility can be a source of status and power and that the curtailment or coercion of mobility may generate social deprivation, untold suffering, and exclusion (Urry 2007, 9; D'Andrea et al. 2011, 158). By criminalizing one of the few economic opportunities for the poor and marginalized in northern Nigeria, the motorcycle ban reduced able-bodied youth to passivity and deprived them of the possibility of being self-determining subjects. One driver noted, "The ban has affected lots of people, such as mechanics, vulcanizers, and boys that provide service support for drivers, helping to wash their machines every evening after work as a source of income. These boys have nothing to do but wash machines in the night 'til morning for, like, N 100 ($0.25) to N 150 (0.38) per bike. *Achaba* drivers and these support people were rendered jobless by the ban." Umar, one of the *achaba* drivers dispossessed by the ban, told me that he bought his *achaba* for N 120,000 just before the ban and was forced to sell it for N 30,000 within a week after the ban. Garba, who used to run an *achaba* business in Yola, told me that following the official ban on motorcycles, "people were in great pain and lots of people had heart attacks and lost their lives, because this is their main means of livelihood for years, and it was stopped abruptly after ten to fifteen years."

Crucially, the ban loosened the grip that many laboring young men felt they had over their life, reducing them to "non-being" (Patterson 1982; Mbembe 2003), a state of "social death" (Borgstrom 2017). The concept of social death is manifested in a series of losses that compromises one's well-being, including loss of social identity, of ability to participate in daily activities, and of social relationships, as well as loss associated with disintegration of the body (Kralova 2015; Norwood 2009). Together, those losses can result in an individual becoming severed from social life. For many *achaba* drivers, the aspirations of physical and social mobility are embodied in their *achabas*. As such, the *achaba*, much like the human body or the relational subject, becomes "a point of overlapping between the physical, the symbolic, and the sociological" (Braidotti 1994, 4). In light of that significance, the motorcycle ban amounts to a loss of social identity and personal agency.

After the ban was announced, many dispossessed *achaba* drivers were forced to leave their states of origin, as a survival strategy (Salaudeen 2018). One driver in the Wulari area in Maiduguri calculated, "If I stay back, what will I be doing? And I cannot steal, so it is better I go back to my state and find something to do to help myself and my family." Other drivers resorted to farming or selling firewood and water as an alternative to driving motorcycles. "I was born here and I grew up here, so where will I go to?" said Sani Bello, a father of six who also holds a national diploma in mechanical engineering. "I have been searching for work for over three years now," he explained, "but I could not find any, and that is why I started driving *achaba*. Now that the government has criminalized our livelihood operations, the only way out for me to live is to enter farming. I cannot buy a tricycle, because it is too expensive. For now, I will be farming to take care of my wife and six children, until I am able to raise enough money to buy a Golf [Volkswagen car], so that I can start traveling long journeys as a transporter." Following the loss of their primary source of income, many *achaba* breadwinners said they endured several sleepless nights thinking about how to provide for their families.

Anecdotal evidence suggests that a handful of *achaba* men committed suicide as a result of severe depression caused by the loss of their means of livelihood. This brings home an important lesson: no matter how resilient, rugged, or resourceful an individual or group (and *achaba* drivers are perhaps the most resilient social category in the Lake Chad region), they cannot always overcome or transform the structural conditions (e.g., exclusions or bans) that traps them in "spaces of vulnerability" (Kihato n.d., 4–5). Some *achaba* drivers shared with me the humiliation of having to postpone their marriage date or cancel it altogether. In the wake of the *achaba* ban, affected cities across northern Nigeria transmogrified into "tinderboxes where hordes of young men . . . face the daily indignities of economic desperation and police harassment in their struggle to get by or make do. And every day, these [marginal men] are confronted by the lavish consumption styles of a stupendously wealthy and corrupt political elite. Rather than addressing these social ills, unscrupulous northern politicians use the reservoir of the jobless youth for recruitment into political thuggery, spreading a taste for violence and easy money across these ravaged communities" (Meagher 2013, 171). Aside from such political instrumentality, the dispossession of *achaba* drivers also played into the waiting hands of Boko Haram leadership, reproducing the insecurity it was intended to forestall. For one thing, the ban meant that many young men lost their social identity, that is, their sense of being "a somebody." Following dispossession, "we sometimes no longer know precisely who we are, or by what we are driven. . . . One can be dispossessed in grief or in passion—unable to find oneself" (Butler and Athanasiou 2013, 3).

The ban allowed Boko Haram leaders to mobilize dispossessed and confused *achaba* drivers searching for living wages and purpose in life. "Before the ban," said Umar, a transport union leader in Yobe State, "if this group called Boko Haram call people to join them, out of every ten people, they hardly get a single person joining them in the insurgency. When people have something doing, most were contented with the little they have from legitimate business. But when there is no means of making ends meet, there were ignorant and jobless men here in Damaturu that were convinced to join the insurgents for lack of something to do." That situation supports the argument that "if we are beings who can be deprived of place, livelihood, shelter, food, and protection, if we can lose our citizenship, our homes, and our rights, then we are fundamentally dependent on those powers that alternately sustain or deprive us, and that hold a certain power over our very survival" (Butler and Athanasiou 2013, 4).

The untold suffering that characterized the lives of dispossessed *achaba* drivers predisposed some of them to Boko Haram's extremist ideas, reinforcing the argument that the interests of the poor lies not so much in ideology as in groups that can directly address their immediate concerns (Bayat 2007, 588). As Joshua Rubin and colleagues note, "in an unstable, violent context, joining an armed group and engaging in warfare becomes a practical means of survival for many young men, even though they may not have a strong ideological stake in the fighting" (Rubin et al. 2019, 431). That point is consistent with empirically grounded research on the questions of who, why, and how individuals in northeast Nigeria join Boko Haram. One study finds that "while religion provides an important backdrop to the activities of Boko Haram, former members themselves did not cite it as a dominant reason for joining Boko Haram." Instead, former Boko Haram respondents referred to the need to be respected and feared (23.52 percent), a need to belong (16.8 percent), and poverty or lack of money

(15.13 percent), as core reasons for joining (Botha and Abdile 2017, 499, 516; see also Mustapha and Meagher 2020).

Following the *achaba* ban, some local residents called attention to the dangerous potentiality of an increased number of idle youths in urban centers. One respondent noted, "If you do not have anything doing and you cannot access any job, conflict is inevitable because an idle mind is the devil's workshop. . . . If they are just idle, it will create opportunity for them to be engaged in violence" (Bansfield et al. 2014, 6). A former *achaba* driver from Adamawa State told me that after the ban, "people remained idle for some time, and some people used that opportunity to join the insurgents to add [to] their strength for want of something to do." That statement was validated by Ibrahim, a mechanic from Damaturu: "Most of those [*achaba*] boys who lost their means of livelihood because of the ban joined Boko Haram, and the insurgency scaled up. Boko Haram sponsors continued to increase in numbers because there was no job for these former *achaba* boys." Grema, the secretary of the *keke napep* union in Damaturu, maintains that prior to the ban, the number of drivers in Yobe State who joined Boko Haram was almost insignificant, amounting to something like one in ten drivers. After the ban, Grema reckons, "there was an increase in the number joining Boko Haram from *achaba* drivers, mechanics, vulcanizers, and even the boys washing machines as their jobs because they do not have anything doing. This swelled the number of insurgents. Today, when you meet young people, you will hear that someone you know has joined the movement. The ban has led to an increase in the number of Boko Haram." As former *achaba* drivers turn to Boko Haram to make ends meet, they, like the migrants in "unhomely spaces," are "forced into situations during which they may re-assess their identity and community and ask questions about their morality and values. They act in ways that diverge from their shared moral values and norms and, hence, force those around them to question expected behaviors and traditions" (Bezabeh 2016, 10).

It is not difficult to see why a number of dispossessed *achaba* drivers turned to Boko Haram for survival and to regain their full manhood as *baaba saare* (in Fulani, "master of the house"): "[Boko Haram] insurgents are relatively well paid for their activities, certainly earning far more money than they would have as farmers, *clando* drivers, or laborers. . . . [Boko Haram] exists in great part because it offers a vision of a better life, the raising up of good Muslims and their triumph over the wicked, to people who see no prospect of a decent or fulfilling life in their present circumstances" (MacEachern 2018, 168, 173). Not all former *achaba* drivers who joined Boko Haram were lured only by material benefits or saw profitable opportunities. Pathways into Boko Haram are rather complex, including (but not limited to) religious convictions, family and friends, opportunistic incentives, and coercion (Ehrhardt 2019, 115–34). As the example of ISIS shows, religion spurs insurgents into action, influencing their willingness to die or kill, as well as their strategic calculations (Hamid 2015).

Checkpoints, Corruption, and Coercion

Northeast Nigeria may be described as a territory of checkpoints. By the term *checkpoint*, I here mean a "governmental or para/shadow governmental apparatus that blocks passage between two points, while imposing criteria—often the checking of 'identity' through the examination of documents and bodies—for passage" (Jeganathan 2018, 403). Checkpoints in northeast Nigeria are best interrogated as "sites of sovereign power" (Amir 2013, 233), places of "emergency" (Adey 2016), and "zones of extrajudicial arrest and subsequent execution following a logic that 'purports' to see 'enemies' of the state everywhere" (Jeganathan 2018, 405). For local populations in conflict-affected zones, passing through a checkpoint is never normal, but it has become part of the everyday that one learns to live with given the constant anticipation of danger. Being at a checkpoint is inherently dangerous, because a checkpoint exists "at the boundaries of a target" and, ipso facto, "delineates and focuses attention on the target" (Jeganathan 2004, 69). Yet the sighting of a checkpoint in conflict zones may also indicate safety, "a place where we who have seen, heard, and felt destruction, terror, pain, and death and who anticipate with uncertain anxiety that which is to come to us and ours, sense for a moment a stilling of that foretelling of death" (Jeganathan 2004, 74).

Studies (from Somalia and the Congo to Iraq and Afghanistan) have shed new light on why and how terrorist/rebel financing often rely on the control and exploitation of checkpoints along strategic routes, sometimes in collusion with state authorities, multinational companies, and aid organizations (e.g., Schouten 2021; Danish Refugee Council 2017; Special Inspector General for Afghanistan Reconstruction 2014). However, an often neglected characteristic of contemporary wars, which I address here, is the transformation of state counterinsurgent forces into highway robbers (coupers de route), in the guise of neutralizing Boko Haram's movement.

The mobilization of mobility in the war against Boko Haram has had a snowball effect on corruption of security forces and on violence and blackmail along transit routes in northeast Nigeria, with abundant stories of security forces who turn checkpoints into private tollbooths. During my fieldwork, road transport workers routinely lamented that security force shakedowns and delays at checkpoints have doubled since the coming of Boko Haram. A bus driver in Yobe told me, "In the past, I know that bribe is taken [by security officers], but it has never occurred that a whopping N 150, 000 ($378) could be made in a day on one lane of the checkpoint. I don't know any business where such a staggering amount could be made in a single day." Another driver pointed out that since the rise of Boko Haram in 2009, commercial drivers have effectively turned into an "ATM machine" for soldiers and traffic police inspectors.

Umar, a *keke napep* driver from Maiduguri, denounced the culture of intimidation, violence, and extortion that has become a trademark of Nigerian security forces: "Boko Haram's coming has amplified practically everything. *The security men have gone commercial on the road.* The lower ranks bribe their superiors to get posted to checkpoints because of its lucrative nature. Officers unable to bribe their way are often posted to a remote place where no vehicles ply the road and there will be nothing for you." In a focus group discussion with a union of tanker drivers in Damaturu, virtually all participants complained bitterly about how corruption impedes their survival and makes it difficult to make headway.

> If you want to go to Maiduguri now, at least you have to set aside N 7,000 ($17.65) to settle [bribe] the road security men, and when you reach there, where will you get the money back? For example, you will encounter bribe-demanding road safety officers and vehicle inspection officers. You must give the Road Safety Officers N 2,000 ($5) just for the load you are carrying, not the issue of vehicle particulars or anything, and when you meet police, they will ask for their own share, and if you cough out N 100 ($0.25), they will complain that it's too small and that you must give them N 1,000 ($2.52). Now if you spend like N 7,000 ($17.65) and bring the stuff you want to sell, you must factor in what you spent on the road. If you don't cooperate with these officers, how can you work?

A truck driver in Damaturu decried the contradiction of giving cash bribes to security operatives on the road, reinforcing the incongruity between signs and their referents.

> You can come to a checkpoint and read a notice: "Don't Give Bribe." But when it gets to your turn and a policeman or a soldier stretched

his hand for something and you don't give, they will ask you to "park well" [pull over], go and sit down under the signpost that reads "Don't Give Bribe." Everybody will pass while you remain stuck there. In this case, your passengers may even say that you have cheated them for not giving out the N 50 or N 100 to enable you to pass and get on. You will be insulted by your passengers that others have given [a bribe] and were allowed to move on while you think you are smart by not giving. There is nothing one can do about it.

Once a response to the widespread criminal activities of smugglers, drug pushers, and armed robbers, the proliferation of checkpoints in northern (especially northeast) Nigeria is now primarily aimed at keeping out Boko Haram insurgents. The checkpoints are typically set up about five to ten kilometers apart and are manned at different points by a hybrid security governance of soldiers, mobile police, vehicle inspection officers, immigration and customs officers, and vigilante militias. At the checkpoints, especially those leading into and out of cities, travelers in public vehicles are forced by military men to part with the sum of N 200 ($0.50) per person for failing to present their national identification cards for clearance at the entrance of the city, according to what the army calls "Operation Positive Identification" (*This Day* 2019).

"This practice has been in place for four to five years," a taxi driver from Maiduguri said, adding that "a combined team of immigration service and the military working at the entrance of this town have been collecting N 200 ($0.50) from all passengers who could not produce their national ID cards. And therefore, we have been suffering delays on our journeys to and from the city." Even in Kaduna, where Boko Haram's attacks have been sporadic, a resident complained, "It is unfortunate that one can no longer freely walk about at night. It is as if one is in a prison in his own town. When you are driving, security people will be stopping you at intervals, asking you for identification [and] your destination, and they will be searching your vehicle as if you are carrying bombs" (National Working Group on Armed Violence 2013, 64). Curiously, few people in Maiduguri have access to the type of national ID required by the soldiers. A bus driver told me, "The authorities here insist on one type of identification cards which many passengers do not possess, and most of the passengers are not willing to pay that N 200 as a fine, and so the authorities would ask the drivers to off-load all the luggage belonging to the erring passenger, which is very difficult and time consuming." A passenger in Maiduguri commented, "Since the road to Gwoza was reopened, I have been paying this N 200 ($0.50) at some checkpoints 'til I reach Gwoza town. I do have two other ID cards, but they only require that specifically, which I couldn't get time to obtain" (Sawab 2019). About the corruption of security forces at checkpoints in Yola in Adamawa State, a *keke napep* driver lamented,

> Before, if I leave here to Gire or Jabbi Lamba, I will meet three checkpoints. Now the checkpoints have increased to ten, and anywhere you go, officers will just stretch their palms in your direction to collect money from you as if it's their right to collect the bribe. If you complain that you don't have lower denomination of currency, they will tell you that they do have change of up to N 1,000 ($2.52). It is just like you are repaying credit, and if you don't give anything, they ask you to park your vehicle and subject you to a time-wasting search. It is always better for you to find something and give them and go ahead while reporting to God.

On the recurring issue of road delays, a *keke napep* driver from Yola told me that drivers have become increasingly reluctant to take passengers on certain routes, due to the presence of several security checkpoints along the way, especially on market days.

> Our main challenge in this business is not Boko Haram. It is checkpoints and the delay tactics of security men on the road, because they are really disturbing us by extorting and collecting money from us by force. If a passenger wants to go to Federal University of Technology, Yola, a *keke* rider will not take you, because at checkpoint the driver will be delayed by security men for three to four hours, so it's better for him not to start what he can't finish.

Another driver made a similar point, going further to argue that the multiplication of highway checkpoints in the name of keeping out Boko Haram is a smokescreen for the corruption of security forces: "We have countless security outfits in this town, but we don't know what the secret is, because we have never heard of interception of anything illegal, yet the checkpoints are multiplying by the day. There is a major road going around the whole town. If one is going out of town through *Hayin Gida*, there is checkpoint in and out. If you are going out to Federal Government Girls College, there is checkpoint in and out. If one is going to Yola, as you leave Bama going to Fufore, there is another checkpoint. *The whole town is surrounded by checkpoints.*" Trucks and drivers have been adversely affected by the corruption and delay tactics of security men. Ahmed, a tanker driver plying the route between Yola and Abuja, told me that the journey is awash with checkpoints that increase danger for drivers: "If you load from here to Abuja, you will be stopped at 'Welcome to Yola' [a signboard] to spend at least five minutes, and the next one is at Ngorore. In short, anywhere you encounter a checkpoint, you must stop and waste your time. When we were young conductors, if you leave Abuja at 6 a.m. you will arrive Yola between 3 to 4 p.m. Today, the story is different. If you leave Yola at 6 a.m. you will arrive Abuja at 10 p.m. if you're lucky. And in the night, you must be alert to robbers and insurgents. At times, if you leave a checkpoint, you can be waylaid by armed robbers within a kilometer from the checkpoint."

Commercial drivers, including truck and tanker drivers, emphasized that the coming of Boko Haram has furnished security personnel with an opportunity to label as Boko Haram any driver who resists their demand for bribes or sample of goods. Bello Idris, a thirty-two-year-old tanker driver from Gwoza, told me, "Our problem are the checkpoints. Sometimes armed personnel will give you signal to pass, but when you approach him, he will ask you who directed you to do so. One can be victimized and humiliated, and when you try to explain, he can even call you a Boko Haram, and there is nothing you can do about that. They can kill you for nothing. This is purely a smear tactic." Similarly, a tanker driver in Maiduguri recalled,

> In the past, if you don't give bribe, nothing serious will happen, but now if you refuse, the whole fight against Boko Haram will be directed at you, which is why we say it has increased. Now you can't exchange words with a security personnel, as he can easily label you as a Boko Haram element, and no one will want that. In the past, a driver can resist paying anything, and a colleague can easily join you and also refuse to pay, but now the officers can threaten you *that* *"You better bring something, or else we finish you and report that we killed Boko Haram. You noticed the vehicle ahead of you has given us something, but you want to prove tough."* I swear to God that I have been threatened like that on numerous occasions by security men, and we all know what Boko Haram has done to this country, and we will not want to be associated with insurgents. Security men now use the name of Boko Haram to intimidate us on the road. (my emphasis)

One form of corruption that has intensified among security forces in the wake of Boko Haram is what road transport workers in northeast Nigeria call "sampling." It occurs when security personnel request to "inspect" portions of the goods transported by long-distance drivers. A man from Maiduguri who drives a petroleum tanker described the problem: "The most annoying thing about passing through numerous checkpoints and roadblocks is the security personnel's constant request for sample of the product that I am carrying. Typically, they will request almost half a gallon as sample, and half a gallon amounts to two liters. When you keep removing two liters at every checkpoint, you will have a shortage on the products you are carrying, and your boss will say that is not his business. It is out of your salary that the amount will be deducted. And if you don't give them the fuel, they delay us for hours. These are some of the problems we face as a result of the coming of Boko Haram." A trucker from Yobe State said, "The [police] always ask for a sample of the products we are transporting." He continued, "Ideally the way we are told by our superiors is to present a small sample in a bottle of small table water for them to be sure of what we are carrying. But when you do that, they can delay you for some hours. To avoid that, you have to give them some money, N 500 ($1.26) to N 1,000 ($2.52), so that they can allow you to continue your journey."

Those challenges notwithstanding, road transport workers in northeast Nigeria believe they are best positioned to expand the state's limited surveillance of Boko Haram activities, on account of their dwelling in motion. However, the government rarely consults with drivers on security matters related to Boko Haram. A trucker in Maiduguri explained, "The ways in which drivers can assist the state on issues of insurgency are many, but it is like the government doesn't recognize the importance of us drivers. Drivers are the ones always on the road and on the move. And the security men are always in a specific checkpoint, and the information we have is necessary for them to have it. Which means it is the driver who is mobile that will relate this sensitive info to them. But we are not so important to them; that's why they don't contact us. What we only do is to inform our colleagues and the public whenever we discover that the road is not safe at a given time." Drivers recognize that effective counterinsurgency should rest on the networked and surveillant capacity of a mobile, rather than moored, population.

Conclusion

Toward a Mobile Logic of Insurgency and Counterinsurgency

The changing character of wars in the contemporary era—particularly the emergence of insurgents and nonstate armed groups, coupled with their readiness to use terror and other irregular methods of fighting—underscores the need for a new mobilities paradigm that attends to the spatial and temporal dynamics of insurgencies, as well as the structural conditions that produce and sustain violence along transit routes and in people's lives (Vogt 2018, 4; Gill et al. 2014, 5). Such a paradigm elides with a growing scholarly interest in approaches that reject a "sedentarist metaphysics" (Malkki 1992), in favor of a "nomadic metaphysics" (Cresswell 2006).

At the same time, a mobilities paradigm articulates a contradiction between, on the one hand, the increasing movement of people and, on the other, more forceful forms of exclusion and dispossession evidenced by securitarian policies that limit people's mobility and their capacity to move. As Paul Virilio ironically puts it, "The time has come, it seems, to face the facts: revolution is a movement, but movement is not a revolution" (1986, 18). Virilio's perspective suggests that mobility is not invariably coterminous with freedom and progress. The freedom of movement is key to social stratification in today's globalizing world and is a powerful mediator of social inclusion and exclusion (Bauman 1998, 9). Zygmunt Bauman observed,

> The present-day combination of annulment of entry visas and the reinforcement of immigration controls has profound symbolic significance. It could be taken as the metaphor for the new, emergent

stratification. It lays bare the fact that it is now the "access to global mobility" which has been raised to the topmost rank among the stratifying factors. (1998, 87)

Although the new mobilities paradigm has become an increasingly mainstream notion in the social sciences (especially in the field of geography and urban studies), it remains a secondary concern in critical security studies (Leese and Wittendorp 2017; Guittet 2017). Mobility is still considered in "separate spheres" (Sheller and Urry 2006, 212), precluding the analytical insights of interdisciplinary approaches. However, that segregation of mobility is gradually changing, in favor of more hybrid approaches. In Africa, empirical studies have begun to examine the relationship between mobility, thuggery, and entrepreneurship (Mutongi 2006), crime and lawlessness (Oteng-Ababio and Agyemang 2015), the control of women and their access to public space (Adamu 2008), collective organizing (Ezeibe et al. 2017; Beekers 2008), "automobilization" of religion (Klaeger 2009), and electoral violence (Agbiboa 2018b).

This book resulted from the observed disconnect between mobility, insurgency, and counterinsurgency in the understanding of conflict dynamics in contemporary Africa. Its primary purpose is to reclaim the logic of mobility in matrices of armed conflicts, using the argument that despite the centrality of mobility to the tactics deployed by state security forces, nonstate armed groups, and civilians in conflict, mobility concerns have remained tangential to how we analyze contemporary wars. The extant literature focuses rather exclusively on the roots of internal wars, while glossing over its routes and trajectories. Specifically, this book interrogates how movement and stasis are intertwined with the logic of insurgency and counterinsurgency, through a focused study of Boko Haram, a Salafi-jihadi sect that has killed thousands and displaced millions across northeast Nigeria and the Lake Chad region. The book provides a textured analysis of the micropolitics of automobility, making an analytical distinction between the multiple and intersecting mobilities in the volatile region, on the one hand, and the precise paradigm of mobilities that drive the Boko Haram insurgency, on the other.

Building on the move from spatial turn to mobilities turn in the social sciences, it is apparent that the dialectic of mobility and immobility, and the tension between fixity and motion, not only are rooted in the longue durée perspective on the history of northeast Nigeria and the Lake Chad region (a poor region where farming, herding, hunting, and trade revolve around movement) but also take center stage in studying why Boko Haram exists and how the Nigerian government has responded. Demonstrating that an understudied dimension of the war against Boko Haram— Operation "Lafiya Dole," Nigeria's counterinsurgency response since 2015—exemplifies how the state mobilizes against, and polices, mobility in its war on terror, the book considers the ramifications of that mobilization and policing for the livelihoods of mobile subjects (e.g. transport operators) who are caught in the crossfire and dangerous interstices between militants and military. It makes an important contribution by recognizing that patterns of mobility and moorings have real implications for violent insurgencies and that all mobilities are not necessarily insurgency-related. Some historically innocuous patterns of mobility and categories of mobile workers that predate Boko Haram (e.g., the *almajiri*) have become unduly pathologized as susceptible to rage and as potential terrorists. The analysis in this book was inspired partly by Mirjam de Bruijn's call for scholars to consider multiple forms of mobility as crucial for shaping societies and governance in Africa.

> Mobility has always shaped African societies. These mobilities encompass all types of movement including travel, explorations, migration, tourism, refugeeism, pastoralism, nomadism, pilgrimage, and trade. In these forms, mobility is essential to many people and is even a means of survival for some. It is culturally and socially embedded in society and in each individual's actions. Being mobile, or living in a culture where many people are mobile, is a fact of life and with it goes an enormous cultural, social, and economic flexibility. (de Bruijn 2007, 112)

Going beyond the relative "a-mobile" nature of conflict and security studies, this study began from the major premise that mobility in its many forms has always been fundamental to social transformations (de Bruijn 2007, 125). By introducing a "new mobilities paradigm" to the rapidly growing literature on Boko Haram, the supposedly immobile is demonstrated to have a "hidden . . . history of trajectories of movement and social relations" (Adey 2010, 26). For example, through the reimagining of both, the micropolitics of insurgency/counterinsurgency is indissolubly linked to control over movement. Furthermore, the symbiotic relation between mobility and immobility are shown to be at the core (in both positive and negative ways) of insurgent zones, terrains where "movement begets constraint, constraint begets movement, and movement occurs within constraints and constraints within movements" (Gill et al. 2011, 302).

Far from treating space as a neutral and vacuous "container" for mobile identities and practices, this book takes seriously the manner in which space is produced by mobility in the context of armed conflict and how mobile subjects are "relationally produced through their entanglements with each other and with spatial forms" (Sheller 2018). In northeast Nigeria, the system of automobility is not passively transporting people but actively changing them (cf. Bissell 2016, 395). For the study of armed conflicts, the book introduces a new framework that treats mobility (e.g., routes and trajectories) as not just the setting but the very medium for the experience and practice of insurgency/counterinsurgency. The book's mobile ethnographic approach invites conflict researchers "to experience, feel and grasp the textures, smells, comforts and discomforts, pleasures and displeasures of a moving life. It means following people around and engaging with their worldviews. *It means focusing on mobility*" (Novoa 2015, 99–100). Through that approach, new light is shed on how civilian populations in conflict zones produce meaning from the dangers and frictions of their mobilities, how they inhabit and socially navigate precarious routes, and how movement and stoppage impinges on their workaday world.

While this book empirically demonstrates how mobility and immobility are intrinsically interwoven in the context of Boko Haram insurgency, state counterinsurgency, and societal response in northeast Nigeria, its mobile logic is generalizable to a broad range of conflict zones, including the Central African Republic (CAR) (Schouten 2021; Schouten and Kalessopo 2017; Lombard 2013), Mali (Retaille and Walther 2013), Liberia (Cheng 2018), Colombia (Idler 2019), Palestine (Bier 2017; Kotef 2015), Afghanistan (Special Inspector General for Afghanistan Reconstruction [SIGAR] 2014), and Sri Lanka (Jeganathan 1997; Hyndman and de Alwis, 2004). In the CAR conflict, for instance, the regulation and control of armed roadblocks and trade routes are key to conflict financing, and affirms the power and currency of "entrepreneurs of imposition"—the rebel militias (i.e., the Séléka alliance) and state soldiers (Schouten and Kalessopo 2017, 17; Schouten 2021). Further, the "politics of pillage" connected to roadblocks in the CAR make it increasingly onerous for people to go to farms and markets.

Similarly, in the Malian conflict, mobile strategies constitute the organizing logic of local Islamist assemblages, including Al-Qaeda in the Islamic Maghreb, Ansar Dine, and the Movement for Oneness and Jihad in West Africa. On the Malian conflict, Denis Retaille and Olivier Walther (2013, v) argue, "For the Islamists, there was no question of saddling themselves with territory and using up their strength in controlling land areas. The control of movement and crossroads is enough to have power in a mobile space since places themselves are mobile."

Further afield, in Sri Lanka's restive northeast region, roads and checkpoints constitute "vectors of capital" (Jeganathan 1997, 222) for both the national army and the Liberation Tigers of Tamil Eelam (LTTE). As Jennifer Hyndman and Malathi de Alwis (2004) point out, "In Sri Lanka, roads are strategic access routes for warring parties, but also the location of checkpoints that control the entrances and exits of civilians based on readings of gender and national identity." Roads and bridges demarcate spaces controlled by the Sri Lankan army during the day and by the LTTE at night. During the day, soldiers patrol the main roads and inspect documents. At night, they return to their base and rebels take control (Hyndman and de Alwis 2004, 548).

While this book advances a "mobilities turn" in analysis of contemporary wars, it is mindful of a caution from Noel Salazar and Alan Smart: "If mobility is the topic of research, there is a great risk that different interpretations of what is going on will be neglected, or that only patterns that fit the paradigm will be considered, or that only extremes of (hyper)mobility or (im)mobility will be given attention" (2011, vi). A case in point is the tendency to reduce the complexity of mobility to migration,[1] particularly the global "ban-opticon" (Bigo 2006) through which undesirable bodies are problematized and apprehended on the move. In the United States, for example, the last two decades have seen the hardening of its borders with Mexico through legislations such as Operation Gatekeeper, Operation Hold the Line, and the Secure Fence Act. Such border rules—mainly targeted at people in transit (Vogt 2018)—have marginalized the study of how the securitization of movement occurs at the local level and especially "how it is invested by 'grassroots' understandings and practices of security" (Ivasiuc 2015, 53). While the biopolitics of modern liberalism is exemplified by walls, checkpoints, and agents patrolling borders (Kotef 2015), we still know little about the embodied realities of mobile subjects in those securitized places, including, for example, "how the actual construction of the border is transforming conditions of life by altering the physical and social geography of communities" (Shapira 2013, 250). Mobility is not an abstract process but a material and embodied one.

The arguments of this book are constructed on the prompting from Stef Wittendorp and Matthias Leese (2017, 2) to marry two related strands of research—(1) inquiries that look into the political regulation of movement and (2) analyses that engage the material enablers and constraints of such movement—in order to properly understand the politics of movement at the core of the production of insecurity and uncertainty. Given that mobility is essentially relational,[2] as every mobility is intertwined with other mobilities that generate "zones of connectivity, centrality and empowerment" (Sheller and Urry 2006, 210), this book articulates the neglected linkages between forms of local immobility and mobilization into armed opposition groups (Boko Haram / ISWAP) and pro-government militias (the Civilian Joint Task Force). By looking at the impact and agency of civilians at the mercy of militants and military, the book illustrates how transit routes and mobile infrastructures constitute a dynamic space accounting for people's daily and defiant struggles to negotiate crisis and impose order and predictability on their lives.

The first chapter of this book explores the emergence and struggles of *achaba* drivers, a cohort of marginalized and stigmatized workers that were among the first subaltern social groups to join Boko Haram. Specifically, the chapter discusses the onset of widespread economic crisis in Nigeria in the 1980s, a period when imported motorcycles became a vital source of survival for youth trapped in waithood, for a population that is constantly on the move, yet stuck.

The second chapter looks at the relationship between local immobility and mobilization of disaffected youth into armed opposition groups, with particular emphasis on the peripatetic Koranic students (*almajirai*). The third chapter revisits the uneasy relationship between the implementation of a state traffic law and the escalation of the Boko Haram conflict, arguing that the transformation of Boko Haram into one of the deadliest insurgencies today owes much to the brutal manner in which a new law requiring commercial motorcyclists and their passengers to wear helmets was brutally enforced by state security services. Chapter 4 examines Boko Haram's mobile warfare, especially how the group deploys speed and increased mobility as a lethal weapon against "enemies of Islam." The analysis extends to the rise of the Civilian Joint Task Force and its mobilization of mobility and local knowledge to extirpate Boko Haram insurgents from their communities and to deny them reentry.

Chapter 5 analyzes how the Nigerian state mobilizes (against) mobility in its counterinsurgency operations (particularly to neutralize the movement and flexibility of armed insurgents) and the ripple effects on mobile communities, individuals, and bodies. The analysis revolves around how the state ban on subversive mobilities such as motorcycles, with its profiling and policing (through fear) of motorists, played into the hands of Boko Haram by allowing the sect to mobilize the new crowd of dispossessed youth, thereby reproducing the very insecurity the ban was meant to prevent. Driven by need and the lack of alternatives, former *achaba* drivers turned to Boko Haram to make ends meet. Also discussed in chapter 5 are corruption of security forces and its adverse effect on the workaday world of road transport workers, especially how Boko Haram's rise has had a snowball effect on extortion and delay tactics by security forces at every checkpoint along major routes in northeast Nigeria; ordinarily, these shakedowns occur within "vertically integrated" networks of corruption (Chayes 2015). The constant interruptions that drivers experience daily is mirrored by what Ghassan Hage (2009) calls "stuckedness," in which drivers must cope with the injustice, frustration, humiliation, and confusion of being ordered to "park" their vehicles and wait for no reason. While stuckedness has been applied to migrants and their precarious lives in transit, it is seldom applied to drivers and their passengers, who traverse dangerous routes and regimes of mobility.

Taken together, the chapters in this book tie together insurgent geographies with mobility studies. Along the way, they underscore mobility as a contradictory resource in violent contexts and encourage us to reimagine the system of automobility as a heuristic revealing sites of both violence and precarity, as well as resistance and agency. That reimagining reinforces the thesis that mobility as a resource sits cheek by jowl with mobility as a burden (Cresswell 2006; Hoechner 2015). This book helps us not only to think through the multiple interacting mobilities that govern conflict but also to home in on how mobile subjects in extremis experience and articulate their world as they move through it. By foregrounding mobile and immobile practices as dynamic technologies of contemporary wars, the book unsettles the dichotomy between conflict and mobility. It urges analytical attention to the overlapping mobile logics of different groups—for example, motorists, militants, military—in a conflict terrain where anything can happen.

Notes

Introduction

1. Cited in United States Interstate Commerce Commission. 1937. *Exercises Commemorating the Fifty Years' Service of the Interstate Commerce Commission, April 1, 1937, Departmental Auditorium, Washington DC* (Washington, DC: US Government Printing Office), p. 84.

2. By using the term *terrorists* here, I mean "those who seek to make others afraid: less mobile or less free to move" (Ahmed 2004a, 128). What makes terrorism so terrifying is "its unpredictability, the unexpected, unanticipated registers of the space-time" (Katz 2007, 354).

3. The securitization of fear involves "the rehearsal of looming threats and invasion, particularly in the register of affect, to strategically shift political support for state polices and measures" (Hyndman 2007, 366). Giorgio Agamben (1998) argues that the securitization of fear is a politically powerful resource for states that need legitimate grounds for extraordinary measures, such as violent exclusion from their territories.

4. The term *mobility* first appeared in the sixteenth century, when the Latin phrase *mobile vulgus* described groups of people whose gathering was seen as threatening or dangerous—elements that continue to be reflected in the association of mobile populations with various forms of moral panic.

5. Although the events of 9/11 are not infrequently adduced to justify new modes of policing that combine biometric, biopolitical, racial, social, and spatial profiling technologies, Emily Kaufman (2016, 72), citing the topical work of Allen Feldman (2004, 331), reminds us that "long before 2001 the US had been waging 'deterritorialized wars of public safety' in the form of the war on drugs, campaigns to exclude asylum seekers and immigrants, and zero-tolerance policing targeting Black and Latino inner-city residents."

6. Kaufman (2016, 74) coined the term *bio-spatial profiling* to define "an analytic

that emphasizes the biometric, biopolitical, and spatial tactics by which individuals are profiled, as well as the spatial effects of such targeting."

7. Established by the Terrorism Information and Prevention System and funded by Department of Homeland Security, Highway Watch trained truck drivers to recognize highway dangers and report them to a central dispatch center.

8. The present study uses the definition of insurgency provided in the *Guide to the Analysis of Insurgency* (n.d., 2): "Insurgency is a protracted political-military activity directed toward completely or partially controlling the resources of a country through the use of irregular military forces and illegal political organizations. Insurgent activity—including guerrilla warfare, terrorism, and political mobilization, for example, propaganda, recruitment, front and covert party organization, and international activity—is designed to weaken government control and legitimacy while increasing insurgent control and legitimacy. The common denominator of most insurgent groups is their desire to control a particular area. This objective differentiates insurgent groups from purely terrorist organizations, whose objectives do not include the creation of an alternative government capable of controlling a given area or country." Three aspects of this definition are worth noting here: (1) insurgents engage in a range of activities, most notably guerrilla warfare, but also political mobilization and attendant efforts to attract support from abroad; (2) in this context, terrorism is a specific tactic that insurgents use as part of a broader strategy to control a particular geographic area; and (3) size also matters as a key distinguishing factor. Terrorist groups often consist of a small number of individuals, sometimes no more than a handful. Insurgent organizations, in contrast, number in the thousands (Byman et al. 2001, 5).

9. About the Toyota Hilux trucks, David Kilcullen notes, "They cover the ground incredibly well. They are often used by insurgent forces as a modern version of light cavalry. They move weapons into positions to fire, and can also shift people around very quickly, with a quick dismount. The Hilux is perfectly designed for that. I've seen 20 people and a mounted weapon on one" (Somaiya 2010).

10. The state of emergency had a major impact on social, economic, and political dynamics within the three states. Large numbers of military personnel were deployed to patrol towns, and curfews were imposed. Checkpoints made even short journeys within and between towns long and difficult (Murtala and Abubakar 2017).

11. In Hausa, *tashan* means "station of."

12. The term *salafism* derives from the Arabic *salaf*, meaning "predecessors." The Salafi movement is characterized by a return to what adherents believe to be true Sunni Islam. Northern Nigerian Salafism originated with anti-Sufi scholar and Salafist Abubakar Gumi (Loimeier 1997; Thurston 2018, 19, 23).

13. In *Knowledge/Power*, Foucault observes that certain bodies of knowledge can be subjugated by more powerful actors: "By 'subjugated knowledges' I mean two things. On the one hand, I am referring to historical contents that have been buried and disguised in a functional coherence or formal systemization. . . . By 'subjugated knowledges' one should understand something else . . . , namely, a whole set of knowledges that have been disqualified as inadequate to the task or insufficiently elaborated; naïve knowledges, located down on the hierarchy, beneath the required level of cognition or scientificity. I also believe that it is through the re-emergence

of these low-ranking knowledges, these unqualified, even directly disqualified knowledges . . . , that criticism performs its work" (1980, 81–82).

14. The helmets cost up to US$29 in a country where at least 80 percent of locals live on less than US$1 a day (Friedman 2014).

15. As Alice Wilson argues, "Deserts have a reputation and history of being suitable spaces into which those who want to escape state authority can melt away" (2017, 78).

Chapter 1

1. As used here, the term *youth* implies a "complex, fluid and permeable social category which is historically and socially situated. As such, it is a site for particular and localized framings of human agency constituted by various intersecting and contested discourses" (Gore and Pratten 2003, 215). Beyond a transitional phase from childhood to adulthood, youth often indicates "an indefinitely expandable life state, affected by political instability, economic decline, and shrinking aspirations" (Masquelier 2019, 13). Durham (2004, 589) uses the term *social shifter* to describe the ways in which youth is appropriated by people of widely varying age.

2. More than just referencing un(der)employment or lack of job security, the term *precarity* describes "living with the unforeseeable, with contingency" (Lorey 2015, 1). It evokes the notion of Mirjam de Bruijn and Jonna Both (2018, 186) of duress in the context of enduring hardship in Africa.

3. In their study of the interface between spatial mobility and youth survival in urban Ghana, Thilde Langevang and Katherine Gough argue, "The discrepancy between young people's positive valuations of being on the move and their actual capacity for mobility means that many feel trapped in their neighborhood with limited social and economic opportunities. They see restrictions on their desired movements as blocking their social becoming" (2009, 753).

4. The nomenclature *okada* derives from the now-defunct Okada Air, Nigeria's first private airline, on which only political elites or "big men" could afford to travel.

5. Marginal(ity) invokes notions of exclusion and abjection (Wacquant 2007; Joe Turner 2016, 148).

Chapter 2

1. The aims of Yan Izala were at once theological and political: "Theologically its members argued that practices of possession in Sufism represented 'shirk' (a denial of the oneness of God) and were wholly un-Islamic, and, further they argued against the dependence on sheikhs and in favor of a greater reliance on studying the primary sources of Islamic law: the Qur'an and hadith. They denounced Sufis politically as rich materialists aligned with corrupt royal authorities and agitated for religious and political reform of the traditional aristocratic system that prevailed in the north and ultimately for the institution of an Islamic state" (Larkin 2005, 178; see also Kane 2003; Loimeier 1997).

2. The young men are so named because of the limited equipment they carry (Prothero and Chapman 1985, 16).

3. In the past, rural parents sent their sons to study the Koran during periods when fields lay fallow; the alms *almajirai* received from town dwellers represented

a small wealth transfer from urban to rural areas. However, with the population explosion in northern Nigeria and deterioration of agriculture—related at least partly to climate change—gangs of *almajirai* unable to return to their home villages become additional mouths to feed (Campbell 2018).

4. For about five hundred years in Muslim West Africa, Sufi sects were dominant; they were Africanized, tolerant, and much more accommodating of different sects and of African traditional religions. From the 1970s onward, we observe the transition from Sufism and the increasing emergence of Salafi versions of Islam. Thus, by the 1970s, we begin to see a major challenge to Sufi hegemony by a much more austere version of Islam, Salafism. The Salafi intrusion was contemporaneous with fundamental social and political changes (authoritarian and military regimes, economic crises, environmental and demographic problems). As society was changing, belief systems were also evolving. While Sufism preached self-purification and introspection (changing oneself as a way of changing society), Salafism, at least in the West African version of it, wanted to impose its own will on society, to change society directly. Thus, Salafists wanted a righteous life, not through the person but through acting directly on society. That desire informs their targeting of the state and their efforts to reconfigure it. Boko Haram derives from that intolerant Salafist strand within the evolution of Islamist thinking in the West African Sahel more broadly (Mustapha 2015).

5. The Sokoto Jihad was fought by two distinct sets of young men. On the one hand were professional students and young Islamic converts (often runaway slaves) who took refuge under a sheikh (a Muslim scholar around forty years old or more). On the other were independent, military-minded young men from Fulani pastoralist families who had lost their cattle. Those youths had long gravitated toward Hausa courts (e.g., in Kano) as mercenaries and would-be palace retainers, to earn a livelihood outside the pastoralist economy (Last 2003, 4).

6. Borno State's first governor to serve two consecutive terms (2003–11), Sheriff has been accused of sponsoring Boko Haram (Tukur 2014).

7. Andrew Walker observes, "Unoriginal and uncritical they may have been, Yusuf's words were powerful. His main mode of transmission was through orations which he gave in many towns around the north-east. He was adaptable in his approach, preaching on market days rather than on Fridays as usually acceptable by Islamic authorities" (2016, 145; see also Kassim and Nwankpa 2018).

8. The extent of Boko Haram penetration of the *almajirai* remains contested. Among observers, there is no consensus on whether the *almajirai* are a key recruiting source for radical Islamists.

9. The Arabic word *madrassa* refers to any type of educational institution, secular or religious, whether a school, college, or university. It is variously transliterated *madrasah*, *medresa*, *madrassa*, *madraza*, *medrese*, and so on. In the West, the word usually refers to a specific type of religious school or college for the study of Islam, though that subject may not be the only one studied.

10. While the poor may not necessarily support Boko Haram's violent tactics, they may still join the group for the purpose of survival and recognition and sympathize with its critique of state failure (Meagher 2014, 2).

11. The term *subjectivity* refers to the conscious and unconscious thoughts and

emotions of an individual, one's sense of oneself and ways of understanding one's relation to the world (Weedon 1987, 32–33, cited in Cahill 2000, 272).

12. As of 2016, 43 percent of Nigerians were under the age of fifteen; another 19 percent were under the age of twenty-five (Thurston 2018, 30).

Chapter 3

1. During the 2003 and 2007 regional elections, northern politicians employed the services of local youth militias, such as *dan kalare* in Gombe, *yan sara suka* in Bauchi, "ECOMOG" militias in Borno, *banu isra'il* in Taraba, and *yan shinko* in Adamawa. Adding to that pool are *yan faratua* (local hunters), *yan tauri* (those who use ritual herbal medicine to prevent injuries from weapons), *yan dada* (young marginal toughs), and the *hisba* (religiously based vigilante group). Even prior to 1999, many northern governors treated their office as private entities. For example, Muhammadu Abubakar Rimi, ex-governor of Kano State, gave "substantial amounts of money" to the leader of the Maitatsine uprising, Marwa, to "buy support" (Falola 1998, 148).

2. Sharia was introduced in Borno in 2000 through the Borno Sharia Administration of Justice Law under Alhaji Mala Kachalla, Sheriff's predecessor. In February 2001, Governor Kachalla appointed the Borno Sharia Law Implementation Committee, of which Yusuf was a member, along with other imams (*Vanguard* 2014b).

3. Foi was executed in police custody in July 2009, twenty-four hours after Yusuf met the same fate. In Brigaglia's view, "the two killings might have been the result of an order to silence the two men [Foi and Yusuf] who, more than anybody else, could provide first-hand information about the genesis of the group and its (local and international) protectors" (2012b, 35).

4. One of the preconditions given by Boko Haram in 2011 for dialoguing with the Nigerian government was that Sheriff and his top security officials be prosecuted. The sect's leaders warned that peace would continue to elude the country unless their conditions were met. Their letter titled "Conditions for Dialogue with President Goodluck Jonathan and Governor Kashim Shettima," signed by Usman Al-Zawahiri noted, "The following people must be prosecuted according to Islamic law for conspiracy which resulted in the killing of late Sheikh Mohammed Yusuf after he was arrested alive by soldiers who handed him over to the police at the 21 Armored Brigade, popularly known as Giwa barracks, in Maiduguri. They include the immediate past Governor of Borno State, Ali Modu Sheriff; the Shehu of Borno, Alhaji Abubakar Ibn Garbai El-Kanemi; former Minister of Police Affairs, Ibrahim Yakubu Lame; former Borno State Commissioner of Police and Director of the State Security Service (SSS), who were in charge of security during the July 2009 violence. Similarly, others that must be prosecuted according to Sharia Islamic law include the security operatives particularly those attached to OF II for causing the first crisis along the custom area in Maiduguri when they shot dead seven of our brothers and wounded 10 others during the commissioning of a Mosque in Monguno local government. We also demand for the immediate arrest and prosecution of those behind the killings of Baba Fugu Mohammed, the father-in-law of our late leader and Alhaji Buju Foi." In addition to calling for the

immediate resignation of Governor Kashim Shettima, the letter demanded, "The All Nigerian Peoples Party (ANPP)-led government in Borno State must resign because its leaders were responsible for the attack on the Ibn Thaimiyya Islamic Center (*Markaz*) and the house of our leader in Maiduguri. We also request for an immediate investigation into the killing of our brothers through food poisoning which was perpetrated by prison warders with connivance of former Governor Ali Sheriff. We challenge the government to seek assistance of FBI, CIA, the Israel Intelligence Agency, MOSSAD [Institute for Intelligence and Special Operations] or INTERPOL and see if these security outfits would stop us from fulfilling our mission" (*Global Intelligence Files*, 2011).

5. In March 2010, police arrested seventeen officers suspected of taking part in filmed executions of Yusuf's followers that later aired on the international news channel Al Jazeera. In April 2010, a Nigerian court ordered the police to pay N 100 million (US$666,400) in damages to the family of Yusuf's father-in-law, Baba Fugu Mohammed, who was killed after surrendering himself to the police in Maiduguri in the aftermath of the July 2009 violence. The court also ordered the police to exhume the body of Baba Fugu from wherever it was buried and to hand it over to the family, for a proper burial in accordance with Islamic rites. The judgment followed a February 2010 suit filed against the police and the late President Umaru Musa Yar'adua by Baba Fugu's eldest son, Babakura Fugu, for the killing of his seventy-two-year-old father (*News24*, 2020). In August 2010, four senior police officers were suspended in connection with the execution of Mohammed Yusuf (BBC 2010).

Chapter 4

1. There are reliable reports that Boko Haram "sent several letters, warning security agencies and the Bauchi State government of their intention that their members would not celebrate the Eid-el Fitr (*Sallah*) in prison. We thought it was a joke but now the reality has dawned on us" (Garba 2010).

2. Since 1991, public transportation has been the target of 20 to 35 percent of worldwide terrorist attacks (Department of Transportation, Office of Intelligence and Security, Briefing Paper, Washington, DC, 1996). From 1991 through 2001, 42 percent of all terrorist attacks worldwide have targeted rail systems or buses (Howitt and Makler 2005, 1).

3. Converting standard pickup trucks into improvised fighting vehicles is a low-cost way to create a multirole vehicle with fast attack capability (http://www.military-today.com/trucks/technicals.htm).

4. The car bomb was fully conceptualized as a weapon of urban warfare in January 12, 1947, when right-wing Zionist guerrillas known as the Stern Gang drove a truckload of explosives into a British police station in Haifa, Palestine, killing 4 and injuring 140. Since then, the car bomb has gained traction (in cities) among terror groups, partly because of its efficiency. Between 1992 and 1999, twenty-five major attacks by vehicle bombing in twenty-two different cities killed 1,337 people and wounded nearly 12,000 (Davis 2007).

5. As a site for the production and transit of globalized manufactured goods and a major consumer of agropastoral produce from Lake Chad region, Nigeria forms

the epicenter of cross-border trade in the Lake Chad Basin (Magrin and Pérouse de Montclos 2018, 53).

6. Prior to the insurgency in 2009, northeast Nigeria did more trade across national borders than it did with the rest of Nigeria. Today, there is little to no trade, as borders remain closed (Mercy Corps 2017, 1).

7. The Janjaweed are "militias composed of men from Arab-speaking nomadic tribes best known for their involvement in the Darfur Crisis starting in 2003. Their international notoriety derives from their central role in attacking non-Arab, black Darfurian communities, mostly sedentary agricultural ones, and hence creating a massive displacement of several million civilians as well as 20,000 deaths" (Alden et al. 2010, 7).

8. As a result of its porous borders, Borno has attracted youths from surrounding countries, who are in even worse stasis than local youth (Paden 2012, 50).

Chapter 5

1. In a typical arrangement, the driver pays a daily fee of N 3,800 to the owner over a twelve-month period, after which the former becomes the owner of the *keke*. However, failure to complete payment in time means that the driver forfeits ownership to the owner.

Conclusion

1. For this book, the concept of mobility was preferred to that of migration because the latter does not cover all types of geographical mobility, nor is mobility limited to the movement of people alone (van Dijk et al. 2000, 9).

2. Peter Adey (2010, 17–18) argues that "mobilities and immobilities are the 'special effects' of a relation: they are an outcome or an accomplishment."

Bibliography

Abbah, T. 2012. "White Paper on Security: Report Links Boko Haram with London Scholar." *Daily Trust*, May 23.

Abbas, B. D. 1999. "Commercial Motorcycles Road Accidents and Casualties in Urban Maiduguri." Paper presented at a Civil Liberty Organization enlightenment campaign to *achaba* riders, Bulunkutu, September 5–7.

Abbink, J. 2005. "Being Young in Africa: The Politics of Despair and Renewal." In Abbink and van Kessel 2005, 1–33.

Abbink, J., and I. van Kessel, eds. 2005. *Vanguard or Vandals: Youth, Politics and Conflict in Africa*. Leiden: Brill.

Abrahams, Ray. 1987. "Sungusungu: Village Vigilante Groups in Tanzania." *African Affairs* 86 (343): 179–96.

Abubakar, U. 2015. "Mpape's Kings of the Roads." *Daily Trust*, December 5.

Abuza, Zachary. 2001. *The Ongoing Insurgency in Southern Thailand: Trends in Violence, Counterinsurgency Operations, and the Impact of National Politics*. Washington, DC: National Defense University Press.

Adam-Hutcheson, G., H. Thorpe, and C. Coleborne. 2017. "Introduction: Understanding Mobilities in a Dangerous World." *Transfers: Interdisciplinary Journal of Mobility Studies* 7 (3): 1–5.

Adamu, Fatima. 2008. "Gender, Hisba and the Enforcement of Morality in Northern Nigeria." *Africa* 78 (1): 136–52.

Adebowale, Yemi. 2019. "Army's Prickly Operation Positive Identification." *This Day*, November 2.

Ademowo, A. J. 2010. "'They Are Poor and Violent': Stereotype and the Ibadan Urban Motor Park Space." *Antrocom* 6 (2): 115–33.

Adepoju, A. 1995. "Migration in Africa: An Overview." In Baker and Aina 1995, 87–108.

Adey, Peter. 2006. "If Mobility Is Everything Then It Is Nothing: Towards a Relational Politics of (Im)mobilities." *Mobilities* 1 (1): 75–94.

Adey, Peter. 2010. *Mobility*. London: Routledge.

Adey, Peter. 2016. "Emergency Mobilities." *Mobilities* 11 (1): 32–48.

Adichie, Chimamanda. 2013. *Americanah*. New York: Random House.

AFP (Agence France-Presse). 2010a. "Jail Attackers Had 'Overwhelming Firepower': Nigerian." September 8.

AFP. 2010b. "Nigeria: Report Gives Details, Says Terrorist Groups Gaining Foothold in Nigeria." January 4.

AFP. 2010c. "Suspected Islamists Attack Prison in Nigeria: Authorities." September 7.

AFP. 2013. "Vigilantes Raise Concern and Hope in Embattled Nigerian City." July 30.

AFP. 2019. "Nigerian Protesters Demand End to Anti–Boko Haram Militia." June 30.

Agamben, Giorgio. 1998. *Homo Sacer: Sovereign Power and Bare Life*. Palo Alto, CA: Stanford University Press.

Agamben, Giorgio. 2005. *State of Exception*. Chicago: University of Chicago Press.

Agbiboa, Daniel E. 2013. "Why Boko Haram Exists: The Relative Deprivation Perspective." *African Conflict and Peacebuilding Review* 3 (1): 144–57.

Agbiboa, Daniel E. 2015. "Resistance to Boko Haram: Civilian Joint Task Forces in North-Eastern Nigeria." Special issue, *Conflict Studies Quarterly*, 3–22.

Agbiboa, Daniel E. 2017. "The Rights Consciousness of Urban Resistance: Legalism from Below in an African Unofficial Sector." *Journal of Legal Pluralism and Unofficial Law* 49 (2): 183–203.

Agbiboa, Daniel E. 2018a. "Eyes on the Street: Civilian Joint Task Force and the Surveillance of Boko Haram in Northeastern Nigeria." *Intelligence and National Security* 33 (7): 1022–29.

Agbiboa, Daniel E. 2018b. "Patronage Politics and Electoral Violence in Lagos, Nigeria: Understanding the Micro-level Dynamics." In *Violence in African Elections: Between Democracy and Big Man Politics*, edited by M. S. Kovacs and J. Bjarnesen, 215–32. London: Zed Books.

Agbiboa, Daniel E. 2020. "The Precariousness of Protection: Civilian Defense Groups Countering Boko Haram in Northeastern Nigeria." *African Studies Review* 64 (1): 192–216.

Agbiboa, Daniel E. 2021. "Out of the Shadows: The Women Countering Insurgency in Nigeria." *Politics & Gender*, 1–32. https://doi.org/10.1017/S1743923X21000283

Aghedo, I., and S. J. Eke. 2013. "From Alms to Arms: The Almajiri Phenomenon and Internal Security in Northern Nigeria." *Korean Journal of Policy Studies* 28 (3): 97–123.

Aguiar, Marian. 2011. *Tracking Modernity: India's Railway and the Culture of Mobility*. Minneapolis: University of Minnesota Press.

Ahmed, Sara. 2004a. "Affective Economies." *Social Text* 22 (2): 117–39.

Ahmed, Sara. 2004b. "Collective Feelings; or, The Impressions Left by Others." *Theory, Culture and Society* 21 (2): 25–42.

Ahmed, Sara. 2015. *The Cultural Politics of Emotion.* New York: Routledge.

Akhlaq, S. 2015. "The Guise of the Sunni-Shiite Use of Excommunication (Takfir) in the Middle East." *Journal of South Asian and Middle Eastern Studies* 38 (4): 1–22.

Alden, C., D. M. Thakur, and D. M. Arnold. 2011. *Militias and the Challenges of Post-Conflict Peace: Silencing the Guns.* London: Zed Books.

Alexander, H. 2013. "Massacre at Fake Checkpoint as Boko Haram Slit Throats of Travellers." *Telegraph*, October 20.

Alfa, Ismail, and Ruth Maclean. 2020. "Executed Nigerian Farmers Were Caught between Boko Haram and the Army." *New York Times*, December 10.

Ali, Rubaba, Federico A. Barrar, Claudia N. Berg, Richard Damania, John D. Nash, and Jason Russ. 2015. "Infrastructure in Conflict Prone and Fragile Environments: Evidence from Democratic Republic of Congo." Policy Research Working Paper, No. 7273. http://cega.berkeley.edu/assets/miscellaneous_files/66_-A BCA-Infrastructure_and_Conflict_(Damania_conf).pdf

Al Jazeera. 2013. "Nigerian President Declares State of Emergency." May 15.

Al Jazeera. 2015. "Boko Haram Fighters on Horseback Kill Villagers." August 31.

Al Jazeera. 2019. "Six Nigerian Soldiers Killed in Borno State Ambush." July 18.

Al Jazeera. 2020. "Attackers Kill, Abduct Dozens in Northeast Nigeria." February 10.

Alozieuwa, S. O. H. 2016. "Beyond Political Islam: Nigeria, the Boko Haram Crisis and the Imperative of National Consensus." *Journal of Retracing Africa* 2 (1): 49–71.

Amin, S. 1995. "Migrations in Contemporary Africa: A Retrospective View." In Baker and Aina 1995, 29–40.

Amir, M. 2013. "The Making of a Void Sovereignty: Political Implications of the Military Checkpoints in the West Bank." *Environment and Planning D: Society and Space* 31 (2): 227–44.

Amir, M., and H. Kotef. 2017. "In-secure Identities: On the Securitization of Abnormality." *Environment and Planning D: Society and Space* 36 (2): 236–54.

Amnesty International. 2015. "'Our Job Is to Shoot, Slaughter, and Kill: Boko Haram's Reign of Terror in Northeast Nigeria." April 14.

Amnesty International. 2018. "'They Betrayed Us': Women Who Survived Boko Haram Raped, Starved and Detained in Nigeria." May 24.

Amnesty International. 2019. "Nigeria: Deadliest Boko Haram Attack on Rann Leaves at Least 60 People Murdered." February 1. https://www.amnesty.org /en/latest/news/2019/02/nigeria-deadliest-boko-haram-attack-on-rann-leaves -at-least-60-people-murdered/

Amoore, L. 2006. "Biometric Borders: Governing Mobilities in the War on Terror." *Political Geography* 25 (3): 336–51.

Anderson, D. M. 2002. "Vigilantes, Violence and the Politics of Public Order in Kenya." *African Affairs* 101 (1): 531–55.

Aniekwe, Chika Charles, and Daniel E. Agbiboa. 2015. "Civic Engagement and Its Role in Mitigating Electoral Violence in Nigeria: Implications for the 2015 General Elections." Working paper, Institute of Development Policy and Management (IOB), February.

Anonymous. 2012. "The Popular Discourses of Salafi Radicalism and Salafi Counter-Radicalism in Nigeria: A Case Study of Boko Haram." *Journal of Religion in Africa* 42 (2): 118–44.

Anyadike, O. 2019. "Reporter's Diary: Boko Haram and the Battle of Ideas." *New Humanitarian*, August 6.

Apard, Elodie. 2015. "The Words of Boko Haram: Understanding Speeches by Mohammed Yusuf and Abubakar Shekau." *Afrique Contemporaine* 255 (3): 41–69.

Appadurai, Arjun. 1996. *Modernity at Large: Cultural Dimensions of Globalization*. Minneapolis: University of Minnesota Press.

Appadurai, Arjun. 2004. "The Capacity to Aspire: Culture and the Terms of Recognition." In *Culture and Public Action*, edited by V. Rao and M. Walton, 59–84. Palo Alto, CA: Stanford University Press.

Apter, A. 2005. *The Pan-African Nation: Oil and the Spectacle of Culture in Nigeria*. Chicago: University of Chicago Press.

Archambault, J. S. 2012. "'Traveling While Sitting Down': Mobile Phones, Mobility and the Communication Landscape in Inhambane, Mozambique." *Africa* 82 (3): 393–412.

Ashforth, B. E., and G. E. Kreiner. 1999. "'How Can You Do It?': Dirty Work and the Challenge of Constructing a Positive Identity." *Academy of Management Review* 24 (3): 413–34.

Associated Press. 2009. "Hundreds Flee Battle in North Nigeria." July 30.

Associated Press. 2014. "Boko Haram Seizing Villages in Nigeria: Witnesses." June 5.

Attoh, Kafui, Patrick Vitale, Hector Agredano, Julie Cidell, and Jacob Shell. 2017. "Transportation and Revolt: Pigeons, Mules, Canals and the Vanishing Geographies of Subversive Mobility." *AAG Review of Books* 5 (2): 138–45.

Audu, O. 2013. "Suspected Boko Haram Members Behead 10 Travellers along Borno-Yobe Highway." *Premium Times*, September 30.

Auge, Marc. 2009. *Non-Places: An Introduction to Super Modernity*. London: Verso.

Auyero, J. 2005. "The Space of Struggles: Topography of Collective Mobilizations." *Social Science Research Proceedings* 160: 122–32.

Bachmann, J., and P. Schouten. 2018. "Concrete Approaches to Peace: Infrastructure as Peacebuilding." *International Affairs* 94 (2): 381–98.

Bærenholdt, J. O. 2013. "Governmobility: The Powers of Mobility." *Mobilities* 8 (1): 20–34.

Bagayoko, N., E. Hutchful, and R. Luckham. 2016. "Hybrid Security Governance in Africa: Rethinking the Foundations of Security, Justice and Legitimate Public Authority." *Conflict, Security and Development* 16 (1): 1–32.

Baker, J., and T. A. Aina, eds. 1995. *The Migration Experience in Africa*. Uppsala: Nordic Africa Institute.

Ballantyne, Tony, and Antoinette Burton, eds. 2009. *Moving Subjects: Gender, Mobility, and Intimacy in an Age of Global Empire*. Urbana: University of Illinois Press.

Ballantyne, Tony, and Antoinette Burton, eds. 2016. *World Histories from Below: Disruption and Dissent, 1750 to the Present*. London: Bloomsbury.

Balzacq, T., T. Basaran, D. Bigo, P.-E. Guittet, and C. Olsson. 2010. "Security Practices." *International Studies Encyclopedia Online*. http://www.open.ac.uk/research projects/iccm/files/iccm/olsson-christian-publication7.pdf

Bansfield, J., C. Nagarajan, and O. Olaide. 2014. *Winners or Losers? Assessing the Contribution of Youth Employment and Empowerment Programs to Reducing Conflict Risk in Nigeria*. Nigeria Stability and Reconciliation Programme, June 30.

Barter, S. J. 2013. "State Proxy or Security Dilemma? Understanding Anti-Rebel Militias in Civil War." *Asian Security* 9:75–92.

Bauman, Zygmunt. 1992. *Mortality, Immortality and Other Life Strategies*. Cambridge: Polity.

Bauman, Zygmunt. 1998. *Globalization: The Human Consequences*. New York: Columbia University Press.

Bauman, Zygmunt. 2000. *Liquid Modernity*. Cambridge: Polity.

Bauman, Zygmunt. 2001. "Wars of the Globalization Era." *European Journal of Social Theory* 4 (1): 11–28.

Bay, Edna. 2006. Introduction to *States of Violence: Politics, Youth, and Memory in Contemporary Africa*, edited by Edna Bay and Donald Donham, 1–15. Charlottesville: University of Virginia Press.

Bayart, J.-F., and S. Ellis. 2000. "Africa in the World: A History of Extraversion." *African Affairs* 99 (395): 217–67.

Bayat, Asef. 1997. "Un-civil Society: The Politics of the 'Informal People.'" *Third World Quarterly* 18 (1): 53–72.

Bayat, Asef. 2000. "From 'Dangerous Classes' to 'Quiet Rebels': Politics of the Urban Subaltern in the Global South." *International Sociology* 15 (3): 533–57.

Bayat, Asef. 2007. "Radical Religion and the Habitus of the Dispossessed: Does Islamic Militancy Have an Urban Ecology?" *International Journal of Urban and Regional Research* 31 (3): 579–90.

BBC. 2009. "Nigeria Sect Head Dies in Custody." July 31.

BBC. 2010. "Fear Reported in Northern Nigeria over Re-emergence of Islamic Sect." September 8.

BBC. 2011. "Abuja Attack: Car Bomb Hits Nigeria UN Building." August 26.

BBC. 2012. "Nigerians Living in Poverty Rise to Nearly 61%." February 13.

BBC. 2013. "Nigeria: 'Cut Off' under Emergency Rule." May 27.

BBC. 2014. "Nigeria Soldiers 'Fire at Army Commander in Maiduguri.'" May 14.

BBC. 2020a. "Nigerian Soldiers and Police Killed in IS Ambush in Borno State." September 27.

BBC. 2020b. "Nigeria's Katsina School Abduction: Boko Haram Says It Took the Students." December 15.

Beauchamp, Tom. 2010. *Standing on Principles: Collected Essays*. New York: Oxford University Press.

Beauchamps, M., M. Hoijtink, M. Leese, B. Magalhaes, S. Weinblum. 2017. "Introduction: Security/Mobility and the Politics of Movement." In *Security/Mobility: Politics of Movement*, edited by M. Leese and S. Wittendorp, 1–13. Manchester: Manchester University Press.

Beck, K. 2013. "Roadside Comforts: Truck Stops on the Forty Days Road in Western Sudan." *Africa* 83 (3): 426–45.

Bedi, T. 2016. "Taxi Drivers, Infrastructures, and Urban Change in Globalizing Mumbai." *City and Society* 28 (3): 387–410.

Beekers, Daan. 2008. "Children of a 'Fallen House': Lives and Livelihoods of Youth in Nigeria." Master's thesis, University of Oxford.

Bellagamba, A., and G. Klute. 2008. *Beside the State: Emergent Powers in Contemporary Africa*. Cologne: Rudiger Koppe Verlag.

Bello, E., and L. Sabo. 2009. "Boko Haram Crisis Wasn't Religious." *Leadership Weekend*, August 8.

Bergen, Peter, and Swati Pandey. 2005. "The Madrassa Myth." *New York Times*, June 14.

Bezabeh, Samson A. 2016. "Africa's Unholy Migrants: Mobility and Migration Morality in the Age of Borders." *African Affairs* 116 (462): 1–17.

Bier, Jess. 2017. "Palestinian State Maps and Imperial Technologies of Staying Put." *Public Culture* 29 (1): 53–78.

Bigo, D. 2002. "Security and Immigration: Toward a Critique of the Governmentality of Unease." *Alternatives* 27: 63–92.

Bigo, D. 2006. "Security, Exception, Ban and Surveillance." In *Theorizing Surveillance: The Panopticon and Beyond*, edited by D. Lyon, 46–68. Uffculme: Willan.

Billig, Michael. 1995. *Banal Nationalism*. Thousand Oaks, CA: SAGE.

BIPSS. 2017. *Local Drivers and Dynamics of Youth Radicalization in Bangladesh*. Dhaka: Bangladesh Institute of Peace and Security Studies. http://bipss.org.bd/pdf/Local%20Drivers.pdf

Bissell, David. 2009. "Conceptualizing Differently-Mobile Passengers: Geographies of Everyday Encumbrance in the Railway Station." *Social and Cultural Geography* 10 (2): 173–95.

Bissell, David. 2014. "Encountering Stressed Bodies: Slow Creep Transformations and Tipping Points of Commuting Mobilities." *Geoforum* 51: 191–201.

Bissell, David. 2016. "Micropolitics of Mobility: Public Transport Commuting and Everyday Encounters with Forces of Enablement and Constraint." *Annals of the American Association of Geographers* 106 (2): 394–403.

Boesen, Elizabeth, Laurence Marfaing, and Mirjam de Bruijn. 2014. "Nomadism and Mobility in the Sahara-Sahel: Introduction." *Canadian Journal of African Studies* 48 (1): 1–12.

Borgstrom, E. 2017. "Social Death." *QJM: An International Journal of Medicine* 110 (1): 5–7.

Botha, Anneli, and Mahdi Abdile. 2019. "Reality versus Perception: Toward Understanding Boko Haram in Nigeria." *Studies in Conflict and Terrorism* 42 (5): 493–519.

Bourdieu, Pierre. 1979. *Outline of a Theory of Practice*. Cambridge: Cambridge University Press.

Bourdieu, Pierre. 1999. *The Weight of the World: Social Suffering in Contemporary Society*. Stanford, CA: Stanford University Press.

Brachet, Julien. 2012. "Geography of Movement, Geography in Movement: Mobility as a Dimension of Fieldwork in Migration Research." *Annales de Geographie* 687–88 (5–6): 543–60.

Brachet, Julien. 2018. "Manufacturing Smugglers: From Irregular to Clandestine Mobility in the Sahara." *Annals of the American Academy of Political and Social Science* 676 (1): 16–35.

Braidotti, Rosi. 1994. *Nomadic Subjects: Embodiment and Sexual Difference in Contemporary Feminist Theory*. New York: Columbia University Press.

Braun, L. N. 2019. "Wandering Women: The Work of Congolese Transnational Traders." *Africa* 89 (2): 378–96.

Brechenmacher, S. 2019. "Stabilizing Northeast Nigeria after Boko Haram." Carnegie Endowment for International Peace, May.

Breen-Smyth, Marie. 2014. "Theorizing the 'Suspect Community': Counterterrorism, Security Practices and the Public Imagination." *Critical Studies on Terrorism* 7 (2): 223–40.

Brenner, L. 1992. "The Jihad Debate between the Sokoto Caliphate and Borno: Historical Analysis of Islamic Political Discourse in Nigeria." In *People and Empires in African History*, edited by J. F. Ade Ajayi and J. D. Y. Peel, 21–43. London: Longmans.

Brigaglia, Andrea. 2012a. "The Career and the Murder of Shaykh Ja'far Mahmoud Adam (Daura, ca. 1961/1962–Kano 2007)." *Islamic Africa Journal* 3 (1): 1–23.

Brigaglia, Andrea. 2012b. "Ja'far Mahmoud Adam, Mohammed Yusuf and Al-Muntada Islamic Trust: Reflections on the Genesis of the Boko Haram Phenomenon in Nigeria." *Annual Review of Islam in Africa* 11: 35–44.

Brigaglia, Andrea, and Fauziyya Fiji. 2008/9. "'We Ain't Coming to Take People Away': A Sufi Praise-Song and the Representation of Police Forces in Northern Nigeria." *Annual Review of Islam in Africa* 10:50–57.

Browne, Deborah, and Andrew Silke. 2011. "The Impact of the Media on Terrorism and Counterterrorism." In Silke 2011, 89–110.

Bukar, K. W. 1982/83. "The Role of Education in an Egalitarian Society." *Intellectual* 1 (2): 33–35.

Burge, Michael. 2011. "Riding the Narrow Tracks of Moral Life: Commercial Motorbike Riders in Makeni, Sierra Leone." *Africa Today* 58 (2): 58–95.

Burns, John F. 2001. "Trucks of the Taliban: Durable, Not Discreet." *New York Times*, November 23.

Butler, Judith. 1999. "Performativity's Social Magic." In *Bourdieu: A Critical Reader*, edited by R. Shusterman, 113–28. Oxford: Blackwell.

Butler Judith. 2004. *Precarious Life: The Powers of Mourning and Violence.* London: Verso.

Butler, Judith. 2009. "Performativity, Precarity and Sexual Politics." *Revista de Antropología Iberoamericana* 4 (3): i–xiii.

Butler, Judith, and Athena Athanasiou. 2013. *Dispossession: The Performative in the Political.* Cambridge: Polity.

Byman, Daniel, P. Chalk, B. Hoffman, W. Rosenau, and D. Brannan. 2001. *Trends in Outside Support for Insurgent Movements.* Arlington, VA: RAND.

Cahill, Caitlin. 2000. "Street Literacy: Urban Teenagers' Strategies for Negotiating Their Neighborhood." *Journal of Youth Studies* 3 (3): 251–77.

Caldeira, Teresa. 2013. "The Paradox of Police Violence in Democratic Brazil." In *Policing and Contemporary Governance: The Anthropology of Police in Practice*, edited by W. Garriott, 97–124. New York: Palgrave Macmillan.

Campbell, John. 2018. "Mother of Boko Haram Leader Abubakar Shekau Speaks about Her Son." *Africa in Transition* (blog), Council on Foreign Relations, June 29.

Canzler, W., V. Kaufmann, and S. Kesselring. 2008. "Tracing Mobilities: An Introduction." In *Tracing Mobilities: Towards a Cosmopolitan Perspective*, edited by W. Canzler, V. Kaufmann, and S. Kesselring, 1–10. Aldershot: Ashgate.

Capote, Truman. 1966. *In Cold Blood.* New York: Random House.

Carey, Sabine C., Neil J. Mitchell, and Will Lowe. 2013. "States, the Security Sector, and the Monopoly of Violence: A New Database on Pro-Government Militias." *Journal of Peace Research* 50 (2): 249–58.

Carling, J. 2013. "Youth Migration in Africa: Moving Away from Youth." https://jorgencarling.org/2013/08/11/youth-migration-in-africa-moving-away-from-youth/

Casey, Conerly. 2007. "Policing through Violence: Fear, Vigilantism and the Politics of Islam in Northern Nigeria." In *Global Vigilantes: Perspectives on Justice and Violence*, edited by D. Pratten and A. Sen, 33–126. London: Hurst.

Casey, Conerly. 2008. "'Marginal Muslims': Politics and the Perceptual Bounds of Islamic Authenticity in Northern Nigeria." *Africa Today* 54 (3): 67–92.

Cass, N., E. Shove, and J. Urry. 2005. "Social Exclusion, Mobility and Access." *Sociological Review* 53 (3): 539–55.

CBS News. 2014. "Boko Haram Slaughters Hundreds in Northern Nigeria, Witnesses Say." June 5.

Center for Civilians in Conflict. 2018. "Civilian Perceptions of the Yan Gora (CJTF) in Borno State, Nigeria." Washington, DC: Center for Civilians in Conflict.

Center for Civilians in Conflict. 2020. "To Defend or Harm? Community Militias in Borno State, Nigeria." Available at https://civiliansinconflict.org/wp-content/uploads/2020/06/CommunityMilitiasFINAL_June2020lowres.pdf

Cervero, R., and A. Golub. 2007. "Informal Transport: A Global Perspective." *Transport Policy* 146: 445–57.

Chan, Sewell. 2005. "Easing Anxiety on Mass Transit." *New York Times*, July 17.

Chayes, Sarah. 2015. *Thieves of State: Why Corruption Threatens Global Security*. New York: W. W. Norton & Company.

Cheng, C. 2018. *Extralegal Groups in Post-Conflict Liberia: How Trade Makes the State*. Oxford: Oxford University Press.

Choplin, A., and J. Lombard. 2014. "On West African Roads: Everyday Mobility and Exchanges between Mauritania, Senegal and Mali." *Canadian Journal of African Studies* 48 (1): 59–75.

Christensen, Maya. 2015. "The Underbelly of Global Security: Sierra Leonean Ex-Militias in Iraq." *African Affairs* 115 (458): 23–43.

Christensen, Maya, and Peter Albrecht. 2020. "Urban Borderwork: Ethnographies of Policing." *Environment and Planning D: Society and Space* 38 (3): 385–98.

Ciavolella, Riccardo. 2011. "Nomadic Culture Put to the Test of Mobility Capital: The Fulaabe Peuls (Mauritania)." *Mappemonde* 103:1–13.

CISAC (Center for International Security and Cooperation). 2018. "Boko Haram." https://cisac.fsi.stanford.edu/mappingmilitants/profiles/boko-haram#highlig ht_text_11862

Clarke, P. B., and I. Linden. 1984. *Islam in Nigeria*. Zaria: Gaskiya Corporation.

Clifford, James. 1997. *Routes: Travel and Translation in the Late Twentieth Century*. Cambridge, MA: Harvard University Press.

Cohen, Corentin. 2015. "Boko Haram and the Impossible Political Sociology of an Armed Group: Catalyzing Armed Violence Region-wide." *Afrique Contemporaine* 255 (3): 71–87.

Cohen, E., S. A. Cohen, and Xiang (Robert) Li. 2017. "Subversive Mobilities." *Applied Mobilities* 2 (2): 115–33.

Columbijn, F. 2002. "On the Road: The Social Impact of New Roads in Southeast Asia." *Bijdragen tot de Taal-Land-en Volkenkunde* 158 (4): 595–617.

Comaroff, Jean, and John Comaroff. 1993. *Modernity and Its Malcontents: Ritual and Power in Postcolonial Africa*. Chicago: University of Chicago Press.

Comaroff, Jean, and John Comaroff. 1999. "Occult Economies and the Violence of Abstraction: Notes from the South African Postcolony." *American Ethnologist* 26 (2): 279–303.

Comaroff, Joan, and John Comaroff. 2004. "Policing Culture, Cultural Policing: Law and Social Order in Postcolonial South Africa." *Law and Social Inquiry* 29 (3): 513–45.

Comaroff, Joan, and John Comaroff. 2006. *Law and Disorder in the Postcolony*. Chicago: University of Chicago Press.

Comaroff, John, and Simon Roberts. 1981. *Rules and Processes: The Cultural Logic of Dispute in an African Context*. Chicago: University of Chicago Press.

Combes, H., C. Hmed, L. Mathieu, J. Simeant, and I. Sommier. 2011. "Observing Mobilizations: Reflections on the Tricks of the Trade in the Sociology of Social Movements." *Politix* 93: 7–27.

Conley, Jim, and Arlene McLaren. 2016. *Car Troubles: Critical Studies of Automobility and Auto-Mobility*. London: Routledge.

Cooke, J. G. 2016. "Now Comes the Hard Part: Five Priorities in the Fight against Boko Haram." Center for Strategic and International Studies, February 5.

Cooke, J. G., and T. M. Sanderson. 2016. *Militancy and the Arc of Instability: Violent Extremism in the Sahel.* Lanham, MD: Rowman and Littlefield.

Cornwall, A. 2001. "Wayward Women and Useless Men: Contest and Change in Gender Relations." In *Wicked Women and the Reconfiguration of Gender in Africa*, edited by S. W. Ado-Odo, D. L. Hodgson, and S. McCurdy. Portsmouth, NH: Heinemann.

Coulter, Chris. 2008. "Female Fighters in the Sierra Leone War: Challenging the Assumptions?" *Feminist Review* 88: 54–73.

Crang, M. 2000. "Relics, Places and Unwritten Geographies in the Work of Michel de Certeau (1925–86)." In *Thinking Space*, edited by M. Crang and N. Thrift, 136–53. London: Routledge.

Crenshaw, Martha. 1981. "The Causes of Terrorism." *Comparative Politics* 13 (4): 379–99.

Cresswell, Tim. 2006. *On the Move: Mobility in the Modern Western World.* New York: Routledge.

Cresswell, Tim. 2010. "Towards a Politics of Mobility." *Environment and Planning D: Society and Space* 28 (1): 17–31.

Cresswell, Tim. 2011. "Mobilities I: Catching Up." *Progress in Human Geography* 35 (4): 550–58.

Crowder, M. 1962. *A Short History of Nigeria.* Rev. ed. New York: Fredrick A. Praeger.

Curiel, R. P., O. Walther, and N. O'Clery. 2020. "Uncovering the Internal Structure of Boko Haram through Its Mobility Patterns." *Applied Network Science* 5 (28): 1–23.

Cyffer. 2006. "Kanuri and Its Neighbors: When Saharan and Chadic Languages Meet." In *West African Linguistics: Papers in Honor of Russell G. Schuh* edited by P. Newman, and L. M. Hyman, 33–55. Studies in African Linguistics, suppl. 11. Columbus: Ohio State University.

Czarniawska, B. 2007. *Shadowing and Other Techniques for Doing Fieldwork in Modern Societies.* Malmö: Copenhagen Business School Press.

Czegledy, A. P. 2004. "Getting Around Town: Transportation and the Built Environment in Post-Apartheid South Africa." *City and Society* 16 (2): 63–92.

Daily Post. 2015. "Boko Haram: Army Bans Traditional Rulers from Using Horses in Borno." September 5.

Daily Trust. 2009. "Assembly Recalls 'Operation Flush." July 11.

Daily Trust. 2014. "Stephen Davis' 7-Year Secret Deals with Boko Haram." September 7.

Daily Trust. 27 July 2009. "Nigeria: Boko Haram sect leader Ustaz Mohammed vows revenge." July 27.

Daily Trust. 2010. "Nigeria: Borno State Signs Order Declaring Islamic Group Dangerous to Government." May 7.

Daily Trust. 2012. "Kaduna Residents Struggle under Achaba Ban." May 24.

Daily Trust. 2018. "Borno Motorists, NURTW Showdown over Military Escorts, Charges." January 13.

Daiute, Colette. 2006. "The Problem of Society in Youth Conflict." In *International Perspectives on Youth Conflict and Development*, edited by Collette Daiute, Z. F. Beykont, C. Higgson-Smith, and L. Nucci, 3–22. Oxford: Oxford University Press.

Dan-Borno (blog). 2008. "Operation Flush II and Maiduguri People." December 10.

Dan-Borno. 2010. "Okadas after the Exit of Operation Flush II." April 20.

Dan-Borno. 2011. "Bye Bye to Achaba." July 8.

D'Andrea, A., L. Ciolfi, and B. Gray. 2011. "Methodological Challenges and Innovations in Mobilities Research." *Mobilities* 6 (2): 149–60.

Danish Refugee Council. 2017. South and Central Somalia: Security Situation, Al-Shahab Presence, and Target Groups." March. https://www.refworld.org/docid/58cbf55d4.html

Darden, J. T. 2019. *Tackling Terrorists' Exploitation of Youth*. American Enterprise Institute, May. https://www.un.org/sexualviolenceinconflict/wp-content/uploads/2019/05/report/tackling-terrorists-exploitation-of-youth/Tackling-Terrorists-Exploitation-of-Youth.pdf

Das, V., and D. Poole, eds. 2004. *Anthropology in the Margins of the State*. Santa Fe: School of American Research Press.

Daskalaki, M., C. L. Butler, and J. Petrovic. 2016. "Somewhere In-Between: Narratives of Place, Identity, and Translocal Work." *Journal of Management Inquiry* 25 (2): 184–98.

Date-Bah, Eugenia. 1980. "The Inscriptions on the Vehicles of Ghanaian Commercial Drivers: A Sociological Analysis." *Journal of Modern African Studies* 18 (3): 525–31.

Davis, Mike. 2007. *Buda's Wagon: A Brief History of the Car Bomb*. London: Verso.

De Boeck, F. 2015. "'Divining' the City: Rhythm, Amalgamation and Knotting as Forms of 'Urbanity.'" *Social Dynamics: A Journal of African Studies* 41 (1): 1–12.

De Boeck, F., and A. Honwana. 2005. "Children and Youth in Africa: Agency, Identity and Place." In *Makers and Breakers: Children and Youth in Postcolonial Africa*, edited by A. Honwana and F. De Boeck, 1–18. Oxford: James Curry.

Debos, M. 2011. "Living by the Gun: Armed Violence as a Practical Occupation." *Journal of Modern African Studies* 49 (3): 409–28.

de Bruijn, Mirjam. 2007. "Mobility and Society in the Sahel: An Exploration of Mobile Margins and Global Governance." In *Cultures of Migration: African Perspectives*, edited by H. P. Hahn and G. Klute. London: Transaction.

de Bruijn, Mirjam, and Jonna Both. 2018. "Introduction: Understanding Experiences and Decisions in Situations of Enduring Hardship in Africa." *Conflict and Society* 4 (1): 186–98.

de Certeau, M. 1984. *The Practice of Everyday Life*. Berkeley: University of California Press.

Defence Post. 2019. "Nigeria: Dozens Killed in Boko Haram Triple Suicide Bombing in Konduga, Borno State." July 17.

de Sardan, Olivier. 1999. "A Moral Economy of Corruption in Africa?" *Journal of Modern African Studies* 37 (1): 25–52.

Desjarlais, R. 1997. *Shelter Blues: Sanity and Selfhood among the Homeless*. Philadelphia: University of Pennsylvania Press.

de Waal, A., ed. 2007. *War in Darfur*. Cambridge, MA: Harvard University Press.

Dewey, J. 1954. *The Public and Its Problems*. Athens, OH: Swallow.

Dietrich, K. 2015. *"When We Can't See the Enemy, Civilians Become the Enemy": Living through Nigeria's Six-Year Insurgency*. Washington, DC: Center for Civilians in Conflict.

Dikeç, Mustafa. 2001. "Justice and the Spatial Imagination." *Environment and Planning A: Economy and Space* 33 (10): 1785–1805.

Dikeç, Mustafa. 2002. "Police, Politics and Right to the City." *GeoJournal* 58 (2–3): 91–98.

Dirkx, T. 2018. "The Unintended Consequences of US Support on Militia Governance in Kunduz Province, Afghanistan." *Civil Wars* 19 (3): 377–401.

Dixon, Robyn. 2014. "In Nigeria, Child Beggars Are Easy Recruits for Boko Haram Extremists." *Los Angeles Times*, August 14.

Donohue, Laura. 2008. *The Cost of Counterterrorism: Power, Politics, and Liberty*. New York: Cambridge University Press.

Doughty, Karolina, and Lesley Murray. 2016. "Discourses of Mobility: Institutions, Everyday Lives and Embodiment." *Mobilities* 11 (2): 303–22.

Douglas, Mary. 1987. *How Institutions Think*. London: Routledge.

Duodu, Cameron. 2009. "Mohammed Yusuf's Final Days." *Guardian*, August 6, 2009.

Durham, D. 2004. "Disappearing Youth: Youth as a Social Shifter in Botswana." *American Ethnologist* 31 (4): 589–605.

Edensor, T. 2004. "Automobility and National Identity: Representation, Geography and Driving Practice." *Theory, Culture and Society* 21 (4–5): 101–20.

Egbewole, Wahab, and Hanfi Hammed. 2018. "Curbing Religious Extremism of Boko Haram Insurgency in Nigeria: Judicial Interventionism and Human Rights Absolutism." In *Religion, Law and Security in Africa*, edited by M. Christian Green, T. Jeremy Gunn, and Mark Hill, 3–20. Stellenbosch, South Africa: African Sun Media.

Ehrhardt, David. 2019. "Radicalization in Northern Nigeria: Stories from Boko Haram." In *Biographies of Radicalization: Hidden Messages of Social Change*, edited by M. de Bruijn, 115–34. Berlin: Walter de Gruyter.

Eickelman, D., and J. Piscatori. 1996. *Muslim Politics*. Princeton, NJ: Princeton University Press.

Elden, S. 2009. *Terror and Territory: The Spatial Extent of Sovereignty*. Minneapolis: University of Minnesota Press.

Engle, P. 2015. "These Toyota Trucks Are Popular with Terrorists—Here's Why." *Business Insider*, October 7.

Etzold, Benjamin. 2017. "Mobility, Space and Livelihood Trajectories: New Perspectives on Migration, Translocality and Place-Making for Livelihood Studies." In *Livelihoods and Development: New Perspectives*, edited by Leo de Haan, 44–68. Leiden: Brill.

Evans, J., J. O'Brien, B. Ch Ng. 2018. "Towards a Geography of Informal Transport: Mobility, Infrastructure and Urban Sustainability from the Back of a Motorbike." *Transactions of the Institute of British Geographers* 43 (4): 674–88.

Ezeibe, C. C., T. Nzeadibe, A. N. Ali, C. U. Udeogu, C. F. Nwankwo, and C. Ogbodo. 2017. "Work on Wheels: Collective Organizing of Motorcycle Taxis in Nigerian Cities." *International Development Planning Review* 39 (3): 249–73.

Falconbridge, J., and A. Hui. 2016. "Traces of a Mobile Field: Ten Years of Mobilities Research." *Mobilities* 11 (1): 1–14.

Falola, Toyin. 1998. *Violence in Nigeria: The Crisis of Religious Politics and Secular Ideologies*. New York: University of Rochester Press.

Faul, M., and I. Abdulaziz. 2014. "Bridge Blown Up as Efforts to Rescue Kidnapped Nigerian Girls Gets Underway." Associated Press, May 10.

Feldman, Allen. 2004. "Securocratic Wars of Public Safety." *International Journal of Postcolonial Studies* 6 (3): 330–50.

Ferme, M. C. 2004. "Deterritorialized Citizenship and the Resonances of the Sierra Leonean State." In Das and Poole 2004, 81–116.

Fessy, T. 2015. "Boko Haram Attack: What Happened in Baga?" BBC, February 2.

Field, M. J. 1960. *Search for Security: An Ethno-psychiatric Study of Rural Ghana*. London: Faber and Faber.

Fierke, K. M. 2007. *Critical Approaches to International Security*. Cambridge: Polity.

Fishel, S. R. 2019. "Of Other Movements: Nonhuman Mobility in the Anthropocene." *Mobilities* 14 (3): 351–62.

Fleming, L. 2015. "Boko Haram Crisis: The Nigerian Truckers Risking Attacks." BBC, March 9.

Fogle, N. 2011. *The Spatial Logic of Social Struggle: A Bourdieuian Topology*. New York: Lexington Books.

Forsdick, C. 2017. "'Translating Cultures,' Translating Research." Multilingualism: Empowering Individuals, Transforming Societies, Dialogues, November 3. http://www.meits.org/dialogues/article/translating-cultures-translating-research

Foster, D., and D. Milton. 2018. "Children at War: Foreign Child Recruits of the Islamic State." *Combating Terrorism Center Sentinel* 11 (6): 11–17.

Foucault, Michel. 1976. *Society Must Be Defended*. Lectures at the College de France. New York: Picador.

Foucault, Michel. 1978. *The History of Sexuality*. Vol. 1, *An Introduction*. Translated by Robert Hurley. New York: Pantheon.

Foucault, Michel. 1980. *Power/Knowledge: Selected Interviews and Other Writings, 1972–1977*. Edited by Colin Gordon. New York: Pantheon.

Foucault, Michel. 1984. "Right of Death and Power over Life." In *The Foucault Reader*, edited by P. Rabinow, 258–72. New York: Pantheon.

Foucault, Michel. 1986. "Of Other Spaces." *Diacritics* 16 (1): 22–27.

Foucault, Michel. 1997a. "The Birth of Biopolitics." In *Ethics, Subjectivity, and Truth*, edited by P. Rainbow and J. D. Faubion, 73–79. New York: New Press.

Foucault, Michel. 1997b. *The Politics of Truth*. Cambridge, MA: MIT Press.

Foucault, Michel. 2008. *The Birth of Biopolitics: Lectures at the College de France, 1978–79*. New York: Palgrave Macmillan. First published 2004.

Friedman, Uri. 2014. "The Bike-Helmet Law That Helped Trigger an Insurgency in Nigeria." *Atlantic*, May 22.

Fuller, M. G., and M. Low. 2017. "Introduction: An Invitation to Spatial Sociology." *Current Sociology* 65 (4): 469–91.

Gartenstein-Ross, D., H. Hagerty, and L. MacNair. 2018. "The Emigrant Sisters Return: The Growing Role of the Islamic State's Women." *War on the Rocks*, April 2.

Garba, Ali. 2010. "Boko Haram: How Attackers Outwitted Security Agencies." *The Guardian* (Nigeria), September 11.

Gaub, F., and J. Lisiecka. 2016. *Women in Daesh: Jihadist "Cheerleaders," Active Operatives?* Brief 27. European Union Institute for Security Studies, October.

Geschiere, Peter, and F. Nyamnjoh. 2000. "Capitalism and Autochthony: The Seesaw of Mobility and Belonging." *Public Culture* 12: 423–52.

Gewald, J.-B., S. Luning, and K. van Walraven, eds. 2009. *The Speed of Change: Motor Vehicles and People in Africa, 1890–2000*. Leiden: Brill.

Ghannam, F. 2011. "Mobility, Liminality, and Embodiment in Urban Egypt." *American Ethnologist* 38 (4): 790–800.

Giddens, A. 1979. *Central Problems in Social Theory*. Berkeley: University of California Press.

Giddens, A. 1990. *Consequences of Modernity*. Stanford, CA: Stanford University Press.

Gieryn, T. F. 2000. "A Space for Place in Sociology." *Annual Review of Sociology* 26: 463–96.

Gill, N., J. Caletrio, and V. Mason. 2011. "Introduction: Mobilities and Forced Migration." *Mobilities* 6 (3): 301–16.

Gill, N., J. Caletrio, and V. Mason. 2014. *Mobilities and Forced Migration*. New York: Routledge.

Ginsberg, Susan. 2006. *Countering Terrorist Mobility: Shaping an Operational Strategy*. Migration Policy Institute, February. https://www.migrationpolicy.org/pubs/MPI_TaskForce_Ginsburg.pdf

Global Intelligence Files. 2011. "Nigeria - Boko Haram Gives 'Fresh' Conditions for Talks with Government," June 13.

Goldstein, Daniel M. 2010. "Toward a Critical Anthropology of Security." *Current Anthropology* 51 (4): 487–517.

Goldstein, Daniel M. 2016. *Owners of the Sidewalk: Security and Survival in the Informal City*. Durham, NC: Duke University Press.

Goodwin, K. J. 2010. "Reconstructing Automobility: The Making and Breaking of Modern Transportation." *Global Environmental Politics* 10 (4): 60–78.

Gopfert, M. 2016. "Surveillance in Niger: Gendarmes and the Problem of 'Seeing Things.'" *African Studies Review* 59 (2): 39–57.

Gordon, H. M., S. B. Horton, and L. A. Harrison. 2007. "Things Fall Apart: The Endgame Dynamics of Internal Wars." *Third World Quarterly* 28 (2): 321–67.

Gore, C., and D. Pratten. 2003. "The Politics of Plunder: The Rhetorics of Order and Disorder in Southern Nigeria." *African Affairs* 102 (407): 211–40.

Gorman-Murray, A. 2009. "Intimate Mobilities: Emotional Embodiment and Queer Migration." *Social and Cultural Geography* 10 (4): 441–60.

Gough, K. V. 2008. "Moving Around: The Social and Spatial Mobility of Youth in Lusaka." *Geografiska Annaler: Series B, Human Geography* 90 (3): 243–55.

Grace, Joshua. 2013. "Heroes of the Road: Race, Gender and the Politics of Mobility in Twentieth Century Tanzania." *Africa* 83 (3): 403–25.

Graham, Stephen. 2006a. "Demodernizing by Design: Everyday Infrastructure and Political Violence." In *Violent Geographies: Fear, Terror, and Political Violence*, edited by D. Gregory and A. Pred, 309–28. London: Routledge.

Graham, Stephen. 2006b. "Urban Metabolism as Target: Contemporary War as Forced Demodernization." In *The Nature of Cities: Urban Political Ecology and the Politics of Urban Metabolism*, edited by N. Heynen, M. Kaika, and E. Swyngedouw, 245–65. London: Routledge.

Graham, Stephen, and Colin McFarlane, ed. 2015. *Infrastructural Lives: Urban Infrastructure in Context*. London: Routledge.

Green-Simms, L. B. 2017. *Postcolonial Automobility: Car Culture in West Africa*. Minneapolis: University of Minnesota Press.

Grégoire, Emmanuel, and Pascal Labazée, eds. 1993. *Grands commerçants d'Afrique de l'Ouest: Logiques et pratiques d'un groupe d'hommes d'affaires contemporains*. Paris: Karthala-ORSTOM.

Gregory, D. 2007. "Vanishing Points." In *Violent Geographies: Fear, Terror, and Political Violence*, edited by D. Gregory and A. Pred, 207–30. New York: Routledge.

Guardian. 2018. "Boko Haram Land Mines in Nigeria Killed at Least 162 in Two Years." September 23.

Guardian. 2019. "Nigeria Detained Children as Young as Five over 'Boko Haram Links'—Report." September 11.

Guevara, Che. 1961. *Guerrilla Warfare*. New York: Monthly Review Press.

Guide to the Analysis of Insurgency. n.d. Central Intelligence Agency. Available at https://www.hsdl.org/?abstract&did=713599

Guittet, E.-P. 2017. "Unpacking the New Mobilities Paradigm: Lessons for Critical Security Studies?" In Leese and Wittendorp 2017, 209–16.

Gupta, Akhil, and James Ferguson. 1997. *Anthropological Locations: Boundaries and Grounds of a Field Science*. Berkeley: University of California Press.

Gusau, Isa U. 2009. "Maiduguri Shooting: Cops Parade Sect Followers." *Daily Trust*, July 25.

Gusau, Isa U. 2010. "One Year After . . . : The Carnage of Boko Haram Stands Tall in Borno, Yobe." *Daily Trust*, August 8.

Gusau, Isa U., and M. I. Kwara. 2009. "In Maiduguri, Operation Flush Men Brutalize Residents." *Daily Trust*, February 7.

Guyer, J. 1997. *An African Niche Economy: Farming to Feed Ibadan, 1968–88*. Edinburgh: Edinburgh University Press.

Guyer, J. 2011. "Describing Urban 'No Man's Land' in Africa." *Africa* 81 (3): 474–92.

Habib, H. 2010. "In Kano, Rising Threat of Achaba Drivers." *Daily Trust*, June 5.

Hagberg, S. 2019. "Performing Tradition While Doing Politics: A Comparative Study of the Dozos and Koglweogos Self-Defense Movements in Burkina Faso." *African Studies Review* 62 (1): 173–93.

Hage, Ghassan. 2009. "Waiting Out the Crisis: On Stuckedness and Governmentality." In *Waiting*, edited by Ghassan Hage, 97–106. Melbourne: Melbourne University Press.

Hage, Ghassan. 2003. *Against Paranoid Nationalism: Searching for Hope in a Shrinking Society*. Annandale, New South Wales: Pluto.

Hamid, Shadi. 2015. "Does ISIS Really Have Nothing to Do with Islam? Islamic Apologetics Carry Serious Risks." *Washington Post*, November 18.

Hannah, M. 2006. "Torture and the Ticking Bomb: The War on Terrorism as a Geographical Imagination of Power/Knowledge." *Annals of the Association of American Geographers* 96 (3): 622–40.

Hannam, K., M. Sheller, and J. Urry. 2006. "Mobilities, Immobilities and Moorings." *Mobilities* 1 (1): 1–22.

Hansen, Karen. 2005. "Getting Stuck in the Compound: Some Odds against Social Adulthood in Lusaka, Zambia." *Africa Today* 51 (4): 3–16.

Hansen, T. Blom. 2006. "Sounds of Freedom: Music, Taxis, and Racial Imagination in Urban South Africa." *Public Culture* 18 (1): 185–208.

Hansen, William. 2016. "Poverty and 'Economic Deprivation Theory': Street Children, Qur'anic Schools / *almajirai* and the Dispossessed as a Source of Recruitment for *Boko Haram* and Other Religious, Political and Criminal Groups in Northern Nigeria." *Perspectives on Terrorism* 10 (5): 83–95.

Hanson, Susan. 2002. "Transportation: Hooked on Speed, Eyeing Sustainability." In *A Companion to Economic Geography*, edited by E. Sheppard and T. Barnes, 468–83. Malden, MA: Blackwell.

Hanson, Susan, and Perry Hanson. 1980. "Gender and Urban Activity Patterns in Uppsala, Sweden." *Geographical Review* 70: 291–99.

Hart, Jennifer. 2016 *Ghana on the Go: African Mobility in the Age of Motor Transportation*. Bloomington: Indiana University Press.

Haruna, A. 2008. "We Met Borno on the Brink of Collapse—Dibal." *Daily Independent*, November 24.

Haruna, A. 2015. "Joblessness and the State Policy on Violent Crime: Impacts of Motorcycles Banning in Damaturu, Yobe State, Nigeria." *International Journal of Advanced Research in Management and Social Sciences* 4 (10): 152–68.

Haruna, A. 2020. "Special Report: Increasing Boko Haram Attacks on Highways Threaten to Cut Borno Off from Nigeria." *Premium Times*, January 23.

Healey, Patsy. 2000. "Planning Theory and Urban and Regional Dynamics: A Comment on Yiftachel and Huxley." *International Journal of Urban and Regional Research* 24 (4): 917–21.

Healy, H. 2018. "Can Peacebuilding End the War with Boko Haram?" *New Internationalist*, September 1.

Hegel, Georg Wilhelm Friedrich. 1977. *Phenomenology of Spirit*. Translated by A. V. Miller. Oxford: Oxford University Press.

Heidegger, Martin. 1993. *Basic Writings*. London: Routledge.

Herzfeld, M. 1992. *The Social Production of Indifference: Exploring the Symbolic Roots of Western Bureaucracy*. New York: Berg.

Hickey, Raymond. 1984. "The 1982 Maitatsine Uprisings in Nigeria: A Note." *African Affairs* 83 (331): 251–56.

Higazi, A. 2008. "Social Mobilization and Collective Violence: Vigilantes and Militias in the Lowlands of Plateau State, Central Nigeria." *Africa* 78 (1): 107–35.

Higazi, A. 2015. "Mobilization into and against Boko Haram in North-East Nigeria." In *Collective Mobilization in Africa: Contestations, Resistance, Revolt*, edited by M. Cahen, M. E. Pommerrolle, and K. Tall, 305–58. Leiden: Brill.

Hinshaw, D. 2013a. "Hundreds Killed in Jails Swelling with Islamist Suspects." *Wall Street Journal*, October 15.

Hinshaw, D. 2013b. "Violence Stalks Drivers on Nigerian Highway." *Wall Street Journal*, October 17.

Hiralal, K., and Z. Jinnah, ed. 2018. *Gender and Mobility in Africa: Borders, Bodies and Boundaries*. Cham, Switzerland: Palgrave Macmillan.

Hoechner, Hannah. 2015. "Mobility as a Contradictory Resource: Peripatetic Qur'anic Students in Kano, Nigeria." *Children's Geographies* 15 (1): 59–72.

Hoechner, Hannah. 2018. *Qur'anic Schools in Northern Nigeria: Everyday Experience of Youth, Faith and Poverty*. Cambridge: Cambridge University Press.

Hoffman, Bruce. 2006. *Inside Terrorism*. New York: Columbia University Press.

Hoffman, Danny. 2007. "The Meaning of a Militia: Understanding the Civil Defense Forces of Sierra Leone." *African Affairs* 106 (425): 639–62.

Hoffman, Danny. 2011. *The War Machines: Young Men and Violence in Sierra Leone and Liberia*. Durham, NC: Duke University Press.

Holston, James. 2008. *Insurgent Citizenship: Disjunctions of Democracy and Modernity in Brazil*. Princeton, NJ: Princeton University Press.

Honwana, Alcinda M. 2012. *The Time of Youth: Work, Social Change, and Politics in Africa*. Sterling, OR: Kumarian.

Howitt, Arnold M., and Jonathan Makler. 2005. "On the Ground: Protecting America's Roads and Transit against Terrorism." Metropolitan Policy Program: The Brookings Institution Series on Transportation Reform. https://www.hks.harvard.edu/sites/default/files/centers/research-initiatives/crisisleadership/files/On%20the%20Ground.pdf

Houreld, K. 2009. "Muslim Clerics Say Authorities Ignored Warnings before Nigeria Clashes Killed 700." Associated Press, August 2.

HRW (Human Rights Watch). 2007. "No One Is Safe: Insurgent Attacks on Civilians in Thailand's Southern Border Provinces." August 27.

HRW. 2012. "Spiraling Violence: Boko Haram Attacks and Security Force Abuses in Nigeria." October 11.

HRW. 2013. "Nigeria: Boko Haram Abducts Women, Recruits Children." November 29.

HRW. 2014. "Nigeria: Boko Haram Kills 2,053 Civilians in 6 Months; Apparent Crime against Humanity." July 15.

HRW. 2016. "'They Set the Classrooms on Fire': Attacks on Education in Northeast Nigeria."

Hughes, Everett C. 1951. "Work and the Self." In *Social Psychology at the Crossroads*, edited by J. H. Rohrer and M. Sherif, 313–23. New York: Harper and Brothers.

Humphrey, Caroline. 2004. "Sovereignty and Ways of Life: The Mashrut System in the City of Ulan-Ude, Russia." In *A Companion to the Anthropology of Politics*, edited by D. Nugent and J. Vincent, 418–36. New York: Blackwell.

Hyndman, Jennifer. 2007. "The Securitization of Fear in Post-Tsunami Sri Lanka." *Annals of the Association of American Geographers* 97 (2): 361–72.

Hyndman, Jennifer, and Malathi de Alwis. 2004. "Bodies, Shrines, and Roads: Violence, (Im)mobility and Displacement in Sri Lanka." *Gender, Place and Culture: A Journal of Feminist Geography* 11 (4): 535–57.

ICG (International Crisis Group). 2014. "Curbing Violence in Nigeria (II): The Boko Haram Insurgency." April 3.

ICG. 2017a. "Double-Edged Sword: Vigilantes in African Counter-Insurgencies." Africa Report 251. September 7.

ICG. 2017b. "Niger and Boko Haram: Beyond Counter-Insurgency." February 27.

ICG. 2018. "Countering Jihadist Militancy in Bangladesh." Asia Report 295.

Idler, Annette. 2018. "Preventing Conflict Upstream: Impunity and Illicit Governance across Colombia's Borders." *Defense Studies* 18 (1): 58–75.

Idler, Annette. 2019. *Borderland Battles: Violence, Crime, and Governance at the Edges of Colombia's War*. Oxford: Oxford University Press.

Idris, H. 2009. "Crash Helmet Crash: How Two Died in Biu." *Daily Trust*, October 24.

Idris, H., and S. Dauda. 2010. "Boko Haram Snipers Kill 3 Policemen." *Daily Trust*, August 26.

Idris, H., and I. Sawab. 2013. "Women as Boko Haram's New Face." *Daily Trust*, July 6.

Iliffe, J. 1987. *The African Poor: A History*. Cambridge: Cambridge University Press.

Ingold, T. 2000. *The Perception of the Environment: Essays in Livelihood, Dwelling and Skill*. London: Routledge.

Institute for Autonomy and Governance. 2017. "Research on Youth Vulnerability to Violent Extremism in the Autonomous Region in Muslim Mindanao."

https://iag.org.ph/images/pdf/Research_on_Youth_Vulnerability_to_VE_in
_the_ARMM.pdf
International Commission on Intervention and State Sovereignty. 2001. *The
Responsibility to Protect: Report of the International Commission on Intervention and
State Sovereignty*. Ottawa: International Development Research Centre.
IRIN (Integrated Regional Information Networks). 2013. "Civilian Vigilante
Groups Increase Dangers in North-Eastern Nigeria." December 12.
IRIN. 2016. "They're Defeating Boko Haram but Are They Nigeria's Next Secu-
rity Threat?" August 22.
Isin, E. F. 2002. "Ways of Being Political." *Distinktion* 3 (1): 7–28.
Ismail, S. 2006. *Political Life in Cairo's New Quarters: Encountering the Everyday State*.
Minneapolis: Regents of the University of Minnesota.
Ivasiuc, A. 2015. "Watching over the Neighborhood: Vigilante Discourses and
Practices in the Suburbs of Rome." *Etnofoor* 27 (2): 53–72.
Iweze, D. O. 2014. "Insurgency in the North-East of Nigeria and Its Implications
on Interstate and Trans-Border Mobility." https://t2m.org/wp-content/uploa
ds/2014/09/Daniel%20Olisa%20Iweze_Insurgency%20and%20Risks%20of
%20Travels%20and%20Mobility.pdf
Iwilade, Akin. 2014. "Networks of Violence and Becoming: Youth and the Politics
of Patronage in Nigeria's Oil-Rich Delta." *Journal of Modern African Studies* 52
(4): 571–95.
Jackson, Emma. 2012. "Fixed in Mobility: Young Homeless People and the City."
International Journal of Urban and Regional Research 36 (4): 725–41.
Jackson, Michael. 2010. "From Anxiety to Method in Anthropological Fieldwork:
An Appraisal of George Devereux's Enduring Ideas." In *Emotions in the Field:
The Psychology and Anthropology of Fieldwork Experience*, edited by James Davies
and Dimitrina Spencer, 35–54. Stanford, CA: Stanford University Press.
Jackson, Richard. 2012. "Unknown Knowns: The Subjugated Knowledge of Ter-
rorism Studies." *Critical Studies on Terrorism* 5 (1): 11–29.
Jaffe, Rivke. 2018. "Cities and the Political Imagination." *Sociological Review* 66 (6):
1097–1110.
Jaffe, Rivke, Christien Klaufus, and Freek Colombijn. 2012. "Mobilities and Mobi-
lizations of the Urban Poor." *International Journal of Urban and Regional Research*
36 (4): 643–54.
Jansen, S. 2014. "Hope for/against the State: Gridding in a Besieged Sarajevo Sub-
urb." *Ethnos: Journal of Anthropology* 79 (2): 238–60.
Jardine, E. 2014. "The Insurgent's Dilemma: A Theory of Mobilization and Con-
flict." PhD diss., Carleton University.
Jeganathan, Pradeep. 1997. "All the Lord's Men? Recollecting a Riot in an Urban
Sri Lankan Community." In *Sri Lanka: Collective Identities Revisited*, edited by M.
Roberts, 221–45. Colombo, Sri Lanka: Marga.
Jeganathan, Pradeep. 2000. "On the Anticipation of Violence: Modernity and
Identity in Southern Sri Lanka." In *Anthropology, Development, and Modernities:*

Exploring Discourses, Counter-Tendencies, and Violence, edited by N. Long and A. Arce, 111–25. London: Routledge.

Jeganathan, P. 2004. "Checkpoint: Anthropology, Identity, and the State." In Das and Poole 2004, 67–80.

Jeganathan, P. 2018. "Border, Checkpoint, Bodies." In *Routledge Handbook of Asia's Borderlands*, edited by A. Horstmann, M. Saxer, and A. Rippa, 403–10. London: Routledge.

Jensen, Ole B. 2009. "Flows of Meaning, Cultures of Movements—Urban Mobility as Meaningful Everyday Life Practice." *Mobilities* 4 (1): 139–58.

Jentzsch, C., S. N. Kalyvas, and L. I. Schubiger. 2015. "Militias in Civil Wars." *Journal of Conflict Resolution* 59 (5): 755–69.

Jirgi, H. 2019. "Borno Govt Bans Keke Napep on Maiduguri Highways." Al Jazeera, December 3.

Jones, R. 2008. "State Failure and Extra-Legal Justice: Vigilante Groups, Civil Militias and the Rule of Law in West Africa." Research Paper 66, UNHCR, October.

Jones, Marian Moser, and Ronald Bayer. 2007. "Paternalism and Its Discontents: Motorcycle Helmet Laws, Libertarian Values, and Public Health." *American Journal of Public Health* 97 (2): 208–17.

Jones, Mayeni. 2019. "Nigeria's 'Torture Houses' Masquerading as Koranic Schools," BBC News, 28 October.

Jónsson, Gunvor. 2008. "Migration Aspirations and Immobility in a Malian Soninke Village." IMI Working Papers 10, International Migration Institute, Oxford.

Jorgensen, M., and L. Phillips. 2002. *Discourse Analysis as Theory and Method*. London: SAGE.

Jose, B., and P. A. Medie. 2016. "Understanding Why and How Civilians Resort to Self-Protection in Armed Conflict." *International Studies Review* 17 (4): 515–35.

Justino, P. 2009. "Poverty and Violent Conflict: A Micro-Level Perspective on the Causes and Duration of Warfare." *Journal of Peace Research* 46 (3): 315–33.

Kah, H. K. 2017. "Boko Haram Is Losing, but So Is Food Production: Conflict and Food Insecurity in Nigeria and Cameroon." *African Development* 42 (3): 177–96.

Kain, John. 1968. "Housing Segregation, Negro Employment, and Metropolitan Decentralization." *Quarterly Journal of Economics* 82 (2): 175–97.

Kaldor, Mary. 1999. *New and Old Wars: Organized Violence in a Global Era*. Cambridge: Polity.

Kalyvas, S. N. 2001. "'New' and 'Old' Civil Wars: A Valid Distinction? *World Politics* 54 (1): 99–118.

Kane, O. 2003. *Muslim Modernity in Postcolonial Nigeria: A Study of the Society for the Removal of Innovation and Reinstatement of Tradition*. Leiden: Brill.

Kano State Motor Vehicle Statistics. 1986. Kano: Government Printers.

Kaplan, Robert. 1994. "The Coming Anarchy: How Scarcity, Crime, Overpopulation, Tribalism, and Disease Are Rapidly Destroying the Social Fabric of Our Planet." *Atlantic*, February.

Kasfir, Nelson, Georg Ferks, and Niels Terpstra. 2018. "Introduction: Armed Groups and Multi-Layered Governance." *Civil Wars* 19 (3): 257–78.

Kassim, A., and M. Nwankpa, eds. 2018. *The Boko Haram Reader: From Nigerian Preachers to the Islamic State*. Oxford: Oxford University Press.

Katz, Cindi. 2007. "Banal Terrorism: Spatial Fetishism and Everyday Insecurity." In *Violent Geographies: Fear, Terror, and Political Violence*, edited by D. Gregory and A. Pred, 349–61. London: Routledge.

Kaufman, Emily. 2016. "Policing Mobilities through Bio-Spatial Profiling in New York City." *Political Geography* 55 (1): 72–81.

Kaufmann, Vincent, M. M. Bergman, and D. Joye. 2004. "Motility: Mobility as Capital." *International Journal of Urban and Regional Research* 28 (4): 745–56.

Kelly, F. 2019. "Nigeria: 'Boko Haram' Convoy Ambush between Sabon Gari and Damboa Kills at Least 20." *Los Angeles Times*, May 26.

Kelly, Robert 1992. "Mobility/Sedentism: Concepts, Archaeological Measures, and Effects." *Annual Review of Anthropology* 21: 43–66.

Kenyon, S., G. Lyons, and J. Rafferty. 2002. "Transport and Social Exclusion: Investigating the Possibility of Promoting Inclusion through Virtual Mobility." *Journal of Transport Geography* 10: 207–19.

Khalili, L. 2011. "Gendered Practices of Counterinsurgency." *Review of International Studies* 37 (4): 1471–91.

Khalili, L. 2014. "The Uses of Happiness in Counterinsurgencies." *Social Text* 118 (32): 23–43.

Khan, M. 2018. "'Blood Neighbors' and Border Enemies: Transport, Trade, *Talibee* Networks and the Gambia-Senegal Relations, 1960–2015." Master's thesis. University of Edinburgh.

Khanna, Rajanna. 2009. "Disposability." *Differences: A Journal of Feminist Cultural Studies* 20 (1): 181–98.

Kihato, Caroline Wanjiku. n.d. "Community Resilience in the Twenty-First Century." A Response Paper Prepared for the Comparative Urban Studies Project, Woodrow Wilson International Center for Scholars and the Fetzer Institute Seminar. https://www.wilsoncenter.org/sites/default/files/media/documents/publication/Kihato.pdf

Kilcullen, D. 2006. "Twenty-Eight Chapters: Fundamentals of Company-Level Counterinsurgency." *Military Review* 86: 103–8.

Kirk-Greene, A. H. M., and C. Sassoon. 1956. *The Cattle People of Nigeria*. Oxford: Oxford University Press.

Kirsch, S. 2002. "Rumor and Other Narratives of Political Violence in West Papua." *Critique of Anthropology* 22 (1): 53–79.

Klaeger, G. 2009. "Religion on the Road: The Spiritual Experience of Road Travel in Ghana." In *The Speed of Change: Motor Vehicles and People in Africa, 1890–2000*, edited by J.-B., Gewald, S. Luning, and K. van Walraven, 212–31. Leiden: Brill.

Klem, Bart. 2011. "Islam, Politics and Violence in Eastern Sri Lanka." *Journal of Asian Studies* 70 (3): 730–53.

Klute, George. 1996. "The Corning State: Reactions of Nomadic Groups in the Western Sudan to the Expansion of Colonial Powers." *Nomadic Peoples* 38:49–71.

Klute, George. 2009. "Speed and Mobility in Contemporary 'Small' Wars." In *The Speed of Change: Motor Vehicles and People in Africa, 1890–2000*, edited by J.-B. Gewald, S. Luning, and K. van Walraven, 191–211. Leiden: Brill.

Knowles, C. 2011. "Cities on the Move: Navigating Urban Life." *City* 15 (2): 136–53.

Kopytoff, Igor. 1986. "The Cultural Biography of Things: Commodization as Process." In *The Social Life of Things: Commodities in Cultural Perspectives*, edited by A. Appadurai, 64–91. Cambridge: Cambridge University Press.

Kopytoff, Igor, ed. 1987. *The African Frontier: The Reproduction of Traditional African Societies*. Bloomington: Indiana University Press.

Kotef, Hagar. 2015. *Movement and the Ordering of Freedom: On Liberal Governances of Mobility*. Durham, NC: Duke University Press.

Kotef, Hagar, and Merav Amir. 2012i. "Between Imaginary Lines: Violence and Its Justifications at the Military Checkpoints in Occupied Palestine." *Theory, Culture and Society* 28 (1): 55–80.

Koultchoumi, B. 2014. "Boko Haram au lac Tchad: La vie socioéconomique de Kofia à l'epreuve de l'insécurité." In *Effets economiques et sociaux des attaques de Boko Haram dans l'Extrême-Nord du Cameroun*, edited by Saïbou Issa, 135–57. Cameroon: University of Marou.

Kowalewski, D. 1991. "Counterinsurgent Vigilantism and Public Response." *Sociological Perspectives* 34 (20): 127–44.

Kralova, J. 2015. "What Is Social Death?" *Contemporary Social Science* 10:235–48.

Krueger, A. B., and J. Maleckova. 2003. "Education, Poverty, and Terrorism: Is There a Causal Connection?" *Journal of Economic Perspectives* 17 (4): 119–44.

Kumar, Deepa. 2018. "See Something, Say Something: Security Rituals, Affect, and US Nationalism from the Cold War to the War on Terror." *Public Culture* 30 (1): 143–71.

Kusenbach, M. 2003. "Street Phenomenology: The Go-Along as Ethnographic Research Tool." *Ethnography* 4 (3): 455–85.

Kwaru, Mustapha Isah, and Ahmad Salkida. 2009. "Funeral Procession Tragedy—Police Shoot 17 in Maiduguri." *Daily Trust*, June 12.

Kyari, M. 2007. "Man and Environment in Borno: A Historical Account." *FUTY Journal of the Environment* 2 (1): 21–32.

Kyari, Mohammed. 2014. "The Message and Methods of Boko Haram." In *Boko Haram: Islamism, Politics, Security and the State in Nigeria*, edited by M.-A. Pérouse de Montclos, 9–32. Ibadan: IFRA.

Lahav, G. 2013. "Mobilizing against Mobility: Immigration Politics in a New Security World." In *Critical Mobilities*, edited by O. Soderstrom, S. Randeria, D. Ruedin, G. D'Amato, and F. Panese, 123–52. Lausanne: EPFL.

Langan, C. 2001. "Mobility Disability." *Public Culture* 13 (3): 459–84.

Langevang, T., and K. V. Gough. 2009. "Surviving through Movement: The Mobility of Urban Youth in Ghana." *Social and Cultural Geography* 10 (7): 741–56.

Larkin, Brian. 2005. Review of *Muslim Modernity in Postcolonial Nigeria: A Study of the Society for the Removal of Innovation and Reinstatement of Tradition*, by Ousmane Kane. *Journal of Religion* 85 (1): 178–79.

Larkin, Brian. 2008. *Signal and Noise: Media, Infrastructure, and Urban Culture in Nigeria*. Durham, NC: Duke University Press.

Larkin, Brian. 2013. "The Politics and Poetics of Infrastructure." *Annual Review of Anthropology* 42: 327–43.

Last, Murray. 1990. "The Power of Youth, Youth of Power." Paper presented at the International Conference, Paris, December 6–8.

Last, Murray. 2003. "Towards a Political History of Youth in Muslim Northern Nigeria, 1750–2000." https://www.ascleiden.nl/pdf/conference24042003-last.pdf

Last, Murray. 2005. "Towards a Political History of Youth in Muslim Northern Nigeria." In Abbink and van Kessel 2005, 37–54.

Last, Murray. 2012. "Nigeria's Boko Haram: The Anatomy of a Crisis." *E-International Relations*, January 30.

Last, Murray. 2014. "From Dissent to Dissidence: The Genesis and Development of Reformist Islamic Groups in Northern Nigeria." In *Sects and Social Disorder: Muslim Identities and Conflict in Northern Nigeria*, edited by Abdul Raufu Mustapha, 18–53. London: James Currey.

Lawuyi, Olatunde. 1988. "The World of a Yoruba Taxi Driver: An Interpretative Approach to Vehicle Slogans." *Africa* 58 (1): 1–13.

Lebbe, C. 2011. "The Ban-Opticon in the Schengen Area: The Ambivalent Meaning of Mobility." *Open!* May 9. https://onlineopen.org/the-ban-opticon-in-the-schengen-area

Lecocq, Baz, and Paul Schrijver. 2007. "The War on Terror in a Haze of Dust: Potholes and Pitfalls on the Saharan Front." *Journal of Contemporary African Studies* 25 (1): 141–66.

Lee, R. 2011. "'Death on the Move': Funerals, Entrepreneurs, and the Rural-Urban Nexus in South Africa." *Africa* 81 (2): 226–47.

Leese, Matthias, and Stef Wittendorp, eds. 2017. *Security/Mobility: The Politics of Movement*. Manchester: University of Manchester Press.

Lefebvre, Henri. 1976. *The Survival of Capitalism: Reproduction of the Relations of Production*. Translated by F. Bryant. London: Allison and Busby.

Lefebvre, Henri. 1991. *The Production of Space*. Translated by D. Nicholson-Smith. Oxford: Blackwell. Originally published as *La production de l'espace* (Paris: Éditions Anthropos, 1974).

Lewis, Oscar. 1966. "The Culture of Poverty." *Scientific American* 215 (4): 19–25.

Linebaugh, Peter, and Marcus Rediker. 2000. *The Many-Headed Hydra: Sailors, Slaves, Commoners and the Hidden History of the Revolutionary Atlantic*. Boston: Beacon.

Loimeier, Roman. 1997. *Islamic Reform and Political Change in Northern Nigeria*. Evanston, IL: Northwestern University Press.

Lombard, Louisa. 2013. "Navigational Tools for Central African Roadblocks." *Political and Legal Anthropology Review* 36 (1): 157–73.

Lombardo, N. 2017. "Controlling Mobility and Regulation in Urban Space: Muslim Pilgrims to Mecca in Colonial Bombay, 1880–1914." *International Journal of Urban and Regional Research* 40 (5): 983–99.

Lonsdale, John. 1986. "Political Accountability in African History." In *Political Domination in Africa: Reflections on the Limit of Power*, edited by Patrick Chabal, 126–57. Cambridge: Cambridge University Press.

Lorey, I. 2015. *State of Insecurity*. London: Verso.

Low, Setha, and Denise Laurence-Zuniga, eds. 2003. *The Anthropology of Space and Place: Locating Culture*. Oxford: Blackwell.

Lubeck, P. M. 1981. "Islamic Networks and Urban Capitalism: An Instance of Articulation from Northern Nigeria." *Cahiers d'études africaines* 21 (81–83): 67–78.

Lubeck, P. M. 1985. "Islamic Protest under Semi-Industrial Capitalism: 'Yan Tatsine Explained." *Africa* 55 (4): 369–89.

Lubeck, P. M. 2010. *Nigeria: Mapping the Shar'ia Movement*. Working paper, Center for Global, International and Regional Studies, University of California, Santa Cruz.

Lubeck, P. M. 2011. "Nigeria: Mapping a Shari'a Restorationist Movement." In *Shari'a Politics: Islamic Law and Society in the Modern World*, edited by R. Hefner, 244–79. Bloomington: Indiana University Press.

Lugalla, J. 1995. *Crisis Urbanization and Urban Poverty in Tanzania: A Study of Urban Poverty and Survival Politics*. Lanham, MD: University Press of America.

MacEachern, Scott. 2018. *Searching for Boko Haram: A History of Violence in Central Africa*. New York: Oxford University Press.

Macek, Steve. 2006. *Urban Nightmares: The Media, the Right, and the Moral Panic over the City*. Minneapolis: University of Minnesota Press.

Magrin, G., and M.-A. Pérouse de Montclos, eds. 2018. *Crisis and Development: The Lake Chad Region and Boko Haram*. Paris: Agence française de développement.

Mahmood, Saba. 2005. *Politics of Piety: The Islamic Revival and the Feminist Subject*. Princeton, NJ: Princeton University Press.

Mains, Daniel. 2011. *Hope Is Cut: Youth, Unemployment, and the Future in Urban Ethiopia*. Philadelphia: Temple University Press.

Mains, Daniel. 2012. "Blackouts and Progress: Privatization, Infrastructure, and a Developmentalist State in Jimma, Ethiopia." *Cultural Anthropology* 27 (1): 3–27.

Mains, Daniel, and E. Kinfu. 2016. "Making the City of Nations and Nationalities: The Politics of Ethnicity and Roads in Hawassa, Ethiopia." *Journal of Modern African Studies* 54 (4): 645–69.

Malkki, L. H. 1992. "National Geographic: The Rooting of Peoples and the Territorialization of National Identity among Scholars and Refugees." *Cultural Anthropology* 7 (1): 24–44.

Manderscheid, Katharina. 2009. "Integrating Space and Mobilities into the Analysis of Social Inequality." *Distinktion: Scandinavian Journal of Social Theory* 10 (1): 8–27.

Manderscheid, Katharina. 2014. "The Movement Problem, the Car and Future

Mobility Regimes: Automobility as Dispositif and Mode of Regulation." *Mobilities* 9 (4): 604–26.

Mann, Michael. 1984. *The Autonomous Power of the State*. Oxford: Blackwell.

Marama, N. 2015. "Suicide Bombers Kill 14 in Biu." *Vanguard*, February 17.

Marama, N. 2014. "22 Die in Two Separate Boko Haram Attacks in Borno." *Vanguard*, July 5.

Marama, N. 2019. "Boko Haram Abducts Several Passengers on Damaturu-Biu Road." *Vanguard*, February 1.

Marama, N. 2020. "Breaking: Again Boko Haram Attacks Borno Governor's Convoy." *Vanguard*, September 27.

Marfaings, Laurence, and Steffen Wippel, eds. 2004. *Les relations transsahariennes à l'epoque contemporaine: Un espace en constante mutation*. Paris: Karthala-ZMO.

Mark, M. 2015. "Yola: The City Where People Fleeing Boko Haram Outnumber 400,000 locals." *Guardian*, January 28.

Masco, Joseph. 2014. *The Theater of Operations: National Security Affect from the Cold War to the War on Terror*. Durham, NC: Duke University Press.

Mashal, M., and T. Shah. 2017. "Without a Motorcycle in Kandahar, 'You Are Like a Prisoner.'" *New York Times*, April 13.

Masquelier, Adeline. 2000. "Of Headhunters and Cannibals: Migrancy, Labor, and Consumption in the Mawri Imagination." *Cultural Anthropology* 15 (1): 84–126.

Masquelier, Adeline. 2001. "Behind the Dispensary's Prosperous Façade: Imagining the State in Rural Niger." *Public Culture* 13 (2): 267–91.

Masquelier, Adeline. 2002. "Road Mythologies: Space, Mobility, and the Historical Imagination in Postcolonial Niger." *American Ethnologist* 29 (4): 829–56.

Masquelier, Adeline. 2019. *Fada: Boredom and Belonging in Niger*. Chicago: University of Chicago Press.

Massey, D. 1984. "Introduction: Geography Matters." In *Geography Matters! A Reader*, edited by D. Massey and J. Allen, 1–11. Cambridge: Cambridge University Press.

Massey, D. 1993. "Power-Geometry and a Progressive Sense of Place," in *Mapping the Futures: Local Cultures, Global Change*, edited by J. Bird, B. Curtis, T. Putnam, G. Robertson, and L. Tickner, 59–69. New York: Routledge.

Massey, D. 1994. *Space, Place, and Gender*. Minneapolis: University of Minnesota Press.

Massey, D. 2005. *For Space*. London: SAGE.

Matfess, Hilary. 2017. *Women and the War on Boko Haram: Wives, Weapons, Witnesses*. London: Zed Books.

Maxwell, Andrew H. 1998. "Motorcyclists and Community in Post-Industrial Urban America." *Urban Anthropology and Studies of Cultural Systems and World Economic Development* 27 (3/4): 263–99.

Mbembe, Achille. 1992. "Provisional Notes on the Postcolony." *Africa* 62: 3–37.

Mbembe, Achille. 2001. *On the Postcolony*. Berkeley: University of California Press.

Mbembe, Achille. 2002a. "At the Edge of the World: Boundaries, Territoriality, and

Sovereignty in Africa." In *Beyond State Crisis: Postcolonial Africa and Post-Soviet Eurasia in Comparative Perspective*, edited by M. R. Bessinger and C. Young, 53–80. Washington DC: Woodrow Wilson Press.

Mbembe, Achille. 2002b. "On the Power of the False." *Public Culture* 14 (3): 629–41.

Mbembe, Achille. 2003. "Necropolitics." *Public Culture* 15 (1): 11–40.

Mbembe, Achille. 2018. "The Idea of a Borderless World." *Africa Is a Country*, November 11.

Mbembe, Achille, and Sarah Nuttall. 2004. "Writing the World from an African Metropolis." *Public Culture* 16 (3): 347–72.

Mbembe, Achille, and J. Roitman. 1995. "Figures of the Subject in Times of Crisis." *Public Culture* 7 (2): 323–52.

Mburza, A., and N. B. Umar. 2008. "Causes of Accidents among Commercial Motorcyclists (Achaba) in Borno State: Implications for Counseling." *Nigerian Journal of Guidance and Counseling* 13 (1): 171–79.

McCall, J. C. 2004. "Juju and Justice at the Movies: Vigilantes in Nigerian Popular Videos." *African Studies Review* 47 (3): 51–68.

McDonald, Matt. 2008. "Securitization and the Construction of Security." *European Journal of International Relations* 14: 563–87.

McDonald-Walker, S. 1998. "Fighting the Legacy: British Bikers in the 1990s." *Sociology* 32 (2): 379–96.

McDougall, James, and Judith Scheele, eds. 2012. *Saharan Frontiers: Space and Mobility in Northwest Africa*. Bloomington: Indiana University Press.

McIntyre, J. 2014. "Mobility in the Hausa Language." *Canadian Journal of African Studies* 48 (1): 101–17.

Meagher, Kate. 2007. "Hijacking Civil Society: The Inside Story of the Bakassi Boys Vigilante Group of South-Eastern Nigeria." *Journal of Modern African Studies* 45 (1): 89–115.

Meagher, Kate. 2012. "The Strength of Weak States? Non-State Security Forces and Hybrid Governance in Africa." *Development and Change* 43 (5): 1073–1101.

Meagher, Kate. 2013. "The Jobs Crisis behind Nigeria's Unrest." *Current History* 112 (754): 169–74.

Meagher, Kate. 2014. *Beyond Terror: Addressing the Boko Haram Challenge in Nigeria*. NOREF Policy Brief, Norwegian Peacebuilding Resource Centre, November.

Meagher, Kate. 2018. "Complementarity, Competition and Conflict: Informal Enterprise and Religious Conflict in Northern Nigeria." In *Creed and Grievance: Muslim-Christian Relations and Conflict Resolution in Northern Nigeria*, edited by A. R. Mustapha and D. Ehrhardt, 184–222. London: Boydell and Brewer.

Mele, M. L., and B. M. Bello. 2007. "Coaxing and Coercion in Roadblock Encounters on Nigerian Highways." *Discourse and Society* 18 (4): 437–52.

Menkhaus, K. 2006–7. "Governance without Government in Somalia: Spoilers, State Building, and the Politics of Coping." *International Security* 31 (3): 74–106.

Menoret, Pascal. 2014. *Joyriding in Riyadh: Oil, Urbanism, and Road Revolt*. Cambridge: Cambridge University Press.

Menoret, Pascal. 2019. "Learning from Riyadh: Automobility, Joyriding, and Politics." *Comparative Studies of South Asia, Africa and the Middle East* 39 (1): 131–42.

Mercy Corps. 2016. *"Motivations and Empty Promises": Voices of Former Boko Haram Combatants and Nigerian Youth*. April. Retrieved from https://www.mercycorps .org/research/motivations-and-empty-promises-voices-former-boko-haram -combatants-and-nigerian

Mercy Corps. 2017. *Northeast Nigeria Joint Livelihood and Market Recovery Assessment*. November 3.

Merriman, Peter, Rhys Jones, Colin Divall, Gijs Mom, Mimmi Sheller, and John Urry. 2013. "Mobility: Geographies, Histories, Sociologies." *Transfers: Interdisciplinary Journal of Mobility Studies* 3 (1): 147–65.

Merry, S. E. 2006. "Transnational Human Rights and Local Activism: Mapping the Middle." *American Anthropologist* 108 (1): 38–51.

Meyer, Birgit, and Peter Geschiere. 1999. Introduction to *Globalization and Identity: Dialectics of Flow and Closure*, edited by Birgit Meyer and Peter Geschiere, 1–16. Oxford: Blackwell.

Mill, John Stuart, 1986. *On Liberty*, edited S. Collini. Cambridge, UK: Cambridge University Press.

Mitchell, D. 2003. *The Right to the City: Social Justice and the Fight for Public Space*. New York: Guilford.

Mkandawire, Thandika. 2002. "The Terrible Toll of Postcolonial 'Rebel Movements' in Africa: Towards an Explanation of the Violence against the Peasantry." *Journal of Modern African Studies* 40 (2): 181–215.

Molz, J. G., and S. Gibson. 2007. *Mobilizing Hospitality: The Ethics of Social Relations in a Mobile World*. Aldershot: Ashgate.

Momoh, A. 2000. "Youth Culture and Area Boys in Lagos." In *Identity Transformation and Identity Politics under Structural Adjustment in Nigeria*, edited by A. Jega, 181–203. Uppsala: Nordic Africa Institute.

Monroe, K. 2009. *Mobile Citizens: Space, Power, and the Remaking of Beirut*. New Brunswick: Rutgers University Press.

Morley, David. 2000. *Home Territories: Media, Mobility and Identity*. London: Routledge.

Mountz, A. 2014. "Specters at the Port of Entry: Understanding State Mobilities through an Ontology of Exclusion." *Mobilities* 6 (3): 317–34.

Muhammad, M. 2015. "Boko Haram Insurgency Gnawing at Nigeria's Food Supply." *Bloomberg*, February 1.

Mukhtar, Y., and W. A. Gazali. 2000. "The Dynamics of Fish Trade in North-East Nigeria: A Case Study of Doron Baga." *Berichte des Sonderforschungsbereichs 268* (14): 83–91.

Münkler, H. 2005. *The New Wars*. Cambridge: Polity.

Murphy, William. 2003. "Military Patrimonialism and Child Soldier Clientalism in the Liberian and Sierra Leonean Civil Wars." *African Studies Review* 46 (2): 61–87.

Murtala, Zainab and, Abubakar Bashir. 2017. "State Governance and Coordination of the Humanitarian Response in North-East Nigeria." *Humanitarian Practice Network*, October.

Muscati, Samer, and Tirana Hassan. 2015. "Anatomy of a Boko Haram Massacre." *Foreign Policy*, June 10.

Mustapha, Abdul Raufu. 1991. "Structural Adjustment and Multiple Modes of Social Livelihood in Nigeria." In *Authoritarian Democracy and Adjustment: The Politics of Economic Reform in Africa*, edited by P. Gibbons, Y. Bangura, and A. Ofstad, 188–216. Uppsala: Nordic Africa Institute.

Mustapha, Abdul Raufu. 2012. "Boko Haram: Killing in God's Name." *Mail and Guardian*, April 5.

Mustapha, Abdul Raufu. 2014. "Synthesis Paper on Lessons Learned from Responses to Violent Conflicts in Nigeria since 2009: With Special Reference to Northern Nigeria." Nigeria Stability and Reconciliation Programme.

Mustapha, Abdul Raufu. 2015. "Overcoming Boko Haram." Paper presented at the Center of African Studies Seminar, University of Edinburgh, November 18.

Mustapha, Abdul Raufu, and M. Ismail. 2016. *Sharia Implementation in Northern Nigeria over 15 Years: The Case of Hisbah*. Policy Brief 2, Nigeria Stability and Reconciliation Programme.

Mustapha, Abdul Raufu, and Kate Meagher, eds. 2020. *Overcoming Boko Haram: Faith, Society and Islamic Radicalization in Northern Nigeria*. Woodbridge: James Currey.

Mutongi, K. 2006. "Thugs or Entrepreneurs? Perceptions of Matatu Operators in Nairobi, 1970 to the Present." *Africa* 76 (4): 549–68.

Nagarajan, C. 2017. "Gender Assessment of Northeastern Nigeria." Managing Conflict in North East Nigeria, June.

Nation. 2011. "Boko Haram Vows to Continue Bombings." September 28.

Nation. 2013. "Almajiris and the Scourge of Boko Haram." May 16.

National Working Group on Armed Violence. 2013. *The Violent Road: An Overview of Armed Violence in Nigeria*. http://aoav.org.uk/wp-content/uploads/2013/12/The-Violent-Road.pdf

Nayar, Pramod K. 2017. "Mobility and Insurgent Celebrityhood: The Case of Arundhati Roy." *Open Cultural Studies* 1:46–54.

Ndimele, M. 2016. "Civilian JTF Member Held for Borno IDP Camp Bomb Attack." *Legit*, March 21.

Nellemann, C., Henriksen, R., Pravettoni, R., Stewart, D., Kotsovou, M., Schlingemann, S.M, and Reitano, T., eds. 2018. "World Atlas of Illicit Flows: A RHIPTO-INTERPOL-GI Assessment." RHIPTO-Norwegian Center for Global Analyses, INTERPOL and the Global Initiative Against Transnational Organized Crime.

News24. 2020. "Nigeria Cops to Pay for Killing," April 14.

Newman, Edward. 2004. "The 'New Wars' Debate: A Historical Perspective Is Needed." *Security Dialogue* 35 (2): 173–89.

Newman, Paul. 2013. "The Etymology of Hausa *Boko*." Mega-Chad Research Network.

Newsdiary. 2020. "The Almajiri Crisis in the North: A Cry for Our Children by Nigerian Mothers." January 24.

Nieman Reports. 2014. "Missing the Story: What Nigeria's Kidnapping Crisis Says about Awareness versus Understanding." https://niemanreports.org/articles/missing-the-story/

Nigerian Bulletin. 2013. "Boko Haram: Borno Empowers 800 Youths for Civilian JTF." September 27.

Nigeria Research Network. 2013. *Almajirai in Northern Nigeria: A Collective Responsibility*. Policy Brief 2, February.

Nolte, Insa. 2007. "Ethnic Vigilantes and the State: The Oodua People's Congress in South-Western Nigeria." *International Relations* 21 (2): 217–35.

Nolte, Insa. 2008. "'Without Women, Nothing Can Succeed': Yoruba Women in the Oodua People's Congress (OPC), Nigeria." *Africa* 78 (1): 84–106.

Nordstrom, Carolyn. 2007. *Global Outlaws: Crime, Money, and Power in the Contemporary World*. Berkeley: University of California Press.

Norwood, F. 2009. *The Maintenance of Life: Preventing Social Death through Euthanasia Talk and End-of-Life Care; Lessons from the Netherlands*. Durham, NC: Carolina Academic Press.

Novoa, A. 2015. "Mobile Ethnography: Emergence, Techniques and Its Importance to Geography." *Human Geographies: Journal of Studies and Research in Human Geography* 9 (1): 97–107.

NSRP (Nigeria Stability and Reconciliation Programme). 2015. *Violent Radicalization in Northern Nigeria: Economy and Society*. Policy brief. https://www.qeh.ox.ac.uk/sites/www.odid.ox.ac.uk/files/onsa-pb05.pdf

NSRP. 2016. *Masculinities, Conflict and Violence*. Nigeria Country Report, Voices for Change. http://www.nsrp-nigeria.org/wp-content/uploads/2016/06/Masculinities-Conflict-and-Violence-web.pdf

Nugent, P. 2002. *Smugglers, Secessionists and Loyal Citizens on the Ghana–Togo Frontier*. Oxford: James Currey.

Nyamnjoh, Francis. 2012. "Fiction and Reality of Mobility in Africa." *Citizenship Studies* 17 (6–7): 653–80.

Nyers, P. 2004. "Introduction: What's Left of Citizenship?" *Citizenship Studies* 8 (3): 203–15.

Nwosu, Annie. 2019. "Abuja Residents Lament as FCT Bans Commercial Tricycles." *Daily Post*, November 12.

O'Brassill-Kulfan, Kristin. 2019. *Vagrants and Vagabonds: Poverty and Mobility in the Early American Republic*. New York: New York University Press.

Ochonu, Moses. 2006. "Conjoined to Empire: The Great Depression and Nigeria." *African Economic History* 34: 103–45.

Ochonu, Moses. 2009. *Colonial Meltdown: Northern Nigeria in the Great Depression*. Athens, OH: Ohio University Press.

Odua, C. 2018. "VOA Interview: Mother of Boko Haram Leader Speaks Out." *VOA*, June 14.

Odunsi, W. 2013. "Women Civilian JTF Emerges in Borno, Targets Female Boko Haram Members." *Daily Post*, August 24.

Odunsi, W. 2014. "Boko Haram Will Continue to Kill: Full Text of Shekau's Speech Declaring Caliphate in Northern Nigeria." *Daily Post*, August 25.

Odunsi, W. 2015. "Borno: Shettima Salutes Youth Volunteers for Repelling BH." *Daily Post*, February 2.

O'Grady, Siobhan. 2015. "Boko Haram Turns Robin Hood's Strategy on its Head." *Foreign Policy*, March 5.

Ogbu, A., H. Shittu, and M. Olugbode. 2011. "Nigeria: Sheriff Fumes—I Didn't Create Boko Haram." *This Day*, July 14.

Ogene, A. 2014. "Nigerian Vigilantes Aim to Rout Boko Haram." Al Jazeera, May 31.

Ohnmacht, Timo, Hanja Maksim, and Manfred Max Bergman. 2009. *Mobilities and Inequality: An Introduction*. London: Routledge.

Okeowo, A. 2015. "The People vs. Boko Haram." *New York Times*, January 28.

Okereke, E. 2014. "From Obscurity to Global Visibility: Periscoping Abubakar Shekau." *Counter Terrorist Trends and Analyses* 6 (10): 17–22.

Okoh, G. 2017. "Gunmen Kill 10 Members of Civilian Joint Task Force." *This Day*, January 16.

Okri, Ben. 1992. *The Famished Road*. London: Jonathan Cape.

Ola, T. 2009. "Bomb Blast Kills One in Borno . . . as Police Burst Islamic Sect Offensive." *Sun*, July 26.

Olaleye, Olawale. 2019. "NYT: Boko Haram Now Stronger, Well Armed with Sophisticated Drones." *This Day*, September 15.

Olofson, H. 1976. "*Yawon Dandi*: A Hausa Category of Migration." *Africa* 6 (1): 66–79.

Olugbode, M. 2018. "Nigeria: Military Reopens Maiduguri–Bama–Banki Road." *This Day*, March 25.

Olvera, L. D., A. Guezere, D. Plat, and P. Pochet. 2016. "Earning a Living, but at What Price? Being a Motorcycle Taxi Driver in a Sub-Saharan African City." *Journal of Transport Geography* 55: 165–74.

Omonobi, K., B. Agande, and N. Marama. 2013. "Scores Feared Dead as Boko Haram Attacks Maiduguri Airforce Base." *Vanguard*, December 3.

Onani, E., and B. Ngwakwe. 2014. "Boko Haram Uses Cows for Bombings." *New Telegraph*, December 5.

Onuoha, F. C. 2013. "Porous Borders and Boko Haram's Arms Smuggling Operations in Nigeria." *Aljazeera Center for Studies*, September 8.

Onuoha, F. C. 2014. "Boko Haram and the Evolving Salafi Jihadist Threat in Nigeria." In *Boko Haram: Islamism, Politics, Security and the State in Nigeria*, edited by M.-A. Pérouse de Montclos, 151–91. Ibadan: IFRA.

Oppong, Y. P. A. 2017. *Moving Through and Passing On: Fulani Mobility, Survival and Identity in Ghana*. London: Routledge.

Osun Defender. 2012. "Lagos–Badagry Expressway: A 'Boko Haram' in the West." October 25.

Oteng-Ababio, Martin, and Ernest Agyemang. 2015. "The *Okada* War in Urban Ghana: A Polemic Issue or Policy Mismatch." *African Studies Quarterly* 15 (4): 25–44.

Owen, Olly. 2012. "The Nigeria Police Force: An Institutional Ethnography." PhD diss., University of Oxford.

Owen, Olly. 2017. "Risk and Motivation in Police Work in Nigeria." In *Police in Africa: The Street Level*, edited by Jan Beek, Micro Göpfert, Olly Owen, and Jonny Steinberg, 149–69. Oxford: Oxford University Press.

Öz, Özlem, and M. Eder. 2018. "'Problem Spaces' and Struggle over the Right to the City: Challenges of Living Differentially in a Gentrifying Istanbul Neighborhood." *International Journal of Urban and Regional Research* 42 (6): 1030–47.

Packer, Jeremy. 2006. "Becoming Bombs: Mobilizing Mobility in the War on Terror." *Cultural Studies* 20 (4–5): 378–99.

Packer, Jeremy. 2008. *Mobility without Mayhem: Safety, Cars, and Citizenship*. Durham, NC: Duke University Press.

Paden, John. 2012. *Postelection Conflict Management in Nigeria: The Challenges of National Unity*. Arlington, VA: George Mason University Press.

Paden, John. 2008. *Faith and Politics in Nigeria*. Washington, DC: United States Institute of Peace Press.

Pahl, Katrin. 2013. *Tropes of Transport*. Evanston, IL: Northwestern University Press.

Pallitto, Robert, and Josiah Heyman. 2008. "Theorizing Cross-Border Mobility: Surveillance, Security and Identity." *Surveillance and Society* 5 (3): 315–33.

Paquette, D., and I. Alfa. 2019. "Suspected Boko Haram Fighters Kill 65 in Attack on Funeral in Nigeria." *Washington Post*, July 29.

Pardo, Italo. 2004. "Introduction: Corruption, Morality and the Law." In *Between Morality and the Law: Corruption, Anthropology and Comparative Society*, edited by Italo Pardo, 1–17. London: Routledge.

Parfitt, T. 2009. "Are the Third World Poor *Homines Sacri*? Biopolitics, Sovereignty, and Development." *Alternatives* 34: 41–58.

Parkinson, J., and G. Akingbule. 2020. "Outside Nigeria's 'Green Zone,' Jihadists Rule the Road." *Wall Street Journal*, November 19.

Parry, Benita. 2004. "The Institutionalization of Postcolonial Studies." In *The Cambridge Companion to Postcolonial Literary Studies*, edited by N. Lazarus, 66-80. Cambridge: Cambridge University Press.

Patterson, Orlando. 1982. *Slavery and Social Death: A Comparative Study*. Cambridge, MA: Harvard University Press.

Peic, Goran. 2014. "Civilian Defense Forces, State Capacity, and Government

Victory in Counterinsurgency Wars." *Studies in Conflict and Terrorism* 37 (2): 162–84.

Peluso, Nancy Lee, and Michael Watts. 2001. eds. *Violent Environments*. Ithaca, NY: Cornell University Press.

Pérouse de Montclos, M.-A. 2014. *Nigeria's Interminable Insurgency: Addressing the Boko Haram Crisis*. Research paper, Chatham House, September.

Pérouse de Montclos, M.-A. 2016. "A Sectarian Jihad in Nigeria: The Case of Boko Haram." *Small Wars and Insurgencies* 27 (5): 878–95.

Perry, D. 2005. "Wolof Women, Economic Liberalization, and the Crisis of Masculinity in Rural Senegal." *Ethnology* 44 (3): 207–26.

Peters, K., and P. Richards. 1998. "Why We Fight: Voices of Youth Combatants in Sierra Leone." *Africa* 68 (2): 183–210.

Pham, Peter. 2006. "In Nigeria False Prophets Are Real Problems." Foundation for Defense of Democracies, October 12.

Pickering, Sharon, and Leanne Weber. 2006. "Borders, Mobility and Technologies of Control." In *Borders, Mobility and Technologies of Control*, edited by Sharon Pickering and Leanne Weber, 1–19. Dordrecht: Springer.

Pieterse, Edgar. 2005. "At the Limits of Possibility: Working Notes on a Relational Model of Urban Politics." In *Urban Africa: Changing Contours of Survival in the City*, edited by A. Simone and A. Abouhani, 138–68. Dakar: CODESRIA.

Pieterse, Edgar. 2010. "Cityness and African Urban Development." *Urban Forum* 21:205–19.

Pillay, A. 2018. "Harnessing Gender Transformative Opportunities within Humanitarian Crises: A Field Note from North-East Nigeria." ACCORD, September 18. https://www.accord.org.za/conflict-trends/harnessing-gender-transformative-opportunities-within-humanitarian-crises/.

Polk, Merritt. 1998. "Swedish Men and Women's Mobility Patterns: Issues of Social Equity and Ecological Sustainability." In *Women's Travel Issues: Proceedings from the Second National Conference*, 187–211. Washington DC: US Department of Transportation. https://www.fhwa.dot.gov/ohim/womens/chap11.pdf

Pooley, Colin. 2017. "Connecting Historical Studies of Transport, Mobility and Migration." *Journal of Transport History* 38 (2): 251–59.

Porter, Gina. 1995. "The Impact of Road Construction on Women's Trade in Rural Nigeria." *Journal of Transport Geography* 3: 3–14.

Porter, Gina. 2002. "Living in a Walking World: Rural Mobility and Social Equity Issues in Sub-Saharan Africa." *World Development* 30 (2): 285–300.

Porter, Gina. 2012. "Reflections on a Century of Road Transport Developments in West Africa and Their (Gendered) Impacts on the Rural Poor." *EchoGeo* 20: 1–14.

Porter, Gina, K. Blaufuss, and F. O. Acheampong. 2007. "Youth, Mobility and Rural Livelihoods in Sub-Saharan Africa: Perspectives from Ghana and Nigeria." *Africa Insight* 37 (3): 420–31.

Porter, Gina, K. Hampshire, A. Abane, A. Munthali, A. Robson, and M. Mashiri.

2017. *Young People's Daily Mobilities in Sub-Saharan Africa: Moving Young Lives.* New York: Palgrave Macmillan.

Porter, Gina, K. Hampshire, M. Mashiri, S. Dube, and G. Maponya. 2010. "'Youthscapes' and Escapes in Rural Africa: Education, Mobility and Livelihood Trajectories for Young People in Eastern Cape, South Africa." *Journal of International Development* 22 (8): 1090–1101.

Pratten, David. 2008. "The Politics of Protection: Perspectives on Vigilantism in Nigeria." *Africa* 78 (1): 1–15.

Pratten, David. 2013. "The Precariousness of Prebendalism." In *Democracy and Prebendalism in Nigeria: Critical Interpretations,* edited by W. Adebanwi and E. Obadare, 243–58. New York: Palgrave Macmillan.

Premium Times. 2014. "How the Seed of Boko Haram Was Sown When I Was a Kid—Ex-Minister Nweke." May 1.

Premium Times. 2017. "Dasukigate: How 1.4 Billion was Allegedly Diverted for National Prayers—Witness." October 19.

Premium Times. 2018. "10 Killed as Soldiers Battle Horse-Riding Boko Haram Fighters—Official." June 3.

Press TV. 2015. "Nigeria Imposes Horse Ban to Stop Boko Haram's Attacks." September 8.

Prothero, M., and M. Chapman, eds. 1985. *Circulation in Third World Countries.* London: Routledge.

Pruitt Dean, and Kim Sung Hee. 2004. *Social Conflict: Escalation, Stalemate, and Settlement.* New York: McGraw-Hill.

Puar, J., L. Berlant, J. Butler, B. Cvejić, L. Lorey, and A. Vujanović. 2012. "Precarity Talk: A Virtual Roundtable with Lauren Berlant, Judith Butler, Bojana Cvejić, Isabell Lorey, Jasbir Puar, and Ana Vujanović." *TDR: The Drama Review* 56 (4): 163–77.

Public Library of US Diplomacy. 2009a. "Nigeria: Borno State Residents Not Yet Recovered from Boko Haram Violence." November 4. https://wikileaks.org/plusd/cables/09ABUJA2014_a.html

Public Library of US Diplomacy. 2009b. "Nigeria: Muslim and Christian Leaders Criticize Boko Haram and GON, Citing Poverty as a Key Issue." August 4. https://wikileaks.org/plusd/cables/09ABUJA1422_a.html

Public Library of US Diplomacy. 2009c. "Nigerian Military Combing for Extremists, Boko Haram Deputy Arrested." July 30. https://wikileaks.org/plusd/cables/09ABUJA1398_a.html

Public Library of US Diplomacy. 2009d. "Nigeria: Yakubu Gowon Discusses Boko Haram, Electoral Reform, PFIZER." August 5. https://wikileaks.org/plusd/cables/09ABUJA1435_a.html

Punch. 2016. "Restriction: Tricycle Operators Protest in Abuja as FCTA Begins Mass Arrest." November 11.

Purvis, Trevor, and Alan Hunt. 1993. "Discourse, Ideology, Discourse, Ideology, Discourse, Ideology . . ." *British Journal of Sociology* 44 (3): 473–99.

Raeymaekers, T. 2010. "Protection for Sale: War and the Transformation of Regulation on the Congo-Ugandan Border." *Development and Change* 41 (4): 563–87.

Rain, David. 1999. *Eaters of the Dry Season: Circular Labor Migration in the West African Sahel.* Boulder, CO: Westview.

Rana, Subir. 2018. "The Micropolitics and Metaphysics of Mobility and Nomadism: A Comparative Study of Rahul Sankrityayan's *Ghumakkar Sastra* and Gilles Deleuze/Felix Guattari's 'Nomadology.'" In *Social Theory and Asian Dialogues: Cultivating Planetary Conversations,* edited by Giri Ananta Kumar, 249–70. London: Palgrave Macmillan.

Ranciere, J. 1999. *Disagreement: Politics and Philosophy.* Minneapolis: University of Minneapolis Press.

Reeves, Joshua. 2012. "If You See Something, Say Something: Lateral Surveillance and the Uses of Responsibility." *Surveillance and Society* 10 (3–4): 235–48.

Renne, E. P. 2014. "Parallel Dilemmas: Polio Transmission and Political Violence in Northern Nigeria." *Africa* 84 (3): 466–86.

Retaille, Denis, and Olivier Walther. 2013. "Conceptualizing the Mobility of Space through the Malian Conflict." *Annales de Geographie* 694 (6): 595–618.

Richards, P. 1996. *Fighting for the Rain Forest: War, Youth, and Resources in Sierra Leone.* London: James Currey.

Rijke-Epstein, Tasha. 2018. "Neglect as Effacement: The Multiple Lives of the Jardin Ralaimongo, Mahajanga, Madagascar." *Africa* 88 (2): 352–84.

Rizzo, M. 2011. "'Life Is War': Informal Transport Workers and Neoliberalism in Tanzania 1998–2009." *Development and Change* 42 (5): 1179–1206.

Rockefeller, Stuart Alexander. 2011. "Flow." *Current Anthropology* 52 (4): 557–78.

Rodgers, D. 2007. "When Vigilantes Turn Bad: Gangs, Violence, and Social Change in Urban Nicaragua." In *Global Vigilantes,* edited by D. Pratten and A. Sen, 349–30. London: Hurst.

Rodgers, D. 2012. "Haussmannization in the Tropics: Abject Urbanism and Infrastructural Violence in Nicaragua." *Ethnography* 13 (4): 413–38.

Roitman, J. 2004a. "Power Is Not Sovereign: The Pluralisation of Economic Regulatory Authority in the Chad Basin." In *Privatising the State,* edited by Béatrice Hibou, 120–46. London: Hurst.

Roitman, J. 2004b. "The Reconstitution of State Power in the Chad Basin." In Das and Poole 2004, 191–224.

Roitman, J. 2006. "The Ethics of Illegality in the Chad Basin." In Comaroff and Comaroff 2006, 247–72. Chicago: University of Chicago Press.

Rosin, R. Thomas. 2000. "Wind, Traffic and Dust: The Recycling of Wastes." *Contributions to Indian Sociology* 33 (3): 361–408.

Rossi, Benedetta. 2015. "Kinetocracy: The Government of Mobility at the Desert's Edge." In *Mobility Makes States: Migration and Power in Africa,* edited by J. Quirk and D. Vigneswaran, 223–56. Philadelphia: University of Pennsylvania Press.

Rubin, Joshua D., S. Fioratta, and J. W. Paller. 2019. "Ethnographies of Emergence: Everyday Politics and Their Origins across Africa." *Africa* 89 (3): 429–36.

Rupesinghe, N., and M. Boas. 2019. *Local Drivers of Violent Extremism in Central Mali*. Norwegian Institute of International Affairs, September 30.

Sageman, Marc. 2008. *Leaderless Jihad: Terror Networks in the Twenty-First Century*. Philadelphia: University of Pennsylvania Press.

Sager, T. 2006. "Freedom as Mobility: Implications of the Distinction between Actual and Potential Travelling." *Mobilities* 1 (3): 465–88.

Saïbou I. 2010. *Les coupeurs de route: Histoire du banditisme rural et transfrontalier dans le bassin du lac Tchad*. Paris: Karthala.

Salaudeen, A. 2018. "The Lagos Motorbike Taxi Drivers Who Survived Boko Haram." *OkayAfrica*, June 25.

Salazar, Noel B., and Alan Smart. 2011. "Anthropological Takes on (Im)mobility." *Identities* 18 (6): i–ix.

Samaila, A. 2015. "Cross-Border Trade in Fairly Used Automobiles (Tokumbo): A Study of the Nigeria North-West Border c. 1973–2013." PhD diss.

Sani, U., and D. Ehrhardt. 2014. "Pathways to Radicalization: Life Histories of JAS Members." Paper presented at the Nigeria Stability and Reconciliation Programme's conference "Radicalization, Counter-Radicalization and De-Radicalization in Nigeria," Abuja, September 14–16.

Sawab, I. 2019. "Boko Haram: Travelers without I.D. Cards forced to part with N200." *Daily Trust*, September 24.

Scheele, Judith. 2012. *Smugglers and Saints of the Sahara: Regional Connectivity in the Twentieth Century*. Cambridge: Cambridge University Press.

Scheper-Hughes, Nancy. 1992. *Death without Weeping: The Violence of Everyday Life in Brazil*. Berkeley: University of California Press.

Schiller, N. G., and Noel B. Salazar. 2013. "Regimes of Mobility across the Globe." *Journal of Ethnic and Migration Studies* 39 (2): 183–200.

Schouten, Peer. 2019. "Roadblock Politics in Central Africa." *Environment and Planning D: Society and Space* 37 (5): 924–41.

Schouten, Peer. 2021. *Roadblock Politics: The Origins of Violence in Central Africa*. Cambridge: Cambridge University Press.

Schouten, Peer, and Soleil-Parfait Kalessopo. 2017. "The Politics of Pillage: The Political Economy of Roadblocks in the Central African Republic." Antwerp: Danish Institute for International Studies.

Scott, James. C. 1972. "Patron-Client Politics and Political Change in Southeast Asia." *American Political Science Review* 66 (1): 91–113.

Scott, James C. 1998. *Seeing Like a State: How Certain Schemes to Improve the Human Condition Have Failed*. New Haven, CT: Yale University Press.

Seignobos, Christian. 2015. "Boko Haram and Lake Chad: An Extension or a Sanctuary?" *Afrique Contemporaine* 255 (3): 89–114.

Seignobos, Christian. 2016. "The Chronicle of a Siege: Boko Haram at Lake Chad, 2015–2016." *Afrique Contemporaine* 259 (3): 139–67.

Senellart, M., ed. 2004. *The Birth of Biopolitics: Lectures at the College de France, 1978–79*. Translated by Graham Burchell. New York: Palgrave Macmillan.

Senema Productions. 2017. "After the Siege: Borno State Road to Recovery, Episode 1." https://www.youtube.com/watch?v=baLbaOxyREA

Sesay, Isha. 2019. *Beneath the Tamarind Tree: A Story of Courage, Family, and the Lost Schoolgirls of Boko Haram*. New York: HarperCollins.

SEU (Social Exclusion Unit). 2003. *Making the Connections: Final Report on Transport and Social Exclusion*. London: SEU.

Shagari, A. S., and J. Boyd. 1978. *Uthman Dan Fodio: The Theory and Practice of His Leadership*. Lagos: Islamic Publications Bureau.

Shapria, H. 2013. "The Border: Infrastructure of the Global." *Public Culture* 25 (2): 249–60.

Shaw, Jon, and M. Hesse. 2010. "Transport, Geography and the 'New' Mobilities." *Transactions of the Institute of British Geographers* 35 (3): 305–12.

Shaw, Jon, and James Sidaway. 2011. "Making Links: On (Re)engaging with Transport and Transport Geography." *Progress in Human Geography* 35 (4): 502–20.

Shaw, Rosalind. 2002. *Memories of the Slave Trade: Ritual and the Historical Imagination in Sierra Leone*. Chicago: University of Chicago Press.

Shell, Jacob. 2015. *Transport and Revolt: Pigeons, Mules, Canals, and the Vanishing Geographies of Subversive Mobility*. Cambridge, MA: MIT Press.

Sheller, Mimi. 2017. "From Spatial Turn to Mobilities Turn." *Current Sociology* 65 (4): 623–29.

Sheller, Mimi. 2018a. "Caribbean Constellations and Mobility Justice." In *Reshaping Global Dynamics of the Caribbean*, edited by A. Bandau, A. Bruske, and N. Ueckmann, 31–46. Heidelberg: Heidelberg University Publishing.

Sheller, Mimi. 2018b. *Mobility Justice: The Politics of Movement in an Age of Extremes*. Brooklyn: Verso.

Sheller, Mimi. 2018c. "Moving Towards Justice." *Verso*, October 31.

Sheller, Mimi, and John Urry. 2006. "The New Mobilities Paradigm." *Environment and Planning A: Economy and Space* 38 (2): 207–26.

Special Inspector General for Afghanistan Reconstruction (SIGAR). 2014. "Quarterly Report to the United States Congress." April 30. http://cdn.govexec.com/media/gbc/docs/pdfs_edit/april2014qr.pdf

Silke, Andrew. 2006. "The Rise of Suicide Politics, Conflict, and Terrorism." *Terrorism and Political Violence* 18 (1): 35–46.

Silke, Andrew. 2008. "Holy Warriors: Exploring the Psychological Processes of Jihadi Radicalization." *European Journal of Criminology* 5 (1): 99–123.

Silke, Andrew, ed. 2011. *The Psychology of Counter-Terrorism*. London: Routledge.

Silvey, Rachel. 2000. "Stigmatized Spaces: Gender and Mobility under Crisis in South Sulawesi, Indonesia." *Gender, Place and Culture: A Journal of Feminist Geography* 7 (2): 143–61.

Simone, AbdouMaliq. 2004. "People as Infrastructure: Intersecting Fragments in Johannesburg," *Public Culture* 16 (3): 407–29.

Sirkeci, I., J. H. Cohen, and P. Yazgan. 2016. *Conflict, Insecurity and Mobility*. London: Transnational Press.

Sivan, E. 1985. *Radical Islam: Medieval Theology and Modern Politics*. New Haven, CT: Yale University Press.

Skeggs, B. 2004. *Class, Self, Culture*. London: Routledge.

Skinner, R. T. 2015. *Bamako Sounds: The Afropolitan Ethics of Malian Music*. Minneapolis: University of Minnesota Press.

Smith, Daniel J. 2004. "The Bakassi Boys: Vigilantism, Violence, and Political Imagination in Nigeria." *Cultural Anthropology* 19 (3): 429–55.

Smith, M. G. 1964. "Historical and Cultural Conditions of Political Corruption among the Hausa." *Comparative Studies in Society and History* 6 (2): 164–94.

Somaiya, R. 2010. "Why Rebel Groups Love the Toyota Hilux." *Newsweek*, October 14.

Sommers, Marc. 2012. *Stuck: Rwandan Youth and the Struggle for Adulthood*. Athens: University of Georgia Press.

Sopranzetti, C. 2014. "Owners of the Map: Mobility and Mobilization among Motorcycle Taxi Drivers in Bangkok." *City and Society* 26 (1): 120–43.

Soyinka, Wole. 1965. *The Road*. London: Oxford University Press.

Sparke, M. 2007. "Geopolitical Fears, Geoeconomic Hopes, and the Responsibilities of Geography." *Annals of the Association of American Geographers* 97 (2): 338–49.

Spelman, Elizabeth. 1998. "Fruits of Sorrow: Framing Our Attention to Suffering." *Hypatia* 13 (2): 162–64.

Spikerman, T. 2001. *Shakespeare's Political Realism: The English History Plays*. Albany: State University of New York Press.

Spinney, J. 2006. "A Place of Sense: A Kinaesthetic Ethnography of Cyclists on Mont Ventoux." *Environment and Planning D: Society and Space* 24 (5): 709–32.

Standing, G. 2011. *The Precariat: The New Dangerous Class*. London: Palgrave Macmillan.

Stasik, Michael, and Sidy Cissoko. 2018. Introduction to "Bus Stations in Africa." Special issue, *Africa Today* 65 (2): vii–xxiv.

Stasiulis, Daiva. 1999. "Relational Positionalities of Nationalisms, Racisms, and Feminisms." In *Between Woman and Nation: Nationalisms, Transnational Feminisms, and the State*, edited by Caren Kaplan, Norma Alarcón, and Minoo Moallem, 182–218. Durham, NC: Duke University Press.

Steedly, Mary Margaret. 1993. *Hanging without a Rope: Narrative Experience in Colonial and Postcolonial Karoland*. Princeton Studies in Culture/Power/History. Princeton, NJ: Princeton University Press.

Steedly, Mary Margaret. 1999. "The State of Culture Theory in the Anthropology of Southeast Asia." *Annual Review of Anthropology* 28:431–54.

Stevenson, L. 2007. "Anthropology in the Margins of the State." *Political and Legal Anthropology Review* 30 (1): 140–44.

Stewart, Scott. 2014. "The Difference between Terrorism and Insurgency." *Stratfor*, 26 June.

Strachan, H., and S. Scheipers. 2011. *The Changing Character of War*. Oxford: Oxford University Press.

Strochlic, A. 2014. "Nigeria's Do-It-Yourself Boko Haram Busters." *Daily Beast*, May 16.

Swindell, K., and M. A. Iliya. 2012. "Time and Timing, Work and Action: Aspects of Rural Livelihoods in Northwest Nigeria." *Canadian Journal of African Studies* 46 (2): 233–50.

Swindell, K., M. A. Iliya, and A. B. Mamman. 1999. "Making a Profit, Making a Living: Commercial Food Farming and Urban Hinterlands in North-West Nigeria." *Africa* 69 (3): 386–403.

Tamuno, T. N. 1991. *Peace and Violence in Nigeria: Conflict Resolution in Society and the State*. Ibadan: Panel on Nigeria since Independence History Project, University of Ibadan Secretariat.

This Day. 2016. "Vigilantes Ponder Future after Fighting Boko Haram." July 7.

Thompson, H. 1966. *Hell's Angels*. New York: Ballantine Books.

Thompson, J. B. 1991. Introduction to *Language and Symbolic Power*, translated by G. Raymond and M. Adamson, 1–31. Cambridge, MA: Harvard University Press.

Thurston, Alex. 2018. *Boko Haram: The History of an African Jihadist Movement*. Princeton, NJ: Princeton University Press.

Tijani, K. 1980. "Political and Administrative Developments in Pre-colonial Borno." PhD diss., Ahmadu Bello University, Zaria.

Tollefsen, A. F., and H. Buhaug. 2015. "Insurgency and Inaccessibility." *International Studies Review* 17 (1): 6–25.

Tonkiss, F. 1998. "Analyzing Discourse." In *Researching Society and Culture*, edited by C. Seale, 405–24. London: SAGE.

Trapido, J. 2015. "Africa's Leaky Giant." *New Left Review* 93:5–42.

Truitt, A. 2008. "On the Back of a Motorbike: Middle-Class Mobility in Ho Chi Minh City, Vietnam." *American Ethnologist* 35 (1): 3–19.

Tsing, Anna L. 1994. "From the Margins." *Cultural Anthropology* 9 (3): 279–97.

Tsing, Anna L. 2005. *Friction: An Ethnography of Global Connection*. Princeton, NJ: Princeton University Press.

Tukur, Sani. 2014. "Ex-Gov Sheriff, Accused of Sponsoring Boko Haram, Ready to Face Justice," *Premium Times*, September 3.

Turner, Joe. 2016. "(En)gendering the Political: Citizenship from Marginal Spaces." *Citizenship Studies* 20 (2): 141–55.

Turner, Jennifer, and Kimberley Peters. 2017. *Carceral Mobilities: Interrogating Movement in Incarceration*. Abingdon: Routledge.

Udo, R. K. 1970. *Geographical Regions of Nigeria*. Berkeley: University of California Press.

Umar, H. 2015. "Boko Haram Seen Striking on Horses." Associated Press, September 2.

Umar, L. Y. 2014. "The Role of the Civilian JTF in Tackling Boko Haram Problems in Borno." *Al-Mahram: International Journal of Center for Trans-Saharan Studies*, vi. http://journals.unimaid.edu.ng/index.php/almahram/issue/view/6

UNDP (United Nations Development Programme). 2009. *Human Development Report 2009: Overcoming Barriers; Human Mobility and Development*. New York: UNDP.

UNDP. 2017. "Journey of Young Africans into Violent Extremism Marked by Poverty and Deprivation." September 7.

UNDP. 2018. *Journey to Extremism in Africa*. September 9.

UNFAO (Food and Agriculture Association of the United Nations). 2009. "Lake Chad Facing Humanitarian Disaster." October 15.

United Nations. 2015. "Violations and Abuses Committed by Boko Haram and the Impact on Human Rights in the Countries Affected." Report of the United Nations High Commissioner for Human Rights, December 9.United Nations. 2016. *The United Nations Motorcycle Helmet Study*. New York: United Nations.

United Nations. 2017. "Borno State LGA's: Baseline Information for Planners." June.

United States Interstate Commerce Commission. 1937. *Exercises Commemorating the Fifty Years' Service of the Interstate Commerce Commission, April 1, 1937, Departmental Auditorium, Washington DC*. Washington, DC: US Government Printing Office.

UN News. 2016. "'Nigeria Faces Worst Humanitarian Crisis on the African Continent,' Warns Senior UN Relief Official." October 26.

UN Security Council. 2017. "Report of the Secretary-General on Children and Armed Conflict in Nigeria." April 10.

Ureta, S. 2008. "To Move or Not to Move? Social Exclusion, Accessibility, and Daily Mobility of Low-Income Population in Santiago, Chile." *Mobilities* 3 (2): 269–89.

Urry, John. 1981. "Localities, Regions and Social Class." *International Journal of Urban and Regional Research* 5 (4): 455–73.

Urry, John. 2002. "The Global Complexities of September 11th." *Theory, Culture and Society* 19 (4): 57–69.

Urry, John. 2003. *Global Complexity*. Cambridge: Polity.

Urry, John. 2004. "The 'System' of Automobility." *Theory, Culture and Society* 21 (4–5): 25–39.

Urry, John. 2007. *Mobilities*. Cambridge: Polity.

US Department of Defense. 2004. *Military Transformation: A Strategic Approach*. Washington, DC: Office of the Secretary of Defense. https://www.hsdl.org/?abstract&did=446223

van Dijk, Rijk, Mirjam de Bruijn, and Jan-Bart Gewald. 2007. "Social and Historical Trajectories of Agency in Africa: An Introduction." In *Strength beyond Structure: Social and Historical Trajectories of Agency in Africa*, edited by Mirjam de Bruijn, Rijk van Dijk, and Jan-Bart Gewald, 1–15. Leiden: Brill.

van Dijk, Han, D. W. J. Foeken, and K. van Til. 2001. "Population Mobility in Africa: An Overview." In de Bruijn, Foeken, and van Dijk 2001, 9–26.

Vanguard. 2009. "Boko Haram Resurrects, Declares Total Jihad." August 14. http://www.vanguardngr.com/2009/08/boko-haram-ressurects-declares-total-jihad/

Vanguard. 2013. "Civilian JTF vs. Boko Haram: Concern, Hope in Embattled Restive City." July 30.

Vanguard. 2014a. "May Day Tragedy: Scores Die in Fresh Abuja Bombing." May 1.

Vanguard. 2014b. "My Boko Haram Story, by Ali Modu Sheriff, ex Borno Gov." September 3.

Van Metre, L. 2019. *From Self-Defense to Vigilantism: A Typology of Framework of Community-Based Armed Groups.* Community Based Armed Groups Series, RESOLVE Network, October.

Vaughan, Olufemi. 2016. *Religion and the Making of Nigeria.* Durham, NC: Duke University Press.

Vigh, Henrik. 2006. *Navigating Terrains of War: Youth and Soldiering in Guinea Bissau.* New York: Berghahn Books.

Vigh, Henrik. 2008. "Crisis and Chronicity: Anthropological Perspectives on Continuous Conflict and Decline." *Ethnos: Journal of Anthropology* 73 (1): 5–24.

Vigh, Henrik. 2009. "Motion Squared: A Second Look at the Concept of Social Navigation." *Anthropological Theory* 9 (4): 419–38.

Vigh, Henrik. 2010. "Youth Mobilisation as Social Navigation: Reflections on the Concept of Dubriagem." *Cadernos de Estudos Africanos* 18/19:140–64.

Vigneswaran, Darshan, and Joel Quirk, eds. 2015. *Mobility Makes States: Migration and Power in Africa.* Philadelphia: University of Pennsylvania Press.

Virilio, P. 1986. *Speed and Politics: An Essay on Dromology.* Translated by Mark Polizzotti. New York: Semiotext(e).

VOA (Voice of America). 2014. "Alleged Boko Haram Gunmen Kill 45 Nigerian Soldiers, Officers." May 27.

Vogt, W. A. 2018. *Lives in Transit: Violence and Intimacy on the Migrant Journey.* Oakland: University of California Press.

Wacquant, Loïc. 2007. *Urban Outcasts: A Comparative Sociology of Advanced Marginality.* Cambridge: Polity.

Walker, Andrew. 2012. *What Is Boko Haram?* Special report, United States Institute of Peace, June.

Walker, Andrew. 2016. *"Eat the Heart of the Infidel": The Harrowing of Nigeria and the Rise of Boko Haram.* London: Hurst.

Walter, Laura. 2012. "Michigan Repeals Motorcycle Helmet Law." *EHS Today,* June 1.

Walters, W. 2006. "Borders/Control." *European Journal of Social Theory* 9 (2): 187–203.

Walters, W. 2015. "Migration, Vehicles, and Politics: Three Theses on Viapolitics." *European Journal of Social Theory* 18 (4): 469–88.

Walther, Olivier J., L. Dambo, M. Kone, and M. van Eupen. 2020. "Mapping Travel Time to Access Accessibility in West Africa: The Role of Borders, Checkpoints, and Road Conditions." *Journal of Transport Geography* 82:1–10.

Walther, Olivier J., and William F. S. Miles. 2018. "Introduction: States, Borders and Political Violence in West Africa." In *African Border Disorders: Addressing*

Transnational Extremist Organizations, edited by Olivier J. Walther and William F. S. Miles, 1–14. New York: Routledge.

Walther, Olivier J., and D. Retaille. 2017. "Mapping the Sahelian Space." https://arxiv.org/pdf/1906.02223.pdf

Watts, Michael. 2015. "A Tale of Two Insurgencies: Oil, Authority and the Spectre of Terror in Nigeria." In *States of War since 9/11: Terrorism, Sovereignty and the War on Terror*, edited by Alex Houen, 103–29. London: Routledge.

Watts, Michael. 2018. "Frontiers: Authority, Precarity, and Insurgency at the Edge of the State." *World Development* 101: 477–88.

Weedon, C. 1987. *Feminist Practice and Poststructuralist Theory*. Oxford: Blackwell.

Weizman, E. 2007. *Hollow Land*. London: Verso.

Whatmore, S. 2002. *Hybrid Geographies: Natures, Cultures, Spaces*. London: SAGE.

Whitehouse, Bruce. 2012. *Migrants and Strangers in an African City: Exile, Dignity, Belonging*. Indiana: Indiana University Press.

WikiLeaks. 2009. "Nigeria: Police Shoot 17 in Maiduguri, Tensions Remain High." June 12. https://wikileaks.org/plusd/cables/09ABUJA1053_a.html

Williams Oluwaseun, Idris Lawal, Oluronke Dorcas Popoola, and Abdullahi Usman Kofar Na'isa. 2019. "Creativity and Social Identity in Urban Transport: Tricycle Decoration in Kano Metropolis." IFRA-Nigeria Working Papers Series 51, IFRA-Nigeria, April.

Wilson, Alice. 2017. "Ambivalences of Mobility: Rival State Authorities and Mobile Strategies in a Saharan Conflict." *American Ethnologist* 44 (1): 77–90.

Winton, Alice. 201Laha5. "Violence, borders and boundaries: Reframing young people's mobility." In *Movement, Mobilities and Journeys: Geographies of Children and Young People*, edited by Caitriona Ni Laoire, Allen White, and Tracey Skelton. Singapore: Springer.

Wlodarczyk, Nathalie. 2009. *Magic and Warfare: Appearance and Reality in Contemporary African Conflict and Beyond*. New York: Palgrave Macmillan.

Wolf, D. R. 1991. *The Rebels: A Brotherhood of Outlaw Bikers*. Toronto: University of Toronto Press.

Wood, R. M. 2010. "Rebel Capability and Strategic Violence against Civilians." *Journal of Peace Research* 47 (5): 601–14.

Wood, R. M., J. D. Kathman, and S. E. Gent. 2012. "Armed Intervention and Civilian Victimization in Intrastate Conflicts." *Journal of Peace Research* 49 (5): 647–60.

World Bank. 2016. "International Development Association Project Paper on a Proposed Additional Credit and Restructuring in the Amount of SDR 70.6 Million (US\$ 100 Million Equivalent) to the Federal Republic of Nigeria for a Youth Employment and Social Support Operation." Report PAD1826, May 24.

Woroniecka-Krzyzanowska, D. 2014. "The Meanings of Ordinary in Times of Crisis: The Case of a Palestinian Refugee Camp in the West Bank." *Polish Sociological Review* 187: 395–410.

Xiao, Allen H. 2018. "Interfered Rhythms, Navigating Mobilities: Chinese Migrants on the Roads in Lagos, Nigeria." In *Transport, Transgression and Politics in African Cities: The Rhythm of Chaos*, edited by D. E. Agbiboa. London: Routledge.

Yahaya, Ibrahim. 2010. "The Ultimate Mowing Machine." *Inspire*, October.

Ya'u, Y. K. 2000. "The Youth, Economic Crisis and Identity Transformation: The Case of the Yandaba in Kano." In *Identity Transformation and Identity Politics under Structural Adjustment*, edited by A. Jega, 178–99. Uppsala: Nordic Africa Institute.

Yu, W.-Y., C.-Y. Chen, W.-T. Chiu, and M.-R. Lin. 2011. "Effectiveness of Different Types of Motorcycle Helmets and Effects of Their Improper Use on Head Injuries." *International Journal of Epidemiology* 40 (3): 794–803.

Yusuf, M. 2009. *Hadhihi 'Aqidatuna wa-Manhaj Da'watina*. Maiduguri: Maktabat al-Ghuraba.

Zenn, J., A. Barkindo, and N. A. Heras. 2013. "The Ideological Evolution of Boko Haram in Nigeria: Merging Local Salafism and International Jihadism." *RUSI Journal* 158 (4): 46–53.

Zhukov, Y. M. 2012. "Roads and the Diffusion of Insurgent Violence." *Political Geography* 31 (3): 144–56.

Zulaika, Joseba. 2012. "Drones, Witches and Other Flying Objects: The Force of Fantasy in US Counterterrorism." *Critical Studies on Terrorism* 5 (1): 51–68.

Index

Ja'far Mahmoud Adam, 64–66
Jama'at Izalat al Bid'a Wa Iqamat as
   Sunna, 60
Jama'atu Nasril Islam, 58
Janjaweed, 120, 183n7
jihad, 65, 72, 84, 92; Sokoto (Fulani), 67
Jihadist movements, 58. *See also* Islamist
   organizations
joint task force (JTF), 124–25
Jonathan, Goodluck, 93, 181–82n4

Kachalla, Alhaji Mala, 181n2
Kallil, Abba Aji, 136
Kallon, Edward, 113
Kamajors, 127, 141, 142
Kane, Ousmane, 57
Kaplan, Robert, 78
Katiba Machina, 58
Katz, Cindi, 121
Kaufman, Emily, 177n5
Kaufmann, Vincent, 8
Kawu, Alhaji Bulama, 107
Keke Napep Association in Yobe, 155,
   157
Keke Napep Owners and Riders Asso-
   ciation, 153, 154
keke napeps (tricycle taxis): advantages of,
   158–59; ban on, 159–60; and check-
   point corruption, 167; code numbers
   for drivers, 159; drivers of, 42–44,
   54, 154–55, 165, 167, 183nn1(ch.5);
   owners of, 54, 155, 183nn1(ch.5); state
   sanction of, 32, 154–55; weaponiza-
   tion of, 159
Khan, Mariama, 55
Khmer Rouge, 26
Kilcullen, David, 178n9
kinetocracy, 146
Klute, George, 22
Koglweogos, 142
kombi taxis, 5, 55
Kony, Joseph, 127
Kopytoff, Igor, 13
Koranic schools, 56, 74, 76, 78. See also
   madrassas
Kotef, Hagar, 2, 4
Kurdistan Workers' Party (PKK), 26
Kwankwaso, Rabiu, 80
Kyari, Mohammed, 138

labor migration, 10. *See also* migration
Lake Chad Basin: Boko Haram in, 9,
   19–20, 30, 122–23; cross-border
   trade in, 114, 122–23, 154, 182–83n5,
   183n6; as frontier spaces, 120–21;
   gangs and bandits in, 71; inaccessibil-
   ity in, 26; mobility in, 6, 17; mobi-
   lization of youth in, 90; rainfall and
   climate change in, 123; smuggling in,
   32, 120–21; territoriality in, 9; youth
   precarity in, 72. *See also* Cameroon;
   Chad; Niger
Lame, Ibrahim Yakubu, 181–82n4
Land Cruisers, 21
land mines, 115, 119, 132
Langevang, Thilde, 179n3
Last, Murray, 57, 62, 66
Lawuyi, Olatunde, 13
Leese, Matthias, 22, 174
Lefebvre, Henri, 96
Lemarchand, Rene, 58
Lewis, Oscar, 77
liberalism, 2–5, 174
Liberation Tigers of Tamil Eelam
   (LTTE), 174
Liberia, 55, 82, 173
Libya, 20
Linebaugh, Peter, 23
Lord's Resistance Army (LRA), 127

MacEachern, Scott, 69
madrassas, 79, 180n9. *See also* Koranic
   schools
Mahdist movement, 59
Maiduguri, Babagana, 159
Maiduguri Railway Terminus, 69–70
Mains, Daniel, 34
Maitatsine movement, 67, 76, 83
Maitatsine Uprising, 58–62
Mali, 7, 22, 173–74
Mao Tse Tung, 20
marabouts, 49–50
martyrdom, 92, 110, 111, 139
Marwa, Muhammed (Maitatsine), 59–60,
   83, 181n1
Masquelier, Adeline, 35, 39, 72, 76
Massey, Doreen, 51
Maxwell, Andrew, 54–55
Mbembe, Achille, 45, 111

Printed and bound by CPI Group (UK) Ltd, Croydon, CR0 4YY

09/06/2025

14685641-0004